MIKE REILLY

FINDING MY VOICE

Tales from IRONMAN,
the World's Greatest Endurance Event

MIKE REILLY

FINDING MY VOICE

Tales from IRONMAN,
the World's Greatest Endurance Event

BY MIKE REILLY
WITH LEE GRUENFELD

A Steeplechase Book

Steeplechase Publishing, Ltd.

A division of Steeplechase Run, Inc.

New York, New York

San Diego, California

First Steeplechase hardcover edition March 2019

Steeplechase Publishing, Ltd.® is a trademark of
Steeplechase Run, Inc.

Manufactured in the United States of America

1 3 5 7 9 10 8 6 4 2

Library of Congress Cataloging-in-Publication Data Available

Reilly, Michael J.
MIKE REILLY: Finding My Voice: Tales from IRONMAN, the World's
Greatest Endurance Event
by Mike Reilly with Lee Gruenfeld
Steeplechase Publishing non-fiction original hardcover
1. Reilly, Michael. 2. Triathlon (Sports) — United States — Biography
I. Gruenfeld, Lee. II. Title.

Front cover photo of John Misner by Nils Nilsen
Back cover photo by Robbie Little/FinisherPix

ISBN

978-1-7337478-2-0 (Hardback)

978-1-7337478-5-1 (Paperback)

978-1-7337478-8-2 (ebook)

978-1-7337478-1-3 (audiobook)

———————

For Rose, my high school sweetheart and love of my life.

Erin, Andy, Andrew and Briana,
who keep me grounded with their honesty and love,

and the boys, Graham and Leo.
Papa loves you to the moon and back.

Serenata Families Forever

And the closest sibs a guy could ever have,
Judith, Donald, Patrick, Kathleen and Margaret Mary.

———————

An IRONMAN triathlon is generally considered to be the toughest and most popular one-day sporting event in the world. It's a 140.6-mile triathlon consisting of three disciplines, done consecutively, with no breaks:

1. Swim: 2.4 miles (3.8 km) in open water

2. Bike: 112 miles (180.2 km)

3. Run: 26.2 miles (42.2 km), a standard marathon

IRONMAN 70.3 is also a triathlon, with each leg half the distance of a full-distance IRONMAN race.

What started out as a private challenge for 15 individuals in 1978 has since grown into the largest series of endurance racing events in the world. There are 41 full-distance events in 24 countries, and 116 half-distance races in 46 countries. Some 200,000 people enter an IRONMAN or IRONMAN 70.3 race every year.

Both series have their own World Championship races. The IRONMAN contest, often referred to simply as "KONA," takes place in Kailua-Kona, Hawai'i, every October. The IRONMAN 70.3 World Championship is held in a different country each year.

Both of these premier events are open only to athletes who have qualified, generally by placing at the top of their age groups in an individual event or, for professionals, by placing high in qualifying races.

"Getting a slot to KONA" is the Holy Grail of the triathlon world.

Contents

I couldn't do it and, to be honest, I'm not quite sure how *he* does it. Imagine being at a microphone for 19 hours in a row, a dozen times a year all over the globe, and doing that for the better part of three decades. That to me is mind boggling. I know my voice— and my will—would cash in their chips just a few hours in.

Then imagine not just being at a microphone, but creating a life-altering moment for thousands of people who have overcome seemingly insurmountable obstacles just to get to the start line, have been racing for as many as 17 hours, and are counting on you to provide the ultimate finishing touch to a day that will stay with them forever.

Welcome to the world of a man I love like a brother.

Mike Reilly is one of the most recognizable figures in the endurance sports world. For over thirty years he has been the "Voice of IRONMAN," having called over 350,000 athletes across the finish lines of more than 180 IRONMAN races around the globe. In all that time it's always been about the athletes for Mike, and he's been careful to make sure that they're the stars of every race.

During those three decades the two of us have stood together on stages at the IRONMAN World Championship, at the Challenged Athletes Foundation (CAF) "Best Day in Triathlon" and at the Competitor Magazine Endurance Sports Awards.

During that time we have laughed together, shed tears together, and shared magic moments together. There is a chemistry between us that is indescribable; sometimes we even seem to read each other's minds.

Before Mike Reilly came into the picture, race announcers were all about giving the audience and the participants the facts. *The water temperature is 68 degrees, aid stations will be serving two flavors of Gatorade on the course today, don't forget to turn in your special needs bags, here comes number three eighty-seven, let's give him a big round of applause,* etc., etc.

Nothing wrong with any of that, but not quite the three-ring circus that Mike is able to create. When I finished my first IRONMAN race in the middle of the night way back in 1980, there was only one other person in Kapiolani Park, not even connected with the race, and that was it. No sound system, no music, no excitement.

When you are at a Mike Reilly finish line, that sacred last fifty yards to nirvana includes high intensity music that gives you goosebumps, thrilling interaction with the crowd and an atmosphere that you have to be immersed in to understand. Mike personally honors each finisher as if he were the *only* finisher, and ensures that his achievement is enthusiastically celebrated by the spectators. Ask anyone who's crossed a Mike Reilly finish line and they'll tell you: Mike creates the world's best party, *you* are the guest of honor, and he revels in your accomplishment as much as you do. Ask Mike how he can possibly get more and more energized as his 19-hour day progresses, and he'll tell you. "How could I possibly not!"

Nils Nilsen

And ever since he took the gloves off and let his energy and his passion spill out over the finish area, announcers all over the world have tried to follow his lead.

I have watched people coming down Ali'i Drive in Kailua-Kona at 11:45 pm on race day. They have spent their day dealing with salt water, swells, wind and heat and, after nearly 17 hours of swim, bike and run, they are barely moving.

Then, suddenly, they hear that amazing voice:

"Come on, everybody!" Mike is shouting. By this time at night he's down from the tower and right on the finish line, dancing, waving a towel, whatever it takes to rev up the crowd. "Let's help this next champion get to the finish! She needs our help...let's bring her in!"

The sound of that voice drives our finisher to suddenly, out of nowhere, get up on her toes and actually start *sprinting*. As she comes into the light, she hears the sweetest sound ever, the one she's been waiting for all day, all year:

"Sally Johnson……YOU…ARE…AN IRONMAN!"

A T LONG LAST, in response to entreaties from athletes all over the world, Mike is opening up about what the sport has meant to him and why he remains so passionate about it. Over the years he's met thousands of competitors and their families, listened to their stories, and amassed a treasure trove of tales about the joy of competing, the triumph of succeeding, and the transformative power of pushing yourself past the edge. He has been witness to extraordinary feats of personal redemption, recovery from overwhelming tragedy, and superhuman displays of perseverance in the face of seemingly impossible odds.

In chronicling these stories, Mike shows us the profound impact IRONMAN can have on the lives of those who make the decision to step up to the start line and find out what they're truly capable of. Mike's passion for the sport and his deep affection for its participants come through on every page. And, born entertainer and accomplished storyteller that he is, he'll keep you enthralled from the very first sentence.

If you have already been brought across an IRONMAN finish line by Mike Reilly, congratulations!

But if you haven't taken the plunge and signed up for an IRONMAN race yet, here is my challenge to you. Find an event where Mike Reilly will be announcing, sign up and get ready for a race day and finish line experience unlike any other.

That finish line and Mike Reilly will change your life forever.

And if you don't believe me now, you will by the time you finish this book.

I guarantee it.

Bob Babbitt

IRONMAN Hall of Fame
USA Triathlon Hall of Fame
Competitor Magazine Co-Founder
Challenged Athletes Foundation Co-Founder

E *komo mai.* An interesting Hawaiian phrase. It's loosely translated as "Welcome," which is why the pre-race ceremony at the IRONMAN World Championship on the Big Island is called the "E Komo Mai (Welcome) Party."

But the true meaning is deeper than that. It translates literally as an invitation to approach the speaker, and what it means in modern terms is: *Please come into my space.*

That's what I'm inviting you to do with this book: *Come into my space.*

During forty years on the microphone at endurance events, it's been all about the athletes for me. You'll rarely hear me say "I" or "me" because I consciously avoid inserting myself into the process, so as not to divert attention from those who have worked so hard and accomplished so much. I've also gotten used to dodging a lot of questions about what I do, how my role evolved and, most importantly, what it all means to me.

So, in one fell swoop with one swell book, I'm going to let it all hang out. I'm going to take a couple hundred pages to answer some questions and tell some stories, and hope that I'm able to convey the depth of my passion for this sport we all love so dearly. There will be a lot of "I" and "me" and then it's back to the microphone and all about the athletes again, as it should be.

There's a common theme that runs through a lot of conversations I have with race volunteers. And there are a lot of race volunteers: It's not unusual to have as many as four *thousand* of them supporting a race, doing everything from checking competitors in to handing out water bottles, directing athletes in and out of the transition areas, delivering supplies to aid stations, and holding up finishers on the verge of collapse and walking them to the medical and massage areas.

The common theme goes like this: *We accidentally bumped into the race during a port stop on our cruise (or a vacation in the Adirondacks or Chattanooga or Australia or Frankfurt...) and were completely hooked. We've been coming back every year for the last umpteen years. We'd sooner miss Christmas than miss IRONMAN. It's the high point of our year.*

I know exactly how they feel. I called my first IRONMAN race in 1989, which was also the first time I'd ever seen one in the flesh. Living an endurance sports lifestyle in San Diego, I'd been around triathletes for years, and was very familiar with IRONMAN. All the greats like Scott Tinley, Paula Newby-Fraser and Mark Allen trained near where I lived, and every year they'd trek to Kailua-Kona to race the World Championship. I was so jealous, and began training in earnest to do it myself, but events conspired to have me announce one before I could compete in one.

I was in complete awe, and as I watched finishers on television coming to the line in various stages of agony, exhilaration, exhaustion, and delirium– often all of those at once–a single thought kept running through my head:

Hell or high water, I've got to become a part of this.

In a later chapter I'll talk about how some people have the good fortune to discover, through design or happenstance, what they were meant to do. There is not a doubt in my mind that being an IRONMAN race announcer is what I was born for. It's the perfect fit for my skills and temperament and, aside from being with my family, I'm never happier than when I'm on the mic shepherding athletes through their race and welcoming them home when their day is done. (Later on, I'll tell you how I got started announcing races.)

With each passing year my passion for the sport only increases. Being a race announcer is about a whole lot more than calling out names, and the work extends well before and after race day. I have a unique vantage point that affords me the opportunity to meet all kinds of people, including not just the athletes but their friends and families and the staff and volunteers who take care of them. I often think of myself as a kind of entertainer, not in the sense that I take the stage and belt out a few songs (I couldn't carry a tune if you put it in my backpack), but as someone who makes sure the athletes and audience are the stars. In what other sport does the guy calling the plays mingle with the public, the fans, the families of the athletes? You don't see a baseball broadcaster out in the stands mixing it up with the public. But I can't imagine doing it any other way.

I've also had the pleasure of swapping stories and sharing experiences with many other announcers. There are 41 full-length IRONMAN events around the world and 116 IRONMAN 70.3 races (half the distance of a full-distance IRONMAN race). I wish that I could call them all myself but I can only manage about a dozen or so a year. I've worked alongside many of the other announcers and we've learned a great deal from each other, all in the interest of improving the experience for the athletes.

As with every announcer, my race starts about 7-10 days before the actual event. One of the most important things I do is read every athlete's name and their personal stories. It's not a memorization exercise but a way of becoming familiar with the unique spirit of each event. I'll go through the whole data base five or six times, so when race day rolls around, seeing names pop up on the computer displays will trigger my memory. *Hey, she's got a special story.* If there aren't too many other athletes coming through at the same time, I can take a few seconds to fill the spectators in, which makes for a richer experience for everybody.

Staging an IRONMAN triathlon is like launching a D-Day invasion. The logistics are complex and daunting, and you never have it nailed down because the process is constantly evolving. Every race is followed by a formal, very intense post mortem analysis of how it could have been done better. That means it's going to be different next time.

A few years ago the organizers of the World Championship in Kailua-Kona (often abbreviated by triathletes to just "KONA") wanted to do something to improve the spectators' view of the swimmers coming out of the water. Athletes entered on the east side of a pier in full view of the crowd but exited on the west side in full view of nobody. Race director Diana Bertsch had the idea of building a stairway on the east side and having the athletes enter and exit the water from the same spot. Construction Director Rocky Campbell thought about that and came up with a way to do it. And it is a sight to behold indeed.

But that presented a challenge for me. I'd been completely comfortable with the original exit and now I had to figure out how to switch gears. And there's no way to rehearse. The pier in Kailua Bay is a very lively place all year 'round so you don't get to put up race-day structures and gather a few hundred of your friends to make test runs. You work from planning sketches and maps and try to anticipate as best you can.

Diana's idea worked beautifully. Spectators were thrilled to be able to see all those athletes hit the stairs and climb up to the pier. And, without moving, they could also see cyclists exiting transition on their way out to the 112-mile bike leg.

I set up my little command center just off the top of the stairs next to the timers, out of the way of the athletes but with a good view of the whole area. I could stand on

Lee Gruenfeld/IRONMAN

the pier and announce to the crowd who they were seeing—people with swim caps and goggles are hard to identify from a distance—and I could move up and down the stairs to call the action. With just a few steps I could also get close to athletes running under showerheads to rinse off the salt water.

To the spectators it all looked effortless, which is exactly how it should look. But it was pretty nerve-racking getting that all squared away and hoping it would work.

This is one of the reasons I thank the heavens I have an announcer's mic in my hand and not a race director's clipboard and radio. Producing an endurance event the size of IRONMAN is a Herculean task and, even after having experienced over 180 of them (and counting), I still don't know how they do it. The complexity is absolutely mind-boggling, and it takes a unique set of talents and skills to pull it off. Recurring events like the World Championship and dozens of other races are tough enough. But how race organizers can parachute into a brand new city and put on a near-flawless race right out of the gate is utterly beyond me.

Anyway, T1 (swim-to-bike transition) and T2 (bike-to-run) in Kona are now one and the same, right at the pier. It took some very creative planning and juggling to make that work, but it was a tremendous improvement. In combination with a new route for the bike leg that makes two passes through town before it heads out to the lava fields, it's now possible for a spectator to get *nine* bird's eye views of the athletes without walking more than about a hundred yards during the day.

So deciding how announcers position themselves and the rest of the announcing crew is part of the planning process. We don't just work the finish line. To the extent possible, we want to spend the day encouraging the racers as they bike and run. If we're lucky enough to have a multi-loop course, we can stay in one spot and shout out to the same athlete two or three times.

IRONMAN Lake Placid is like that. It's a logistical madhouse but it works and it's well worth the trouble. There's a "hot corner" on the run that the athletes pass five times before they head into the Olympic speed skating oval for the finish. It's perfect for announcing and spectating. IRONMAN Arizona is particularly wild: It's like one of those old demolition derbies that's shaped like a figure-eight with athletes crossing in the middle!

Announcers also have to figure out how to move equipment from place to place, taking into consideration the many barriers and fences that define the race course and spectator areas.

KONA is pretty easy because I can stay inside a small, walkable radius. But at other venues announcers might have to use bikes, cars, handcarts and a lot of muscle. The timing is important so that we don't miss anything. Again, all of this must be largely invisible and seamless.

Sachin Shrestha/IRONMAN

At IRONMAN Mont-Tremblant, it takes special transportation to get us from the race start to the swim exit.

I mentioned the rest of the announcing crew. This is not a solo job. In addition to the people who help move us around, there is also someone to man the two computers that display athletes' names and particulars as they cross timing mats. Where there are no mats, we have spotters out on the course who radio names in time for us to bring them up on the computers so we're ready when the athlete passes.

I don't like to take breaks. I figure, if the athletes can go seventeen hours of constant effort, I can surely go nineteen since I'm not swimming, biking or running. However, while I'm happy to be on the mic all that time, I do have to occasionally answer nature's call. And, while experienced triathletes have learned to pee while competing, doing it while announcing probably wouldn't be equally praiseworthy. I'm happy to pee into an empty bottle if I have to—and believe me, I've had to—but it's better to dash off to the Porta-Potty and keep things civil. Fortunately, at many events I have great announcing help to take over for a time, people like Tom Ziebart, Paul Kaye, Dave Downing, Pete Murray, Eric Gilsenan, Alain Cyr and Cameron Harper, to name just a few.

Another pre-race activity is planning for and hosting the welcome party, which was sometimes called the carbo-load party in the old days. This is an exciting gathering, especially for newbies getting their first taste of the extraordinary energy surrounding an IRONMAN race. People start showing up at the airport days before race day and, as the clock winds down, the buzz becomes palpable. The welcome banquet is kind of a clarion call that, yes, it's really happening, you're really here, this is IT!

The race announcer is typically the master of ceremonies at the festivities, doing everything he can to make the experience memorable. It's different at each race, but usually there are welcome speeches by IRONMAN officials and local notables, including mayors and governors. Special athletes like the oldest and youngest are introduced and interviewed, and a professionally produced video or two of previous races or inspirational stories are shown.

One of the things I like to do after I welcome everyone is say something like, "Tonight is for you, to inspire you, to entertain you, and to relax you. Sit back and enjoy the show, and on Sunday...you will be an IRONMAN!"

And that brings me to one of my favorite parts of the evening, when I ask every first-timer to stand. There are always hundreds of them at a full-distance event and I never fail to get goose bumps when they rise and the crowd showers them with applause and shouts of encouragement. Nobody enters an IRONMAN race casually. By the time they arrive on site they're already intimately familiar with every aspect of the race. They talked with coaches, joined triathlon clubs, endlessly buttonholed veterans for tips and insider information, heard and read and dreamt about doing this race for months or even years. And now they're actually *here*, and the guy introducing them is the same guy who, if all goes well, is going to tell them what they've been aching all that time to hear and that their lives are about to be changed forever.

It's the emcee who keeps it moving and lively, and he ensures that all the athletes and their families and friends are able to gorge out on all things IRONMAN. If we do our jobs, by the time the evening is over everyone is so excited they can hardly sleep, and race week is officially *on*.

Sometimes, we create excitement we didn't intend to. One of my oldest buddies is Bob Babbitt, co-founder of the Challenged Athletes Foundation, a six-time IRONMAN finisher and someone who's been in the sport of triathlon longer than just about anybody. He's without doubt the best story teller I've ever met, with a knack for finding the human interest everywhere he looks and a gift for communicating it. Bringing him up on stage at the Kona banquets to tell a few tales is a great treat for both the audience and me.

A few years ago my beautiful daughter Erin got married, and the family was very honored to have Bob officiate the ceremony. He did it masterfully, of course, and when I introduced him at the welcome banquet in Kona a few months later, I told the crowd how proud I was that he'd just married my daughter. There was an audible gasp followed by very lusty applause, and I didn't think much of it except that it was all pretty cool.

After the banquet dozens of people began rushing up to me.

"That's so great about your daughter, Mike!"

Why, thank you.

"And Babbitt. Wow!"

Yeah, pretty great.

"How does it feel to have him in the family now?"

I'm sorry; what?

"I can't believe he and your daughter got married!"

Wait! What? No, wait…!

"Babbitt's your son-in-law? Holy smokes!"

No, no, no, no, no…!

As more well-wishers pumped my hand and my shock began to wear off, I looked wistfully back at the stage. I wanted to run back up and explain, but the lights had come up and people were already drifting out. Maybe it wouldn't be so bad…?

"Hey, Mike!"

Oh no. I know that voice. I turned to see Bob's wife Heidi heading towards me. "Thanks for letting everyone know my husband has another wife!"

Okay, that's it. I started for the stage…just in time to see a crewman yank the mic out of its holder and begin coiling the wire.

I had to live with that piece of misinformation flying around until the awards banquet, where I corrected the record to raucous laughter that had me blushing and shaking my head.

(It didn't quite end there. After the awards banquet an athlete came up to me and told me that he'd really been in some hurt around mile 80 of the bike and then he started thinking about what I'd said. "I couldn't get it out of my mind," he told me. "I kept thinking, How the hell did Reilly let Babbitt marry his daughter!" I said, "Really? That's what you were thinking about out there?" He said yes, he really was. "And before I knew it, I was dismounting my bike in T2 and barely remembered those last 32 miles!" Glad I could help, buddy!)

We do other things during race week as well. One of my favorites takes place in Kona, stopping by the Iron Gents and Ladies dinner where I get to meet the 60-and-over athletes. Some of these people have been racing IRONMAN for decades and make no mistake about it: These folks are not there as a novelty act trying to finish. They've already finished plenty of races and that's no longer an issue. Every time I get up in front of this audience it's a bit daunting. They are in essence the leaders of our sport, the ones who have guided us with their lasting performances, the ones who never fail to tell us like it is, and the ones who have never, ever given up.

One time I asked the 70+ people to raise their hands. About half the room did so. I said, "I'm wondering: When one of you finishes the race and then a 38-year-old finishes behind you, do you think I should say to that guy, "You are an IRONMAN, but hey, buddy...you just got beaten by a 76-year-old!" I would never actually do that—I was just trying to get a laugh—but Lew Hollander, who was 82 at the time, stood up, pointed to me and yelled, "Hell, yes!" They are truly IRONMAN's greatest generation.

RACE MORNING FOR ANNOUNCERS starts about two hours before the cannon goes off (hence, the 19-hour day). We're on the mic well before dawn, shepherding athletes through check-in, body marking, bike prep and swim staging. Athletes arrive at various times, so we have to make sure that everybody hears announcements, delivered in a calming voice, about changes, weather updates and procedure reminders. I always find it funny to be reminded of just how nervous and distracted the assembling racers can be. It's not unusual for me to say something like, "There are plenty of bicycle pumps in barrels placed at every aisle in transition," and then have an athlete come up a few seconds later and ask, "Uhhh, are there any pumps in transition?" Pre-race is just that intense.

If you think back to a race you were in or watched, you might recall that you pretty much heard only one voice over the PA the entire day. This is purposeful. There is a vast organization behind each race and one of the announcer's jobs is to be the face of that organization, a single point of contact and recognition for the athletes to focus on. The announcer is a source of both comfort and authority for the athletes, something to latch on to when things get confusing or chaotic.

I often tell people that the start of the race is fifty percent of my day. It's the announcer who sets the tone for how the day is going to go, and it's a responsibility we take very seriously. If we're competent and confident, the athletes will relax (at least a little), knowing that everything is under control. If we hem and haw or give wrong or conflicting information or get annoyed or lose our cool, the effect can be striking. And when one of your key tasks is making sure the race starts on time, it can be a tricky balancing act.

One of the toughest jobs is herding the swimmers at the start. Everyone is amped up and nervous. Inevitably, swimmers toward the front creep forward slowly, unconsciously, making a mess of what we hoped would be an orderly start line. You'd think that a 10-yard lead in a 140.6-mile race isn't going to make much of a difference, but it's not a lead the athletes are worried about: It's getting kicked in the face or losing your goggles amid the frenzy of 2,500 hyper-adrenalized swimmers who've been waiting for this moment for a year, and sometimes far longer than that. Race organizers have experimented with several "safe start" methods which put age group athletes into the water according to their predicted swim finish times. This has made for a lot less shoving and kicking but it's still a jungle out there.

It's the announcers who call out pleas to stay back, along with directions to the supporters on surfboards and kayaks to try to maintain some control. It never works, but you hope that a soothing tone and easygoing body language will at least keep it from going completely out of control.

And, boy, can things go out of control. Remember those little experiments I mentioned before? One of them was tried—*once*—at the start of the 2001 World Championship. Somebody had the idea that we should give the athletes a five-minute pre-start heads up with an air horn. I was a little apprehensive about that because most endurance events are started with an air horn.

The rationale was that the IRONMAN World Championship in Hawai'i has always been started with a cannon. "Everybody knows that," I was told. NBC often captures that moment when a perfect O-ring emerges from the mouth of the cannon as the calm blue waters of Kailua Bay underneath it are instantly churned into white foam.

Except…not *everyone* knows that. And many that do also know that we have an air horn on standby in case the cannon malfunctions. But, the athletes were told about the warning horn during the mandatory race meetings so what could possibly…etc.

I didn't have time to think about it because I was pretty busy as the start approached, and it was such a beautiful morning, and the athletes seemed unusually calm as they entered the water from the small beach alongside the pier. (The locals call it "Dig Me Beach," because of all the insanely fit people who parade around on it in swimsuits about as substantial as dental floss.)

The introductory speeches and the blessing by the Hawaiian *kahu* (priest) were all on time, the national anthem was played, the NBC camera crews were making last-minute equipment checks and the helicopters were starting to move into position. After a thumbs-up that we were good for an on-time start from then-director Sharron Ackles, I got ready to say a few encouraging words to the athletes to start them on their way.

By the time I raised the mic to begin speaking I'd forgotten completely about the air horn, and was so startled when it went off that I almost dropped the mic as I ducked reflexively and put both hands on top of my head. It lasted only a second but by the time I looked back up, the pros up front had taken off and the age groupers were following close behind. I could see some swimmers partway back hesitate, probably because they'd remembered about the five-minute warning, but as soon as they saw the rest of the field face down and stroking and kicking, they took off as well. And it was spreading rapidly towards the back of the pack.

It was a disaster in slow motion unfolding right in front of me. Spectators were clapping and cheering wildly because they had no idea that something had gone wrong, but I only had a moment to listen because my earpiece suddenly exploded with what sounded like a thousand voices: timers were screaming that they hadn't started the clocks, camera crews hadn't filmed the swimmers taking off, the choppers weren't in position overhead, the close-in safety crews on surfboards hadn't yet jumped out ahead of the racers…

I was trying to figure out whether to just let it go when I felt a tug on my sleeve. It was Sharron, who was by now standing next to me. She probably saw the panicked look on my face and decided she needed to be the cool-headed one.

"Mike," she said calmly, "you have to stop them."

Stop them? How the hell was I supposed to…

"Figure out a way," she said before I could even get the question out.

It seemed like an eternity had passed, but it had probably only been five or six seconds since the horn had sounded. Yet it had been enough for all 2,000 souls to now be flailing their way towards open water.

"STOP!" I yelled at the top of my lungs, something I never do. "Everybody stop! You have to go back!"

How lame was that? A few swimmers whose heads were out of the water paused to look my way, and maybe wondered what that crazy guy waving his arms was all about, but they quickly got back to work and kept swimming.

I looked out and saw that the leaders had already shot past the close-in surfboarders. But I noticed a group of about ten swim safety people sitting on paddle boards some fifty yards ahead. They were back-paddling with their hands, somewhat tentatively, swiveling their heads back and forth between me and this mass of humanity headed towards them. They were well aware of the five-minute warning blast and didn't know what they were supposed to do now that the race seemed to be underway.

I got the idea that, if we could contain the lead swimmers, maybe the rest would follow suit and at least start slowing down enough for us to get their attention.

"Paddle boarders, can you hear me!" I shouted.

They raised their hands and nodded emphatically, eager to get some instructions.

The swimmers were now within twenty yards of them. "We have to stop the swimmers!" I called out. "It was a false start! We have to stop them!"

They instinctively began turning their boards sideways. Good crew!

"Do whatever you have to do!" I continued. "Grab 'em by their swim suits, their caps, their *goggles* if you have to! Whatever it takes!"

I gave this about a ten percent chance of working. Twenty percent, tops. So what happened next just amazed me.

As the three people in the lead got to the boards, the safety guys reached down, took hold of their suits and held on. IRONMAN racers are used to getting kicked, grabbed and scratched in the chaos of a mass swim start, but they'd never experienced somebody hanging on to their swimsuits and pulling them back. They clearly knew something was wrong and came to an immediate halt. They looked up, and at least two of them hurled what I later learned were some choice epithets at the safety guys, quite too pungent to print here.

The swimmers behind the leaders, no longer seeing the toes in front of them that they'd been keying on, hesitated and then stopped, and so did the swimmers behind them. By now the paddle boarders had formed a solid line blocking access to the sea, and as more heads came up out of the water and people were able to hear, I explained that there'd been a false start.

It was a sight I'll never forget, all of those swimmers realizing that something had gone wrong. You could see it moving across the field like a ripple across a pond.

My heart went out to the athletes. To have thought, "This is it! This is finally it!" only to be told they had to go back and start all over again must have been terrible. An awful lot of fists were pounding the water in anger and frustration and disappointment.

Sharron must have known how they were feeling. "You've gotta calm 'em down," she said. "Make this okay."

I said the first thing that popped into my mind. "Sorry, everybody. We just wanted to give you a little warmup!"

That got a few laughs and the tension eased up a bit. I think it might have been because, rather than berate the athletes for forgetting about the warning blast, I made it sound like it was the race officials who'd screwed up. I didn't realize I was doing that, but it worked anyway.

We ended up getting the race going only ten minutes after the scheduled start time...with the cannon. You'd better believe there was no five-minute warning this time. Or ever again. To this day, any time I have to start a race with an air horn, I cringe thinking about that false start.

So that was the start of my day. Three more hours to go before I had to set up at T2 to bring the cyclists in and send the runners out.

People often remark that the World Championship must be my easiest race because there's little to do while the cyclists are out on their 112-mile ride, but it's actually the hardest. The race in Kona is the mother of all IRONMAN races. I love being on the mic, encouraging the athletes and keeping the spectators informed. When I have to stand around for hours because the athletes are miles away, it drives me nuts.

One of the reasons I love KONA so much is the warm humidity. It might be tough on the athletes, but it's heaven on my throat. By the time the day is done I've spoken the equivalent of two or three good-sized novels over the PA, and all that moist, warm air makes a huge difference. Contrast that with IRONMAN Arizona and its dry desert air: By the time that one's done I feel like I've swallowed sandpaper. Two years ago, heading home, I pulled into the drive-thru lane of an In-N-Out Burger. I hadn't spoken in a few hours and when I tried to talk into the speaker, nothing came out but a weak, incomprehensible rasp. I had to go inside and write my order down. (I'm still amazed when athletes come up to me and ask about my voice. The first time it happened, I was floored. "My voice?" I responded. "You're asking about my voice? Never mind my voice…how are your legs!") The supply of throat lozenges and honey I carry around with me all day helps a little, but it's ultimately a losing battle.

Which I can't afford to lose. I'll talk later about what the finish line is like, but race day isn't the end for announcers. We've still got to preside over the awards banquet the next day, and that's a key event in the overall experience for the athletes and their families. By the time that rolls around, most of the pain and suffering of the previous day have given way to deep-seated feelings of accomplishment, triumph and a quiet kind of contentment. As IRONMAN co-creator John Collins put it, pain is temporary but the memories will last a lifetime. All of the uncertainties about getting through the race have been resolved; everyone who finished now has bragging rights for life.

IRONMAN isn't just something you do; it's something you become. And our job at the awards banquet is to help drive it home for every person in attendance.

I tend to a get a little contemplative when preparing for that celebration. I think it's because, all during my adult life, I've become increasingly convinced that we are the cause of our own experiences to a far greater degree than we might think. Of course, there are strong external forces that shape us, and we're often dependent on others for our successes and failures. We've all known people who just seem to run into dead ends all the time. They seem perfectly ordinary on the face of it, but they're always getting fired or butting heads with people and just can't seem to get anywhere. Then there are those who seem to land in roses no matter what they try. They're always getting the promotions, closing the sales, making the right decisions.

I don't think the first guy is unlucky and the second one especially fortunate. I think they're causing their successes and failures, sometimes in subtle ways we don't always understand.

Which is not to say that everything is under our control. Of course it isn't. If you want to become a bestselling novelist, you can write a wonderful book but then you have to rely on someone else to sell it to a publisher, someone else to edit it, someone to market it and a demanding public to buy it. Want to be a Super Bowl MVP? You can have all the talent and drive in the world but you have to get noticed and drafted, get past others competing for the same position as yours, beat the other team and have a lot of plays go your way.

So I'm not trying to oversimplify the idea of being the cause of your own experiences. There are plenty of obstacles and dependencies you can't control yourself. But there are also a lot of tipping points that you can push your way based on how you manage your life. If you truly believe that you are the cause of your own experiences, and work from that premise every day, a lot of the obstacles that confront other people are not going to find you.

What's all this got to do with IRONMAN and the awards banquet? Simply this: Of all the truly momentous, life-changing things it's possible for you to achieve, IRONMAN is one of the rare ones that, barring an accident or bad weather, is virtually 100% within your control.

Sure, you have to organize your life so you can train. That's all part of the commitment you have to make. But there are no obstacles to signing up. There is nothing to stop you from getting up two hours earlier every day so you can swim, bike and run. Nobody can interfere with eating properly and, if they try, it's in your control not to let them.

If you do the work, and fully commit to getting to the finish, you can be an IRONMAN. And that's one of the clearest examples of being the cause of your own experience that I can think of. The best part of the awards banquet for me is looking out over that sea of blissed-out faces and thinking, *Every one of those people made it happen for themselves.*

S o, that's a little taste of what it's like behind the mic for that whirlwind of activity we call "race week." I look forward to race day the way a little kid looks forward to Christmas morning, but I look at all those other things wrapped around the main event as additional opportunities to make IRONMAN the experience of a lifetime for the athletes.

And I'm the luckiest guy in the whole bunch, because there are few more fortunate circumstances in life than being in love with your job and having the chance to make someone else's life just a little happier. A competitor gets to feel the IRONMAN magic maybe once or twice a year or, for many, once in an entire life. I get to experience it more than a dozen times a year.

The best part is, I get to hang out with the greatest people in the world. I feel a part of both their struggles and their triumphs. I love listening to their stories, and every tale they tell makes me even more passionate about the part I play in the IRONMAN *ʻohana*, that extended family of people who have done it, or seen it, or just plain *get it*. Being able to enhance the experience for them a little is the deepest professional satisfaction I know.

The chapters to come are my chance to share some of those stories, to tell you how I see this unique slice of the world I love so much, and hopefully to convey why I continue to be so knocked out by IRONMAN. In a way, this book is my gift to every athlete I've ever called across the line and everyone who loved and supported these amazing creatures who walk among us.

E komo mai.

CHAPTER 2

Tony Svensson/IRONMAN

I played NFL football for fourteen years but IRONMAN was by far the hardest thing I've ever done in my life. The last five miles of the race I actually thought I was going to die. As I struggled closer to town, I could hear Mike Reilly faintly, declaring each finisher an IRONMAN. All through my training, the sweat, the pain, I'd thought about Mike saying that to me. Right now that was all I could think about, and it motivated me to take one more step, then another, then another. My heart was beating out of my chest but as I got closer to town and the finish line and could hear Mike's voice getting louder and louder, I found a new burst of adrenaline and the intense pain seemed to go away for the few more moments it took me to reach the ramp crossing the finish line. As I hit the top I heard that amazing voice and those unbelievable words, "Hines Ward…you are an IRONMAN!" I felt like Rocky Balboa running up the stairs in Philly with my hands up in the air, like the touchdown pass I caught to win the 2005 Super Bowl. Hearing Mike Reilly declare me an IRONMAN was one of the greatest moments of my life.

--Hines Ward, Super Bowl XL MVP

To understand my perspective on this phrase I've uttered some 400,000 times now, listen in on what I try to keep in mind when I say it:

"You are an IRONMAN" is not an endorsement of what you did today; it's a certification of what you've become. It's the last step of a rite of passage that has changed you forever and stamped you as special. You are no longer among those who have never known the gratification of an immensely difficult task done well. You've stepped through a doorway and joined a very special, very exclusive club, and no matter how the rest of your life goes, you will always be an IRONMAN.

Doing the race was your initiation.

"You are an IRONMAN!" was your swearing in.

I'M ACUTELY AWARE THAT ATHLETES treat this pronouncement as the official declaration that they've passed from the realm of ordinary mortals and joined the pantheon of the extraordinary. And I cherish my role as the symbolic focal point of their singular achievement.

So I'd like to tell you that I sat down one day and wracked my brain to come up with a phrase that would perfectly capture the true meaning of such a life-changing accomplishment. I'd like to tell you that I experimented with dozens of variations, tested them out at races, agonized over it and finally decided on just the right one.

But...it didn't happen that way at all. It was pure serendipity, and the only credit I take is for recognizing it when it did happen.

By 1991 I'd announced in Kona twice. I'd used every form of congratulations imaginable as athletes finished, including *Well done!* and *Way to go!* and *Atta girl!* and *You did it!* and, of course, plain old *Congratulations!*

A couple of days before the '91 World Championship I ran into a friend of mine on Ali'i Drive named Dan Trone. We'd done some group runs together around Mission Bay in San Diego and he was headed to Kona. I thought he'd be filled with excitement, but he didn't seem to be looking forward to it at all. In fact, he was downright mopey.

When I asked him what was wrong, he just kind of shrugged. I knew that he'd not done as well as he'd have liked in the previous year's race and figured maybe that was what was bothering him. I tried to buck him up a little, but the guy was so down on himself and full of self-doubt that it didn't seem to do any good.

The day before the race I saw him again during the bike check-in at the pier. He didn't look any more confident or jazzed than he had earlier in the week. He needed something...

"Dan, listen to me," I said as I grabbed him by both shoulders. "Tomorrow, you will be an IRONMAN! I promise!"

The next day, I made sure I was on the mic when Dan came down the final stretch. He looked good, and he was clocking a great time. Mindful of the promise I'd made, I called out, "Dan Trone, you are an IRONMAN!"

It was the first time I'd ever said it. It was no big deal, really, just me recalling our conversation and kind of giving him a little I-told-you-so, like *Ha, I was right, see? You really are an IRONMAN!*

Dan looked up at me in the tower, smiled brightly and pointed at me. I pointed back, but got a little distracted because the crowd was roaring louder than they had been all day. I looked around to figure out why, but all I could see were people clapping and cheering for Dan...who, frankly, was nobody particularly special to any of the onlookers.

Hmmm...

When the next finisher hit the line, I said it again: "You are an IRONMAN!"

The crowd went nuts.

Then it happened again. And again.

And it hit me: They're all an IRONMAN, every last one. And they deserved to hear it. So I did it for every finisher, right up until the midnight cutoff.

FUNNY CODA TO THIS STORY: As Dan was walking away from the finish area, he heard me call the next athlete across with the same phrase. And the next, and the next. Later in the evening when I came down from the tower and started announcing from the floor, he came up to me with a disappointed look on his face.

"Gee whiz, Reilly," he said. "I thought that was just for me!"

As a matter of fact, at the time it *had* been just for him. But then it took on a life of its own.

"IRONMAN" includes women, by the way. About four or five finishers after Dan, a woman approached the line, and I was momentarily stymied. *What should I say?* Should I call her an "Iron Woman," which she certainly was? I only had a few seconds to think about it, because she was almost there.

Then I thought, *This is an IRONMAN event, and that means everyone, regardless of sex.* So I called her an IRONMAN, held my breath, and was thrilled when she beamed a brilliant smile and the reaction from the crowd was the same as before.

Later she told me that she'd heard the previous calls as she was coming down Ali'i Drive. It gave her a shot of adrenaline and, as she picked up the pace, she thought, *Please, please let him call me that, too!* It never entered her mind to be called anything else.

At the next race, a woman came up to me before the swim start and said, "Will you say that for me when I finish?"

I asked her what she meant.

"C'mon, you know…" She looked around a little sheepishly, then leaned in and whispered, "*You are an IRONMAN!*"

No exaggeration, that happened thirty or forty more times that morning.

In all my years, I have never heard even a single female athlete say that she'd prefer anything other than IRONMAN. Not ever. In fact, the once or twice when I heard something like that proposed, the chorus of female voices rising to crush it was so loud that the concept died aborning. The word IRONMAN is definitively gender-neutral!

I HAD A LOT OF TIME TO THINK about it later, about what it all meant. I had called a great number of endurance events prior to that night in Kona—many marathons, half marathons, shorter distance triathlons—and always tried to make everyone feel welcome, feel like the champions they are.

But when I declared Dan an IRONMAN that night, it was different. Those four simple words carried a lot of emotional power, bottling up accolades that could fill a book and bestowing them on the finisher in no more time than it took to raise their arms in the air.

The crowd that night had understood way before I did that the spectators at an

IRONMAN finish line aren't cheering an accomplishment; they're celebrating a transformation. That heretofore ordinary human being passing under the arch is ordinary no longer.

He or she is an IRONMAN.

And I'm the lucky guy who gets to tell them so.

THE QUESTION I GET ASKED most often is this: "How can you keep doing this without growing complacent?"

It's a reasonable question. Part of the answer is that I often find out only after a finisher comes in that there was a particularly special story behind his or her race. A few years ago a guy's bike seat broke in a crash out on the Queen Ka'ahumanu Highway (known as the "Queen K") in Kona. Undeterred, he used one of his biking tools to slice a thick plastic water bottle in half vertically, then laid it sideways on top of the seat tube and rode home that way. Another athlete's bike broke out by the airport and he *carried* it six miles into T2, in his stocking feet.

Then there was Petri ("Pete") Rautapuro, a 52-year-old aerospace systems engineer from Finland. It took him seventeen years and thirteen IRONMAN races to get to the World Championship in Kona on a special "legacy" qualifying program. Three months before his race he had a horrific bike crash that tore off part of his scalp. Blood gushing, he drove himself to the hospital with his left eyeball hanging halfway down his cheek owing to the fracture of his eye socket. He had reconstructive surgery three weeks later to get a titanium cheek, eye socket and frontal sinus installed. Alarmed by his low 30 beats-per-minute heart rate, the surgeons tried to raise it, despite Pete having told them that he was a veteran endurance athlete and that a low heart rate was normal for him. They succeeded in getting it to 70 BPM, and drove him into cardiac arrest in the process. His heart stopped for fifteen minutes: the white light, soothing voices calling him…the whole near-death experience. When he woke up, he arrested again.

Nine weeks later I called him across the line in Kona. I had no idea what he'd gone through, but later he sent me a letter telling me about it. He also said something that stuck with me, that you can't tell just by looking at someone if they're having the race of their lives under extraordinary circumstances. It's something I try to keep in mind when I'm calling people across the line.

And then there's Angie Polizzi.

It's well-established that girls who grow up with strong fathers who are deeply involved in their lives are far more likely to grow into strong, self-confident and successful women than those who didn't have such an influence.

Which didn't bode well for Angie. Her father was an addict who was rarely around, and when he was, it would have been better had he stayed away. There were no games of catch or swimming lessons or even a little encouragement to participate in sports. Her mother was her hero and the family's savior, but Mom didn't know anything about athletics. By the time Angie finished high school, she couldn't hit a softball, serve a volleyball or kick a soccer ball had her life depended on it.

Later in life, after her father passed, some friends encouraged her to try a triathlon. Something about it spoke to a deep-seated need, and she jumped into it with a vengeance. The better she got, the better she felt, and her life was changed forever. She got a great kick whenever people who saw how determined and dedicated she was would ask, "So which sport did you come from?" She'd answer, "None of them," and then enjoy the startled looks on their faces.

You've heard this story before, people with no athletic background who discover the joys of participating and competing and eventually set themselves the goal of completing an IRONMAN triathlon. It's a monumental challenge that not only speaks to who you are but transforms you in the process. Doing triathlons and marathons is an ongoing process for many; for some, doing one is the only goal, the culmination of a lot of hard work and commitment. It feels great to accomplish it, and then you move on.

But when that goal is IRONMAN, it's no longer a local feat you tuck away and think about now and again before it fades into vague memory. IRONMAN is like trekking to the North Pole or scaling Everest. You come out very different from when you went in.

And, like planting the flag at the Pole or getting your picture taken at the roof of the world, you need an official declaration, a moment in the sun.

Which brings us back to Angie. She'd heard of IRONMAN, of course, but it was an otherworldly concept, something "they" did because "they" lived in a rarefied sphere she couldn't even imagine.

Until she could. She found out that other "ordinary people" were doing IRONMAN races, so she looked into it.

(Side note here: You hear a lot about people who "look into it," and wonder, and research, yada yada yada. My feeling? The minute you start "looking into it," it's a foregone conclusion. The challenge is too alluring, the temptation too delicious, the thought of those lifetime bragging rights too irresistible. Sure, go ahead and "look into it," pretend there's some kind of decision to be made, but you're not fooling anybody except yourself. You're toast, and I'll see you at the start line!)

As I said, Angie looked into it, trying to fathom what it would take, until she decided that it might be possible after all. And then she dug in. Putting in the hours, her confidence grew right along with her strength and endurance. At some point in her training she realized that the physical part wasn't the main issue anymore; the commitment was, and she was as committed as they come.

She dreamed about being called an IRONMAN.

At Lake Placid, after months of focused preparation, Angie crossed the finish line in a little over fifteen hours, well ahead of her goal. She nearly broke down when her 13-year-old daughter hugged her fiercely and told her how proud she was. She now knew that she had the motivation and willpower to do anything she set her mind to, and that the result was well worth however tough the effort was. A great day, a great accomplishment…

Except: It seems that Angie had gotten lost in a shuffle of finishers coming across at the same time. Not only did she not hear herself declared an IRONMAN, her name never even got announced.

I don't remember how that got back to me, but several days later I called Angie and apologized. I told her to call her daughter over to the phone, and then I yelled, "You are an IRONMAN!"

I can't even begin to describe the emotion in her voice. Whenever I worry that the call might be getting tedious or mundane, I think of Angie and others like her, people who have never experienced the thrill of athletic success in their lives, always watching the game from the stands and never being on the field. Then they set this absurd goal and cover 140.6 miles under their own steam and nothing will ever be the same.

I couldn't get complacent about that if I did this for another two hundred years.

PEOPLE ENTER IRONMAN RACES for many different reasons: to deal with trauma, to reinvent their lives, to honor a lost loved one, or just because it's the next big challenge in an accomplished life. For some it's a cleansing of the soul; for others, a way to redefine their identity. They throw themselves into the fire to learn something or prove something about themselves, or to finally obliterate self-limiting beliefs that have been holding them back, not just in their athletic endeavors but in their lives. Letters, emails and phone calls with athletes all over the world have driven home for me that IRONMAN is not just a race.

And announcing it is not just a job.

Once I got into it, I took it very seriously. On the advice of my brother Don I joined Toastmasters to improve my public speaking skills. It's a great way to learn how to make sure you're heard and understood. You give short speeches and get a lot of honest and often brutal criticism on the way to helping you figure out how to engage an audience. And those guys were really tough. They had a big metal pail and if any speaker uttered "um" or "er," someone would throw a marble into the pail with a sound like a hammer hitting glass. Breaks you of the habit very quickly.

I worked hard to perfect what I'd learned. Didn't matter if I was announcing a marathon or speaking to one of my kids' school classes; the same rules applied and I practiced every chance I got. I also learned the hard way that I wasn't Robin Williams and didn't try to pretend I was a stand-up comic.

I also began to watch and study public speakers of all types to get a sense of what had the most impact and the kinds of mistakes I wanted to avoid. I'd watch TV newscasts or listen to radio broadcasts registering errors, making notes of what not to do when I'm on a stage or at a finish line. I learned about flow, that the pace and rhythm of what you're saying is as important as the content. I thought back to professors at school who could make even the most fascinating topics as dull as dirt, and others who could grip your very soul talking about double-entry bookkeeping.

My influences were the great sportscasters, like Vin Scully, Dick Enberg, Jack Buck, Joe Buck, Keith Jackson, Ernie Harwell, Al Michaels, Phil Liggett, Chris Berman and Howard Cosell. They could narrate a game or a boxing match or a bike race for three or four hours (or two weeks, in Phil's case!) and never seem repetitive or mundane. They were as eloquent and energetic in the last minute of the game as they'd been in the first. I wasn't sure how they could do that, but soon it became obvious: These guys *loved* the sports they were covering, loved what they did, and their passion fueled their talent.

That's how I came to feel about IRONMAN. And I think that athletes and spectators get it, which is why, after the 1995 IRONMAN Australia, when I was in the airport waiting to board my flight home, an athlete felt perfectly comfortable coming up to me and saying, "You're Reilly, right?"

When I stood up and confirmed that I was, we shook hands. But then he said, "I gotta tell you, mate: Maybe you were on a pee break or something, but I never heard you call me across!"

His wife was standing just behind him, shaking her head. "We were so disappointed," she said. Even their two little kids looked morose.

I let go of his hand and pointed to his bag. "Put that down!" I said. He hesitated but dropped it, then I turned to his wife, who had a video camera sticking out of her carry-on. I waggled my fingers at it and said, "Get that out!"

I waited for her to step aside and start recording, then I shouted his name and stuck my arms in the air. When he did the same, I added—really loudly—"You are an IRONMAN!"

I think that heads turned five gates away. But the guy and his wife were laughing like crazy while the little ones danced around their father. I could tell from some clapping and shouting that there were at least a few people in the vicinity who caught on to what was happening.

I've done the same thing in a café in Frankfurt, on a busy street in New York City, even once on an airplane. I was asked to make an audio recording for a couple getting married where I narrated the march down the aisle like it was the finish to a race and then said, "You are MARRIED!" at the end.

I once did it for a deaf woman. Her name was Stephanie Grover and she finished IRONMAN Arizona in 2018. She had an interpreter at the finish line, but was unable to see her, and of course she couldn't hear me. I used sign language, as I always do for hearing impaired athletes, but she wasn't looking in my direction. A few days later, some friends of hers got in touch with me and told me that Stephanie had missed the experience of being called an IRONMAN. Inconceivable! I asked if she could read lips. She could, so I made a video and sent it to her. You can find a link to it on my website.

There's also a link to a video I did for a couple who threw a little party to announce the sex of the child they were expecting. In one hand I held two helium-filled balloons, one blue and one pink, and in the other, a pin. The idea was to pop the "wrong" one so the one remaining would reveal the gender. The best part was, even the parents didn't know: They'd given their doctor permission to tell me. So when the moment came, I popped one balloon and called out, "You're having a ___!"

You'll have to go see for yourself which one it was.

THE CALL HAS BECOME PRETTY MUCH STANDARD at all IRONMAN races, whether I'm announcing them or not. I like that other announcers have picked it up. I know how much it means for people to hear it, and I can't be at every race, so it all works out.

It's always a professional announcer on the mic, and I've never offered it to a spectator to make the call, except once. It happened at the 2017 World Championship and the spectator was a kid named Nicholas Purschke. He was only 12 years old but had already been battling a very rare and serious genetic disease for most of his life. Nick was an IRONMAN fanatic, and when the Make-a-Wish Foundation approached the family and asked what he would wish for, he didn't hesitate: He wanted to come to Kona and experience it all first hand.

Thanks to the IRONMAN Foundation, which is a charitable organization that donates money to worthy programs in towns that host IRONMAN races, Nick got his wish, and got it in spades. He'd been with us all week, had seen all the backstage preparations, had slapped hands with a bunch of his pro heroes, and now he had a front row seat in the stands not far from me. I'd spotted Nick and his parents many times throughout the day, and tried to enjoy their enjoyment, pushing back any thoughts of the struggles he and his family still had before them.

About 11:30 at night, half an hour before the race cutoff, I was down on the finish line floor and walked over to them. Nick was smiling, as he had been all day. I high-fived him, and then I had an idea:

"Nick...you want to call the next finisher an IRONMAN?"

His eyes widened, then he whipped his head around to his mom. She was already nodding her permission. "Yes, I would!" he exclaimed.

I introduced him to the crowd and told them what I was doing—they were on board in a New York second—then I gave Nick instructions over the PA so everyone could hear. "I'll say the athlete's name, then I'll hand you the mic and you can say it, okay?"

As the spectators cheered, I turned off the mic and said, in a serious, no-nonsense but calming voice, "You have to be loud, you have to bring it from deep down. Just let it loose. You're about to let the whole world know this person is an IRONMAN!"

Several emotions swept over his face. He was elated, and eager, but he was also nervous, and became more so as we waited for the next athlete. It was one of those "sounded good at the time" moments, and I hoped this would happen soon because he wanted to get this right but might second guess himself if the waiting went on much longer.

Nicholas totally nailed it. With a clear voice and an intensity beyond his years, he shouted "You…are…an IRONMAN!" to a woman finishing with only 23 minutes to spare. She raised her arms and got one of the biggest cheers of the night.

Maybe some of it was for Nicholas. The joy on his face was something I'll never forget, and the smile of happiness on his mom's face made me tear up right on the spot.

Like I said, I'm the luckiest guy in the sport.

CHAPTER 3

It's hard to imagine how beating yourself half to death covering 140.6 miles under your own power, and training for months or years over endless miles to be able to do that, can be healing.

Well, it can.

There's always an extra measure of applause from spectators when I announce that a finisher is a member of the US Marines, or the Navy, or the Royal Air Force or any other service branch from any country. I believe that those men and women who have chosen to put themselves in harm's way on foreign soil to protect and serve their country are the bravest who walk among us. Every IRONMAN race has a number of active military people competing, sometimes as many as fifty, and the World Championship even has a separate awards division for service people. It's always fun to watch those athletes knock themselves out trying to make sure their branch is the one atop the podium.

IRONMAN has a rich history of military participation. John Collins was a Navy Commander when he came up with the swim, bike and run distances that are still standard and challenged his military buddies to do it. That first year, third place went to a 22-year-old Marine named Dave Orlowski, who is still a part of the IRONMAN scene today. You can usually see him in Kona wearing the T-shirt that was made up for the first race, or at least what remains of the 40-year-old thing.

Whenever I call someone across who's served, I wonder what his or her story is. A number of challenged athletes were injured in places like Iraq and Afghanistan and I've gotten to know some of those people. One is Melissa Stockwell, who was a platoon leader and convoy commander in Baghdad. Ten minutes into a convoy along what was unaffectionately called IED Alley, a roadside bomb went off underneath her vehicle, turning her into the first American woman ever to lose a limb in active combat. I was thrilled to call her across the line in Arizona in 2013 as only the second female above-the-knee amputee to finish an IRONMAN triathlon. And that was only the latest of a long line of extraordinary athletic accomplishments in the nine years since she was wounded.

But sometimes the trauma isn't visible. We're all familiar—vaguely familiar— with the condition known as PTSD, post-traumatic stress disorder. I say "vaguely" because very few of us, myself included, are aware of the array of specific symptoms lumped into this single diagnosis. It isn't necessarily restricted to people in combat situations. However, active duty service people are the ones most likely to suffer PTSD, because it's their job to walk into the heart of traumatic situations. Even people who grew up in a culture of hyper-realistic violent movies, television shows and video games are unprepared for the grisly realities of war. And for those who do manage to deal with many of war's horrors, the one thing even they can't fight very well is the emotional sucker punch of losing a comrade.

All of which makes me marvel at how my friend Mike Ergo, who lost 29 of his brothers in arms—17 during a single battle in Iraq—found a way to put his life back together after nearly ending it himself.

I became aware of Mike through the IRONMAN Foundation. He was going to be a featured athlete at the 2017 World Championship, so we met in Kona. By that time the 35-year-old had come to terms with his troubles and was willing to talk about it. This was my first real education in how devastating PTSD could be, and also how bad things had to get in order for a tough-ass Marine like Mike to succumb to it.

He didn't start out that tough. A talented musician, he joined the Corps straight out of high school in 2001 because he wanted to be in the storied USMC band. Before he was scheduled to report, 9/11 happened, and he didn't hesitate before switching to the infantry. He did a tour in Iraq, then went back for a second one in 2004, this time as an infantry team leader with the 1st Battalion, 8th Marines. That November, at all of 21 years old, he found himself smack in the middle of the month-long Second Battle of Fallujah, the fiercest and bloodiest fighting faced by U.S. Marines since the 1968 battle for Hue City in Vietnam.

Somewhere during that nonstop firefight, when he started to lose count of the people dying around him, Mike gave up hope of coming home alive. The odds were too stacked against him. But the rounds kept whizzing past his head and hitting other people. Once, when he descended a set of stairs in a house he'd been searching, he got to the bottom just as an enemy soldier was swinging a rifle in his direction and got off a shot. The insurgent missed. Mike fired back and didn't miss.

When the battle ended in late December, Mike had a small piece of shrapnel in his neck, but he was alive. Eighteen of his comrades had perished. Four others had been killed in earlier, separate actions.

Prior to returning home he was deployed to Abu Ghraib prison. There, the reality of all those friends he'd lost began to sink in, and he was wracked with survivor's guilt that seemed to shroud his very soul. On New Year's Eve, just a few weeks after emerging from Fallujah, he put his M-16 rifle into his mouth and his finger on the trigger. Later he'd wonder if he wouldn't have been better off had he pulled it.

Even after his return home it didn't end. One of his buddies drank himself to death. Another died of seizures caused by head wounds he'd suffered in Iraq. Another, he would learn much later, had been captured and tortured to death.

Having reconciled himself to never coming home, he had no idea how to move forward once he got there. He was reluctant to kill himself because of the suffering it would cause his family, especially his wife, Sarah, so he lived recklessly, on the chance that fate might do the job for him and cause the least damage to his surviving loved ones. He rode his motorcycle full throttle while roaring drunk, abused cocaine, and often woke up at home with no idea what had happened or how he'd gotten there. Once, when he was coming down some stairs, something about the light or the sounds or the time of day triggered a panic attack that set him down on the floor, his heart racing and his breath coming in gasps. It took a few minutes for him to realize that his mind had jumped back to the moment when he'd almost been shot coming down another set of stairs.

"I was angry, afraid, and confused," he said. "Some days were like waking up after surgery."

It was a hellish dilemma, trying to get the pain and the memories to stop without hurting his family, and the only way out was to numb himself with drugs, weed and alcohol. But after a while even that option was no longer open to him: Sarah's patience had run out and she put her foot down, telling Mike that he either stop relying on a bottle to suppress his sorrow or she was leaving. She wasn't trying to be cruel, but she wasn't going to stand by while he poisoned himself to death.

He knew she was right, and he wanted to get straight, but how? No amount of psychiatric talk therapy was going to lift him out of that black hole.

He opened up to a neighbor who happened to be a Vietnam vet. "You look and act like I did when I came back from 'Nam," the man said.

He didn't look like that now, Mike noticed. So when the neighbor urged him to get to the Veterans Affairs Center for counseling, he went. They suggested that working out, and doing it hard, had been helpful to a lot of vets.

So Mike tried it.

Mike liked it. Once he got into the swing of gym training and running, he discovered that working out gave him a comfortable feeling he hadn't known in years. It wasn't just the physical action, but the discipline required to do it well. It demanded prolonged concentration, and when he focused on exercising, he didn't have to focus on his memories. And in the quieter times, he didn't feel as anxious to avoid them, as he'd tried to do with booze. Gradually, he found himself able to think the unthinkable thoughts without slipping over the edge.

He got sober. He got therapy. He upped his physical activity. A friend bought him an entry to a half marathon as a birthday present. Mike said to me, "What a crappy present that was! You mean I had to get even fitter?" But he did it, and he also accepted a challenge from another Vietnam vet to swim 1.3 miles from Alcatraz to San Francisco with a group of vets.

Then he and Sarah took a vacation on the Big Island of Hawai'i in 2014. In October. During IRONMAN week. You know where this is going, right?

Bells went off in Mike's head. He wanted to do a triathlon. A big one. He signed up for IRONMAN 70.3 Vineman, then started figuring out how to become a cyclist. While training for Vineman (since rechristened IRONMAN 70.3 Santa Rosa), he did several shorter Olympic-distance triathlons: a 1.5k/0.9-mile swim, 40k/25-mile bike and 10k/6.2-mile swim. He liked them and decided that this was the sport for him.

As he worked at it, Mike began to understand that he'd been thinking outside of himself, afraid to go near the dark places. The harder he trained, the less afraid he became, and he dared to look inside himself more and more. Even better, he felt safe when he was on a triathlon course, safer than any other place he could think of.

It became a self-*constructive* cycle of enjoying the effort, training to keep it going, and getting his mind back to some semblance of normalcy.

He'd also discovered what a lot of people with PTSD come to realize, that structure and routine are powerful remedies. "My condition was like a broken mirror," he told me, "pieces of myself shattered on the floor and no clue where to start to put them all back together."

Sticking to a training schedule was that start. After a while, even nerves didn't scare him anymore. He used to run away from himself every time he felt anxiety threatening to close in, but he learned that some anxieties can be healthy, like the kind you get waiting for the starting cannon to go off. Your heart beating fast and your breath getting a little short doesn't necessarily mean that anything's wrong. It can just mean that you care about what's about to happen and are excited to be where you are.

Mike did other IRONMAN 70.3 races, including Oceanside, where the Marine base at Camp Pendleton hosts part of the course. Then he kicked it up a notch and completed the full-distance IRONMAN Santa Rosa in 2017. Later that year he came to Kona.

Mike believes that IRONMAN saved his life. "Maybe another sport might have helped me," he told me, "but this one had a special pull on me and made me want to try." For him, healing is all about actively moving forward, pushing himself and having a purpose. Once he'd taken off the uniform, his sense of purpose had vanished, and now he was getting it back.

But it wasn't just about racing; it was about racing for a reason. As Mike began healing he looked for ways to help others do the same. He was inspired by an episode that would prove to be a defining moment in his life. A Gold Star mother, who'd lost a son in Iraq, came up to him at a charity function and said how happy she was that he was home safe.

"Here's a mom whose son was killed," he said, wonder in his voice, "and she's telling me she's happy *I'm* home?" Her kind-heartedness and lack of self-pity affected him deeply. He soon became actively involved in representing Gold Star families and raising funds for them.

He also went to work for the VA, counseling soldiers who came back broken and lost. And, I'm proud to call him a fellow ambassador of the IRONMAN

Foundation.

Mike had a special race jersey made up that lists the names of every one of the 29 buddies he lost in Iraq—21 from the 2001 deployment and eight afterwards—and the dates they died. It's a stark, sobering piece of cloth; eighteen of the deaths occurred within a span of two weeks. When he wears it he feels them near, not in some abstract way but as a palpable presence.

Melissa Ergo

Mike raced IRONMAN Santa Rosa in 2018 and carried a large American flag during all 26.2 miles of the marathon. At the finish line he handed it to the mother, wife and daughter of his dear friend, Cpl. Josh Kynoch, who was killed in action in October 2005. Josh's daughter, Savannah, then thirteen, was three days old when Josh was killed.

Mike felt Josh watching, and he remembers exactly what he said to his friend's daughter: "Savannah, when my daughter was born, the shockwave of love hit me so hard. I didn't know it was possible to love someone that much until I saw her. I know your daddy felt the same way and loved you just as much when he saw you. Please know that he still loves you and he is still with you."

Amen to that.

I'M ABLE TO TELL MIKE'S STORY in some detail because we became friends and, over time, he was willing to share the details. But his experience was by no means unique.

I connected with a career soldier named Robert Mann. He was deployed to war zones 35 times over an 11-year period. As he put it himself, "You could say I picked up some demons over that time." Not surprisingly, he took up drinking as a way to cope.

He did what he could to stay fit, but a military parachuting accident, years of wearing heavy body armor and the simple passage of time took their toll. To deal with the constant pain he added pills and upped his drinking.

In 2015 he met a woman who tried to introduce him to endurance sports. He thought she was crazy, along with everyone else who did that stuff. But he really liked her so he gave it a whirl. Like Mike, he discovered that the intense training gave him some peace, and having a difficult goal to focus on allowed him to have what he calls a "mental reset." In 2017 he raced a sprint tri, an international distance, IRONMAN 70.3 Eagleman and, finally, the full-distance in Mont-Tremblant, Canada.

In 2018 he went on another deployment, but didn't let it stop his training. He raced Eagleman again, besting his earlier time by almost thirty minutes, and IRONMAN Maryland.

Robert still has to deal with his PTSD, but he's doing it without drinking or pain pills. He married the crazy woman, and they're going to be honeymooning in Kona in 2019 because she qualified for the World Championship.

Neither Mike nor Robert are "cured." Mike discovered this when he tried to take a break from training after his 2017 IRONMAN finish. It wasn't long before the dark clouds started to gather, but he drove them away by resuming his training.

They're not cured, but what they've done is find a healthier way to cope. How great would it be if others who made sacrifices on behalf of our country and communities and found themselves in similar straits were inspired enough by these stories to try a better way out of their troubles?

IRONMAN Lake Placid – July, 2012

Lake Placid is one of the most beautiful venues on the IRONMAN circuit, five hours and a world away from New York City. Nestled in the heart of the Adirondack Mountains, the town boasts fewer than 3,000 residents but has hosted two Winter Olympic Games, the last one in 1980. The two ski jump towers are still standing and active, and are visible for miles as they rise high above lush alpine scenery.

IRONMAN Lake Placid serves up a truly unique thrill at the finish: The race ends on the same speed skating oval where American Eric Heiden won more gold medals than all but two *nations* in the 1980 Games. It's no wonder that a lot of triathletes have raced here multiple times.

One of those repeat competitors was Chris McDonnell. I met him, his wife Lynn, and their two children a few days before the 2012 event. They were a delightful family from a small town in Connecticut, excited as all get out to be there. But the real charmer in the group was the little girl, all of six years old, bubbly and vivacious, with a smile that could warm a small planet. Within two minutes I could tell that this little kid was wise beyond her years, with plenty of sass and spirit.

Lynn McDonnell

She stepped up without hesitation and said, "Mr. Reilly, would you take a picture with me and my brother?"

"I will if you tell me your name," I answered.

"Grace McDonnell!" she announced, and stuck out her hand.

As I shook it, I leaned over to her mom, Lynn. "She seems a lot older than six."

Lynn rolled her eyes heavenward. "Tell me about it," she said, but with a proud smile. Grace was clearly one of those totally-worth-it handfuls.

While Lynn set up the shot, I asked Grace why they were here.

She pointed at Chris. "My Dad's gonna be an IRONMAN tomorrow, and when he's done, you're gonna say, Chris McDonnell—" She raised her arms above her head "—you are an IRONMAN!"

When she lowered her arms, Lynn snapped the photo.

"Just like you did last time!" Grace added.

"I finished before nightfall, twelve hours and change," Chris explained as he shook his head. It was about 30 minutes slower than his time the year before. "But all Grace remembers is you calling me across the line. She's been talking about it all year."

"Okay, you got your wish," Lynn said to her daughter. "Now what do you say to Mr. Reilly?"

"Thank-You-Mister-Reilly," she forced out through clenched teeth, with comical annoyance at the forced etiquette.

We all laughed, and before they walked off I made sure to give Grace's brother, Jack, a high-five. He hadn't said much, and it had to be tough for an older brother to sit outside the spotlight shining so brightly on his little sister.

I saw the family several times during race day, and I had a special shout out for Chris when he came out of the water. But after nine Lake Placid finishes in a row, this just wasn't his day, and he had to drop out.

I remember hoping that Grace wasn't too disappointed. She was young enough to only remember two or three of her father's races and had no experience of his failing to finish.

She had a keen understanding of how much IRONMAN meant to her dad and, from endless conversations around the dinner table throughout the year and watching how hard he trained, she'd become a great fan of the sport. Lynn told me that a week before the race Grace would already have packed her little travel knapsack, making sure she didn't forget anything so the trip would be perfect. Lynn would buy the kids new clothes and sneakers before every race, and that meant unpacking and repacking the knapsack, which was fine because it gave Grace something to do to help manage her eager anticipation.

Grace also shared her father's dream that he would one day compete in the IRONMAN World Championship. Unlike the other races on the circuit, you can't just sign up and go. It's a true championship, and to make sure that only the best participate, there's a strict qualification protocol in place: You have to finish high atop the leaderboard in your age group at another IRONMAN race in order to gain entry. But, just in case there might be an exception in the rules somewhere, Lynn wrote a letter to IRONMAN requesting an entry for her husband.

Chris was diligent in pursuit of that goal. He trained hard, and his race times kept improving. With the strong support of his family and a little patience, he was pretty sure he could do it.

For her seventh birthday that November Grace asked for, and got, a cake with a purple peace sign and polka dots. Like Grace herself, the cake was both whimsical and serious.

December 14, 2012

As did much of America on that day, I watched, transfixed, as the events in Newtown, Connecticut, played out on network news.

A vile, loathsome creature had emerged from the bowels of hell, walked into the Sandy Hook Elementary School and begun shooting. He started in a hallway, then entered a classroom where a teacher and a therapist caring for a special needs student had heard the shots and herded fifteen kids to the back of the room. The two adults were trying to hide the kids in a bathroom when the shooter walked in and slaughtered them all. He went to another classroom, where a teacher put herself between him and her students. He shot her, along with four children she was trying to protect. Then he saw a teacher's aide who had thrown herself over one of the kids on the floor. He killed them both.

By the time the carnage ended, six adults and twenty children were dead. All of the kids were either six or seven years old.

Being a parent myself, the thoughts and feelings that were running through my mind were probably much the same as those of every other parent watching the horror unfold. Even with live images coming through the television screen, it was still incomprehensible.

S HORTLY AFTERWARDS, I got a call from Tom Begg. He's one of three highly accomplished brothers who are also ardent IRONMAN enthusiasts who like to compete against each other and talk loads of trash while doing it.

There are a ton of wonderful stories about these great guys. In 2009, Tom drove five hours from Westchester, NY, to Lake Placid to pick up his registration packet, then drove five hours back so he could participate in a four-mile charity swim in Long Island Sound *the day before* the IRONMAN race, then drove back to Lake Placid to compete.

Brother Bill is an emergency room physician. Once during a local 5K he turned back to see how his kids were doing. His son told him someone had fallen and wasn't moving. Bill ran over to the man, found him unresponsive, and began administering CPR, saving his life. Later that same year, a runner fell right in front of him. Once again Bill's resuscitative skills saved a life.

Brother Michael was a whole story in himself. He ran his very first triathlon *three weeks* before competing in, and finishing, the 2009 IRONMAN Lake Placid. The whole family is so into it: Bill's wife Leah has competed, as well as his daughter Erin when she was 18, and so did Tom's daughter Caity, who started a triathlon club at Harvard.

It was always fun hearing from these guys, and I was glad to see Tom's name on the caller ID that day.

After I answered the phone and said hello, Tom said my name. It wasn't with the usual upward inflection indicating a question to confirm who answered the call, meaning "Is this Mike?"

It was just "Mike," a single dead, flat syllable.

I knew instantly that something was wrong. Had something happened to one of his brothers? That hit close to home for me; I'm one of three brothers myself, which is part of the reason I felt close to the Begg boys. "Talk to me," I said, bracing for the worst.

There was a pause. Maybe it was just the normal delay of a transcontinental satellite connection.

"Bill was on duty in the ER when they brought the kids in from Sandy Hook," Tom said.

So that was it, I thought. *Bill's traumatized. Must have been overwhelming. He needs someone to talk to. That's fine; I'm more than happy to call him and…*

"Mike…Grace McDonnell is gone."

THERE ARE BAD THINGS that happen in life that we accept as inevitable. The death of a parent, for example, or of an ailing friend. It's sad, sometimes bittersweet, but it's part of the natural order of things and we usually have a long time to prepare. It happens, we mourn, we move on. Very soon, we're able to remember the lost loved one with fondness, and can talk easily about the good memories without re-living the trauma of the passing.

But there's nothing natural about the loss of a child. It's an aberration, an abomination, a punch-to-the-stomach scream that the natural order of things has gone badly off the rails. There is no place in God's own universe where losing a child makes any kind of sense.

When Tom told me about Grace, I went numb. It was a defense mechanism kicking in, because I have kids of my own and my first instinct was to imagine how I'd feel if I'd lost one of them. But I couldn't do it, because the mind just reels at something that abhorrent. Even later I wasn't able to summon up any notion of how deep the pain must be for Grace's parents and brother, what it must be like, in that twilight moment between sleep and wakefulness, to find yourself praying, *Dear God, please tell me it was all a dream…*and then your eyes open and it wasn't. How do you even get out of bed?

As the shock wore off, Chris, Lynn and Jack were all I could think about. How were they dealing with the searing grief of losing Grace? Was it worse because it wasn't due to some disease or accident or other unconscious force but to a deranged madman who made a *choice* to end their daughter's life?

I knew that the loss of a child often caused the surviving family to fall apart. Usually it was because of some guilt, justified or not, self-inflicted or imposed by a damaged and blame-seeking spouse. *Why did you turn your back when the kids were swimming? Why did I let her go to that party? How could we have missed the signs?*

But there was nothing of that for the McDonnells. The only thing they were guilty of was sending their kid off to school that morning. Would that make it easier for them to find a way to carry on?

And I didn't know how to deal with the McDonnell family. I wanted to be helpful and supportive, I wanted to just talk to them, but I had no idea how. Was it okay to call them? Was there a decent interval before I did? Should I ask questions, were some questions off limits, should I stick to the weather, should I not get in touch at all…?

The last part wasn't really an option. I had to at least know how they were doing, even if there was nothing I could do. But that angelic little face kept popping up in my mind, as it must have been doing in theirs, and I was lost.

There was no rule book. But to their everlasting credit, the McDonnells wrote their own. Even in the midst of their unimaginable suffering, they knew they had to make it okay for their friends to still be friends, to see to it that the people around them didn't have to walk on eggshells.

At the time, I wasn't sure that I'd be able to live a normal life if something like that had happened to me. To this day I still don't know, but seeing how the McDonnell family found a way to climb out of that bottomless well of sorrow rekindled my faith in the resiliency of the human spirit.

And I found myself deeply grateful that they–and I–were a part of the IRONMAN family.

Chris and Lynn knew better than to spend energy putting up a false front. They were broken—badly—and a stiff upper lip wasn't going to fix anything.

They were also acutely aware that Jack had lost a piece of his parents along with his little sister. He was too young to pick up the shards alone and was dependent on them to somehow help him find a way to have something close to a normal life.

An important part of how the family tried to move forward was to not give up on their routines and their plans. They also didn't want to avoid thinking or talking about Grace, so they tried to incorporate her memory into whatever they did, and to do as much as possible as a family.

Grace had always wanted to visit Notre Dame, so the three of them did just that. She loved music and art, so Lynn found a way to help art students.

And then there was IRONMAN. Grace hadn't known a time when her father wasn't training for a race or competing. To her, it was as central to her family life as watching television or going to the movies or having meals together. IRONMAN wasn't just what Daddy did; it was part of how they lived, and their year revolved around the annual pilgrimage to Lake Placid.

Chris resumed his training, and while it was somewhat therapeutic, for his family as well as Chris, it just wasn't the same not having his daughter to share it with. His heart wasn't fully in it.

Then Lynn got an idea. Grace and her father had shared a dream of him one day competing at the Big One, the IRONMAN World Championship in Kailua-Kona, Hawai'i. Grace was so convinced it was going to happen that she had a grass hula skirt and a Hawaiian lei hanging on her bedroom wall. They hadn't heard from the IRONMAN organization about Lynn's letter–hundreds of such pleas flood the office each year–but that hadn't deterred Grace in the slightest. It was going to happen; she was sure of it.

When Chris started back into training, Lynn discovered that her brother-in-law had a connection to WTC, the World Triathlon Corporation. Messages flew, and a few days later Lynn got a phone call.

"Is this Lynn McDonnell?" the caller said.

Lynn confirmed that it was indeed she, and asked who was calling.

"This is Andrew Messick."

Andrew Messick? IRONMAN CEO?

"Let me ask you something straight out," Messick said after Lynn found her voice and confirmed that he'd reached the right party. "We'd like your husband to be one of our special interest stories for the NBC show. Does he think he's ready to compete in Kona? Is it too soon?"

It took about a nanosecond for Lynn to gather her wits and respond. "Yes, he's ready!"

"How can he be so sure?"

"Oh, he doesn't even know it yet, but he is!"

That got them both laughing.

And Chris was in.

THERE'S AN OBSCURE LITTLE MOVIE starring Robert Duvall and James Earl Jones called "A Family Thing." Duvall's character has a line in it that's stuck with me since I saw the film over twenty years ago: *Happiness is having something to look forward to.*

Lynn's call with Andrew Messick marked a turning point for the family. Here was something exciting and new they could coalesce around, and Grace would be as much a part of it as her parents and brother.

Lynn tried to come up with a special way to let Chris know the good news. She settled on a surprise box containing the hula skirt and lei, along with a note signed "Peace. Love. Grace."

The invitation to race in Hawai'i had come with a condition, though, which was standard procedure to make sure competitors were ready for the grueling Kona course: Chris had to complete an IRONMAN race that same year before he'd be allowed to register for the World Championship.

The choice of venue was a no-brainer: He'd be going back to Lake Placid.

Chris did his best to get ready, but when we met in Lake Placid in July, which was very emotional for me, he said his training had been difficult. He'd had a lot of hours by himself and couldn't stop his thoughts from drifting back to his lost daughter. He had a successful race, though, and there were brief smiles from Lynn and Jack as I called him across the line, but they were fleeting. Jack in particular seemed to be pulling inside himself, and I found myself praying for this family to make it, to be okay.

Things were much better by the time they got to Kona. Chris had a good race, and I watched as he and Lynn hugged fiercely at the finish line. Then I noticed Jack standing a little off to the side, by himself. I barely had time to think about that when Lynn, without letting go of her husband, put her arm out towards her son. Jack rushed in and joined the embrace. Finish line personnel, who normally hustle athletes out of the area in order to keep things flowing, stood back and let them have their moment.

I had a pretty good notion that the family was going to be okay.

"IRONMAN FILLED A VOID FOR US," Lynn told me recently. "Without it, I don't know if we would have made it."

She said that, with every race since that awful day, she got a piece of her husband back. IRONMAN 2018 in Lake Placid was the best of all.

"It was a happy event for us," Lynn said." She's discovered that she now sheds tears of happiness instead of sadness when Chris starts a race.

"I felt like I had an extra set of legs," Chris said. "Like Grace was right there helping me through the toughest parts of the course."

It gives Chris and Lynn a little bit of peace to know that some good things managed to emerge from their daughter's passing and the family's ongoing

association with the IRONMAN family. The most gratifying is that it has brought them into contact with people who have become close friends. Among these are the Begg brothers. Although they, like Chris, were IRONMAN athletes and lived relatively close to the McDonnells, they'd never met.

And there are small things. At the race in 2018, someone the McDonnells didn't know at all left a bag on Chris's bike. It turns out that I *did* know who it was: a New York State trooper named Kristen Kastrinos, who'd lost her mother earlier that year. There was a state police t-shirt and hat inside the bag.

"We're very alive as a family," Lynn told me before we all had to leave Lake Placid, "and all our memories now are good ones."

I could see in her eyes that this wasn't just wishful thinking. This was the real thing.

To this day, at every race I announce, I wear the wristband that Lynn gave me.

It says, "Practice Aloha" on one side, and "Grace" on the other.

CHAPTER 4

I n the last chapter, I talked about a few of the times I've seen how an intense undertaking like an IRONMAN race can aid in coming back from a potentially crippling emotional trauma. It shouldn't surprise you to learn that it can do the same for physical injuries and other life-threatening conditions as well.

The benefits of exercise and motivation are well-documented critical factors in the healing process. There are some wonderful illustrative stories throughout history, like the one about Glenn Cunningham. His legs were badly burned in an explosion that took the life of his older brother. The doctors wanted to amputate both legs but the eight-year-old Cunningham was so upset at the prospect that his parents relented. Good call: He went on to become a teammate of Jesse Owens at the 1936 Berlin Olympic Games, winning a silver medal in the process, and he held world records in three different running events. The track and field world considers him one of the greatest American milers of all time.

(Interesting side note: My dad, Don Reilly, was the fastest high school miler in Ohio in 1932 and was a teammate of Jesse Owens at Ohio State University in 1933.)

IRONMAN is a very young sport, all of 40 years old as of this writing, but it has more than its fair share of stories every bit as miraculous as Glenn Cunningham's.

B RIAN BOYLE WAS ABOUT AS PERFECT an example of a fair-haired boy that you could ever conjure up. Movie-star good looks, All-American Scholar, star athlete in a handful of sports, a Norman Rockwell family…the works. This kid was headed for the moon and it seemed nothing could stop him. The Hallmark Channel would have salivated over the movie rights.

A few months after high school graduation in 2004, while he was driving home from swim practice, a dump truck slammed into him at an intersection. First responders radioed it in as a fatal accident, because there was no way anyone could have survived it. But, when they finally managed to reach Brian deep in the mangled wreckage, they found a weak pulse and he was breathing. They airlifted him out to a special shock-trauma hospital, because that's what the rules said you had to do if they were breathing, but nobody on the scene thought for a minute it was worth the gas in the chopper.

Later in the OR, one of the trauma surgeon's colleagues came up next to him, took one look and whispered in his ear, "What's wrong with you? You're operating on a cadaver." And he didn't even know this was already the kid's fifth round of surgery.

Brian had been slammed so hard that his heart had been pushed completely into the right side of his chest. He'd lost well over half his blood by the time they got him out. A 15-year veteran of the ER would say later that it was the worst non-fatal trauma he'd ever seen.

"As long as he has a pulse," the surgeon answered, "he's alive and I'm operating."

Bravura attitude, for sure, but he didn't sound very hopeful. Every doctor on the case knew that Brian could die at any second. Technically, he did; eight times over the course of his treatment and recovery. At one point a priest was summoned to give him last rites. This is not the stuff of hope.

The pain was so bad that Brian was put into an induced coma. He stayed that way for two months, during which time he underwent 14 operations, 36 blood transfusions and 13 plasma treatments. When he finally was brought back to consciousness, he'd lost a hundred pounds and was so completely paralyzed he couldn't even blink. But he could hear, and what he heard were words like "vegetable" and "nursing home" being tossed about.

His first instinct was to bring the same drive he'd put into his academic and athletic careers into getting his life back. His family was behind him all the way—how could they not be—but they and the physicians harbored serious doubts about the results he was likely to achieve.

This is the part where the Hallmark camera crew would have packed up and left, because the first two months post-coma, to put it mildly, didn't go well. In awful pain and making little progress, all the gung-ho now knocked out of him, Brian prayed to God to let him die and end the terrible suffering.

As he regained some ability to communicate, his parents learned how he felt and could barely stand to watch his agony. At the same time, they couldn't bear the thought of losing him. After a heartfelt plea from them to keep trying—"You're all we've got" were the exact words—Brian promised to give it a while longer.

I can't even imagine what the ensuing weeks and months must have been like for him. Physical therapy was excruciating, and it was all in service of nothing more ambitious than just getting himself to the point where he could at least move around on his own.

He put everything he had into rehab. Blinking, squeezing a ball, shaking a hand… each of those was a breakthrough. Combing his own hair was a monumental achievement. Standing up in a walker the first time? Like scaling Everest with one hand and no oxygen.

Slowly at first, and then faster, his iron will began winning out over the posted odds. The more progress he made, the harder he worked. Don't ask me how, because I don't know all the details, but a year after the accident, Brian started his freshman year in college. Absurdly, he joined the swim team. Hampered by his damaged lungs, he could only pull himself through laps for twenty or thirty minutes at a time, but he kept at it.

He got stronger. His breathing improved. And that's when he decided he needed a great big goal to work toward because these puny little advances were no longer supplying the motivation his outsized ambition demanded.

"Dad," he said one day, "I'm going to do IRONMAN."

"Sure, kid. What's IRONMAN?"

Brian told him.

Yeah, right. Dad didn't think *anyone* could do an IRONMAN race, much less his badly battered son who just managed to draw a full breath after a year of rehab. *But if it gives you something to shoot for…*

Fast-forward two years to the 2007 World Championship. I became aware of Brian a few weeks before the race when I was sent a list of the special stories that NBC would cover. Each year a few people are singled out for coverage, much like the "Up close and personal" features during the Olympics. I've read a lot of these, and some are truly awe-inspiring, but this one hit me especially hard. It was also a little unsettling, because I couldn't help wonder what it would be like if what happened to Brian were to happen to my own son, Andy. One minute you're a strapping young athlete, and the next, no one even knows if you're going to live. Or what your life will be like even if you do. What was this kid who'd been in a coma two years ago doing on the start line of the toughest endurance event in the world?

During race week I made it a point to meet Brian and his parents, Garth and JoAnne. I wanted to understand how they'd been able to cope with what had happened to their son. How were they able to maintain the necessary positive attitude around him when they were being eaten up inside? Would they even be willing to talk about everything that had happened?

When I finally met the family, I was immediately drawn to them. Despite the intense media attention and the filming and the interviews, they seemed so genuine, and so wide-eyed awestruck about being in Kona. They were also very open to talking about what had happened to them.

It was also obvious that, despite having learned the details of what constituted an IRONMAN triathlon, they really had very little comprehension of what it was going to be like once they got to the Big Island. They hadn't even gotten around to buying any of the IRONMAN-branded clothes everyone else was sporting, just these down-home cutoff shirts that they'd obviously de-sleeved themselves. I tried to make sure that, when they were with just me, they could relax a little and be themselves. And I also wanted to make sure that they weren't too disappointed when this naïve novice didn't even finish the swim before the cutoff because, well, who did Brian think he was kidding?

Brian wasn't troubled by any of the attention and chaos. He connected well with everyone he met, always a big smile on his welcoming face. It was easy to see the attitude that had played such a big part in saving his life. But you need a lot more than a by-golly 'tude to get through an IRONMAN triathlon, especially the tough one in Kona.

He made the swim cutoff. I got reports during the bike and run legs and relayed them to Garth and JoAnne. I would announce special interest story updates to the crowd, but when they were about Brian, I spoke directly to Garth and JoAnne. I still remember the hopeful but confused look on their faces. I don't think they had a clue about what was happening out there, which was just as well or they would have worried a lot more. I've seen parents of perfectly healthy athletes drive themselves nuts when their kids were out on the course. Imagine what the Boyles would have been going through if they truly understood what it was like out there on the lava fields.

I got some reports that Brian was walking when he should have been running and might not make the cutoff at the pace he was holding. I didn't tell his folks because, well, what the heck: Let them be optimistic for another hour before the hammer fell. But after a while a spotter called in to tell me Brian was back up on his toes.

Was it possible...?

It was. He hit the line with time to spare. Mom JoAnne was so emotional seeing her son that I think I had her more in mind than Brian when I called him across. What an extraordinary, life-affirming triumph that finish was. The three of them hugged so tightly I thought one of them would explode.

It was one of the greatest comebacks in sports history, and I remember the thought that ran through my mind as I watched: *I hope Brian continues to be part of our sport. He's too big a champion for us to let him walk away.*

I got my wish. This was not a one-and-done. Brian was completely hooked, and he went on to do all kinds of endurance events, including a bunch more IRONMAN and 70.3 races. He graduated summa cum laude from St. Mary's College in Maryland and went on to pursue a Master's at Johns Hopkins. He's also done a great deal of public service work, most notably with the American Red Cross, for which he's a spokesman.

I made a promise to myself to stay in touch with this family. I was heading up the sales department of a major endurance sports company at the time. The summer after Brian's remarkable achievement at the World Championship, I'd been thinking of ways to motivate the sales force at our annual conference when an idea hit me. I decided to show them a 13-minute video of what Brian had gone through and achieved. I introduced it by telling the sales force that, whenever they felt down, they should think about someone who was *really* down and pulled himself out of it.

Halfway through the video, I could hear sniffles around the room, and by the time it was over, even some of the macho guys (remember, this was a sports company) had given in and were crying.

But showing the video wasn't the whole of my plan. I spoke for a few minutes about how much Brian's story had affected me, how motivating it had been whenever I'd been tempted to get down on myself, and how blessed I felt to have been able to get to know the Boyle family.

"I know you've seen a lot of motivational videos over the years from some pretty famous and amazing people," I said. "But no matter how inspirational it might have been, the effect isn't the same as meeting those people and being able to spend a little time together. I'd like you all to have that experience."

Now they were looking at me, like *What the hell is he talking about?*

"Instead of just hearing his story through a video," I went on, "I want you to hear it from Brian and his parents, Garth and JoAnne."

And with that I opened the door near the front of the room and the three of them walked in. The reaction from the group was explosive. They stood up, clapped, stomped and shouted. Some were so overwhelmed they were visibly shaking and their shouts came out choked. The management team was thrilled, too. They had no idea that I'd flown the Boyles out from Baltimore and they were moved beyond words.

After things settled down, the family took the stage for a no-holds-barred Q&A with the audience. They were frank, open and gracious, well aware of the impact their story could have on people and only too willing to share whatever they could. Questions from the audience flew fast and furious. I had spoken to the Boyles a number of times since the race, but had not seen them again until now. As I listened to them chat with the audience, it seemed to me that their ability to push past the worst of odds had something to do with their humbleness. The rapport they quickly established with the audience was just amazing to see. The sales people seemed to revere them at the same time they wanted to bring them into their family.

Brian and his folks stayed with us the whole day, and joined us on a bay cruise in the evening. They treated everybody like old friends and the sales people just couldn't get enough of them. To this day ex-colleagues of mine from that company tell me that the inspiration they got that day is with them still.

I stayed in touch with the Boyles, and I've brought Brian across many an IRONMAN finish line since his debut in 2007. His commitment to the American

Red Cross has only deepened over time, and he's also written two books. He's married now, and has a beautiful little girl named Clara. This past summer, he and his wife Pamela, a pediatric nurse practitioner, wrote a children's book together called *Swim Bark Run*. They sent a signed copy for my four-year-old grandson and the kid is crazy about it. The first time I read it to him, I got a weird kind of glow. I was trying to get the words out, but at the same time couldn't stop thinking about this teenager who almost died and went on to extraordinary accomplishment. Brian and Pamela's children's book was already inspiring my grandson to read, and it wouldn't surprise me if it also inspired him to become an IRONMAN someday.

P.S. I started writing this chapter a week before IRONMAN Maryland on September 29, 2018. I finished it on the plane home on the 30th, the day after I called Brian across and shouted out his 11:06 finish time. It was a good race, but not his best. At IRONMAN Florida in 2010 he went 10:14. For those of you not familiar with amateur performances for this race, that's a very, very fast time...even for someone who hasn't come back from the dead.

I ran into the Boyle clan a few days before the race. It was more emotional than I was prepared for; seeing Brian is always like running into a long-lost son. We talked, laughed (I never miss an opportunity to kid them about those cutoff shirts), reminisced, hugged a lot. As always, they made me feel a part of the family. Even little Clara showered me with kisses.

At the awards banquet a few days later, it was Brian and his family I was thinking about when I spoke the final words of the ceremony: "Isn't it amazing that IRONMAN beats you up like nothing else in the world, yet it seems to heal us at the same time?"

Boyle Family

I USED THE WORD *MIRACULOUS* BEFORE, but that was a bit of hyperbole. As remarkable as Brian's story is, there's little in it that runs counter to what we know about how the body heals. What was truly remarkable was the strength of his resolve.

But I have no problem using *miraculous* when it comes to Jim Howley. To this day, medical science still hasn't gotten around to figuring out why this guy is alive, much less explaining how he was able to do an IRONMAN race.

Jim was diagnosed HIV positive in the early 1980s. As we near 2020 it's hard for us to recall what that meant back then, so let me refresh your memory: It meant that you were going to die. The presence of the human immunodeficiency virus in your bloodstream inevitably led to acquired immune deficiency syndrome, otherwise known as AIDS. "Immune deficiency" refers to the inability of your body to fight off infections. Catch pneumonia, contract tuberculosis or develop skin cancer or some other serious but otherwise non-fatal "opportunistic" illness, and you were defenseless against it. It might take a year, it might take ten, but you didn't have a chance.

It didn't matter if you had a boatload of money and the best doctors in the world, either. AIDS claimed Rock Hudson, Freddy Mercury, Arthur Ashe, Liberace, Isaac Asimov and countless others. There was simply nothing anyone could do about it.

So when he contracted HIV, Jim Howley had no reason to believe that he might be the first person on earth to beat the reaper. He prepared to die, and his strategy for dealing with it was to draw up his will, pick the music for his funeral and spiral into a deep depression that he treated with drugs and alcohol. Watching friends in New York and L.A. die by the dozens, it didn't take him long to get up to 220 pounds and two packs of cigarettes a day. After all, if he was going to die anyway, what was the point of trying to take care of himself?

On August 21, 1989, he ran into a friend. She was sweating profusely after a ten-mile run and told Jim she was training for something called a triathlon. He'd never met anybody who'd run ten miles, and was impressed, but dismissed this triathlon thing as a curiosity. Besides, he had other things to worry about.

The next day he was diagnosed with "full-blown" AIDS. He'd known it was coming but the news was devastating nonetheless. He was told that his T-cell count was nose-diving and he had 18 months to live, two years if he was lucky. He was 28 years old.

"On paper," Howley said, "I was a corpse."

For some reason, though, the news sparked a bit of a rebellion against his strategy of self-destruction. He wondered if there wasn't something meaningful he could accomplish before he departed, maybe check off something on his bucket list.

Which is when the conversation the day before popped into his head. Should he try a triathlon?

"I couldn't run, swim or bike," he thought, "but why not give it a shot?" After all, aside from the superhuman effort it would take in his condition, what was the downside?

According to his doctors, there might be a pretty significant downside. AIDS sufferers had a terrible time trying to maintain muscle mass. Their appetite dwindled to near zero. If they engaged in intense exercise, that might eat further into their muscle mass. Such effort could also further compromise the immune system and damage an already fragile body in any number of other ways.

It might do any of those things. Or it might not. Back in 1989, nobody had any idea what they were talking about. It was all pure speculation, because there weren't a lot of people with AIDS doing marathons to provide the data. But AIDS was, to a large extent, a disease of wasting; maybe high levels of exercise could increase the appetite and lead to the building of new muscle mass? Some doctors held the view that, if an AIDS patient wanted to try to maintain a high fitness level, might as well go ahead and give it a shot.

Jim gave it a shot. At his first attempt at a jog, he couldn't make it around the block. Eight months after the diagnosis, he competed in a triathlon. Two months after that, he ran a marathon. Over the next four years he did 35 more triathlons and seven marathons and had 180 pounds of solid muscle on his six-foot frame.

During this time, the mid-1990s, AIDS treatment entered its "cautiously optimistic" stage; experimental drug protocols began seeing some success. And Magic Johnson's notable lack of deterioration following his AIDS diagnosis in 1991 lent some credence to the theory that strenuous and prolonged physical activity might also play a large role in staving off the disease's progression.

A normal T-cell count is between 400 and 1,700 per microliter of blood. T-cells are a lymphocyte critical to the body's immune response. Below 200 and you have

AIDS. At the time of his diagnosis, Jim's count was 50, and at one point it dipped to 3. By 1995 it had rebounded to 260 and, to the astonishment of his physicians and the researchers in the drug trials he participated in, the AIDS virus had become undetectable in his bloodstream.

That didn't mean it wasn't there. It was, but at such small concentrations no test could find it. It also didn't mean he was cured. There was no cure in 1995, and there still isn't. Try to think about what all of this meant 25 years ago when the AIDS pandemic was still terrifying people all over the world.

Jim was a true pioneer. He'd stumbled onto a strategy to save his own life and was riding it as hard as he could. Which is why, in 1996, he decided to push in all his chips and accept an opportunity to compete in the IRONMAN World Championship. He'd be the first person in history with AIDS to do it. I'm willing to bet he was the first person with AIDS to even *think* about it.

We met in Kona and I liked the guy right off. I did a public interview with him during race week and I was smitten by his self-confidence, even though there was some nervousness and hesitancy in the crowd of onlookers. They were likely thinking the same thing I was: *How much longer is he going to live?* That made his uplifting tone and positive attitude all the more impressive. It wasn't a put-on, either, or some sort of self-preserving defense mechanism. This was a man who felt he was in control of his life.

I was also impressed with his matter-of-fact approach toward talking about having AIDS. I think that had a lot to do with him being buoyed by the dramatic rise in his T-cell count since he'd started doing endurance events. (After the race I would ask him if he planned on coming back to do it again. He laughed and said, "I go month-by-month, so we'll see." He was optimistic but not unrealistic.)

I spoke to Jim several times during the week. The race itself aside, it seemed to me that he was awed with the whole IRONMAN scene and having the time of his life. But I don't think his dire situation could ever have been far from his mind. I try to remember now how, despite his extraordinary progress, things were still so terribly uncertain for him back then. There was no precedent for what was happening and no way to predict how it would eventually turn out. His disease was a time bomb with a fuse of unknown delay.

Something else was on my mind, though, speaking of "back then." There was still a huge social stigma around AIDS. People thought you could get it from kissing or touching (you can't), and since few sufferers were willing to be open about it, there was a lot of suspicion and fear along with the misconceptions. The media's treatment of it was, understandably, relentlessly negative and often even accusatory. (The Tom Hanks film *Philadelphia* tried to highlight some of the misconceptions. It came out in 1993, the same year that tennis great Arthur Ashe died after contracting AIDS from a blood transfusion.)

So I really had no idea how I was going to handle it when Jim came across the finish line. Do I just call his name, do I tell his story, do I gloss it over by referring to some unnamed "medical issue?" I didn't want to ignore or hide it. It was too significant and historic, and it would hold great meaning and significance for a lot of people. But how would the crowd react if I blurted it out over the PA?

I decided not to decide. I pride myself on being able to read a crowd and know what's going to work and what isn't. I trusted that I would know what to do when the time came.

In 1996 we didn't have announcer timing mats to let us know who was about to come into the finish area. Spotters would radio race numbers into us and we'd type them into laptops to get the names. It so happened that I was up in the booth looking down Ali'i Drive through binoculars when Jim came into view. I recognized him and didn't need to bother with a look-up. That gave me more time to talk about him.

And talk about him I did. There was really no reason not to, and I trusted the audience. I told them about Jim's diagnosis years ago and how miraculous it was that he was even alive, much less finishing IRONMAN right before their eyes. If I'd had any misgivings about their reaction, they vanished just a few seconds after I started speaking. I doubt they even heard the last part because the ear-splitting roar that rose up when they realized what was happening drowned me out completely. The look on his face when he heard that noise was unforgettable, and calling him an IRONMAN was an extraordinary honor.

A week later he ran the New York City Marathon. The following year he took off on a nine-week, 3,500-mile transcontinental triathlon, from Santa Monica to New York, to raise awareness of the power of exercise in fighting disease. The year after that he did it again, this time with a group of physically-challenged athletes.

Jim is one hundred percent convinced that his fitness level is what kept him alive long enough to take advantage of treatments that weren't available when he was first diagnosed. Doctors now are far more encouraging of exercise for their AIDS patients. Some of that has to do with advances in drug treatments that have practically eliminated the lethality of the disease and made quality of life, rather than mere survival, the goal. I believe that the example of people like Jim Howley had a lot to do with opening the medical world's eyes to the benefits of staying fit.

Jim, I'm happy to say, is alive and thriving. He did come back to do the World Championship again, as well as IRONMAN races in Germany and New Zealand. And, just to cap it all off, in 1998 he did Ultraman: a 6.2-mile swim, 261.4-mile bike, and a double marathon of 52.4 miles.

All this from a guy who'd already picked the music for his funeral.

YOU MIGHT WANT TO FASTEN YOUR SEATBELT for this one. Just when you thought you'd heard it all about the astonishing ability of people to come back from a dreaded disease or horrific injury, along comes someone who completely resets the bar.

I first ran into Matt Long at the finish line of an IRONMAN event. Since then he's become a close friend; I call him "my Irish brother from another mother." He's a very special human being and I try to see him every time I'm in New York.

The race where we met was the 2005 IRONMAN Lake Placid. He was introduced to me by New York City firefighter Larry Parker, who said, "Hey, Mike, you gotta come meet this guy." Matt was a fellow firefighter, 35 at the time, and had just crossed the finish line at a very respectable 11:18:01.

We connected immediately. Matt is one of those rare guys who has a happy-go-lucky persona but is serious about how he leads his life. He was a first responder at the World Trade Center during 9/11 and was also credited by the FDNY with an official "save." While fighting a fire at a supposedly vacant tenement, he noticed mail in front of an apartment door. He broke in and discovered a man lying unconscious from the effects of smoke. Matt and a buddy carried him out and he survived. Highly thought of in the department, Matt had been assigned as a health and fitness instructor in a special training program for newcomers. One of eight kids from a blue-collar family in Bay Ridge, Brooklyn, he was a perfect fit for the job, unflappably sunny, but obviously strong and determined as well as confident in his skills and ability to command respect.

He was gregarious and fun loving, a heady combination for a single man living in New York City who, in addition to being a firefighter, co-owned three bars. His personal touch was all over them, starting with the names—each one had "Long" in it—which might explain why they were packed all the time. When I visited one called Third & Long sometime later, it seemed that everyone in the place knew Matt personally.

Matt hung around the finish line at Lake Placid celebrating, and every once in a while when there was a lull in incoming athletes, I'd wander over and chat him up. He told me that he was going to do the New York Marathon in a few months, and also said he was coming back to do IRONMAN Lake Placid again the following year.

He ran the marathon on November 6, clocking 3:13, which got him to his goal of qualifying for the Boston Marathon the following spring, along with three buddies from the department.

Six weeks later, at 3:00 am on December 20, Transport Workers Union Local 100 in New York went on strike against the Metropolitan Transportation Authority, bringing every subway and bus in the city to a halt.

Two days after that, about nine hours before the strike was called off, Matt bundled himself up against the 28°F weather and hopped on his bike to get from his apartment on East 48th Street to the "Rock," the firefighter training facility on Randall's Island where he worked. He had only two days left on the year-long assignment before returning to Ladder Company 43 in East Harlem.

He biked up Third Avenue, eventually pulling alongside a private bus that had been hired by a brokerage firm to transport some if its employees to work during the strike. As they approached 52nd Street, the driver, who'd been brought in from out of town and apparently didn't know buses were prohibited from making turns outside of a designated lane, and who also didn't seem to be aware of the cyclist alongside him, swung sharply to the right and slammed into Matt.

Who wound up underneath the bus. One end of the handlebars jammed into the undercarriage so hard that the other end was driven into Matt's belly and out his back. His innards ripped to shreds, Matt started bleeding. Badly. There was so much blood that a police officer, who later tried to saw the handlebars off the undercarriage, had to wedge his feet against the bottom of the bus to stop from sliding around on the pavement.

It took forty-five minutes to get Matt out from under the bus. His dangerously low blood pressure was the first thing the docs in the ER had to deal with, but there was much more. He had compound fractures of the left femur, tibia and foot. His right shoulder and hip were badly broken and his pelvis had been crushed. Then there was a perforated abdominal wall, and torn organs and extensive nerve damage in his midsection.

At their most optimistic, the doctors gave him a five percent chance of survival. One of the surgeons operating on him had treated U.S. service people wounded in Iraq and said that Matt's injuries were worse than those of soldiers he'd seen who'd been hit by mortar fire. In the first twelve hours of the initial round of surgeries, they pumped forty-eight units of blood into him. That's four times what was normally in his body at any one time. It was so bad that, after the surgeries, they kept Matt in an induced coma for two weeks. Even if he lived, the odds were high that he'd contract a fatal infection from the contents of his intestines that had poured through his peritoneum or be reduced to a vegetative state.

He escaped the infection, but it would be five months and twenty-two surgeries before Matt would leave the hospital, fifty pounds lighter and not even in the neighborhood of back to normal. He was full of metal rods and screws, his right leg had shortened by two inches because of the shattered hip, and half of his abductor muscles—the ones that hold us upright and enable us to walk—had atrophied to uselessness. His doctor told him it'd be two years before he could try walking without crutches.

Reduced from an athletic, man-about-town *bon vivant* to a wheelchair, Matt sank into despair. A lot of his funk had to do with being saddled with a colostomy bag owing to the traumatic loss of the "last mile" of his digestive system. Even if he managed to rehab to the point where he could walk on his own and maybe even jog a few steps, what was his life going to be like hitched to that smelly thing hanging off his belt?

Lousy, that's what. So he chose to go back for one more surgery, a 14-hour reconstructive odyssey followed by two more weeks in the hospital. It worked, and

Matt's spirits brightened. The estimate of how long it would take for him to be able to walk with only a cane turned out to be eerily precise. Two years to the day after the accident, he put aside the crutches. A week later he swam in a pool. An hour after he climbed out he declared to his buds that he was going to run the New York City Marathon, eleven months away. They humored him; privately, they just hoped he'd lose the cane by then.

The press coverage of Matt in New York had been extensive. Even the mayor had spoken about him on television. He needed to get out of the city and all that attention and concentrate on rehabbing. He found some trainers in Tempe, Arizona, who had devised new techniques of working with injuries like Matt's. They were a godsend for him, and then he went back to New York to work with a sports physiologist who specialized in flexibility techniques. It was all difficult and painful, and none of it came with a guarantee. When he started running, that longed-for breakthrough was marred by setbacks, including a tear in the ring of cartilage surrounding his hip socket. There were times he thought he'd never be able to climb his way out of that deep hole.

But Matt soldiered on, and that November he stepped up to the start line of the New York City Marathon with two of his firehouse friends. He grimaced, limped, teetered and wobbled over the 26.2-mile course. His best marathon time ever was 3:13. This day it took him 7:21. As he crossed the finish line he dropped to the ground, but waved off concerned onlookers because he'd gone down to do a dozen celebratory pushups. It was a monumental achievement, a testament to guts, to state-of-the-art medicine and therapeutic techniques, and to the almost unbelievable determination it took to fight off despair and remain hopeful. He'd come back, and now he could declare victory, accept his fate and resign himself to a sedentary but self-sufficient life, with no more need to test himself by pushing his battered body to its severely and irrevocably constrained limits.

Seven months later, Matt stepped up to the start line of IRONMAN Lake Placid.

I'D SEEN HIM THERE THE YEAR BEFORE. He'd come to support some of his friends, but he could pretty much only stand and cheer, because he was still using a cane and had a hitch in his step so pronounced that he looked in danger of falling over with every step.

Sometime toward the end of the evening as the midnight cutoff was approaching, he leaned over the barrier fence and said, "Mike, I'm going to do this race next year."

One never wants to be discouraging, and Lord knows I'm as positive and supporting as anyone, especially when I'm in "IRONMAN mode," but I did a double take before I was able to respond. It was something lame and unintentionally halfhearted, like, "Gee, Matt…that's great."

He saw it, but wasn't offended. "Just between you and me for now, okay?"

Sure, Matt. No problem there. I wouldn't have told anyone anyway, or they would have thought I was as crazy as Matt was. The guy could barely stand upright, and every step looked painfully awkward. When he did the marathon four months later, it was a total shock. I sent him a congratulatory message but never mentioned IRONMAN. Maybe he'd just been feeling the energy in the thin mountain air that evening in Lake Placid and unwisely voiced a momentary fantasy. No sense bringing it up and making him feel bad about it. Even though he'd finished a marathon, he hadn't warmed up with a 2.4-mile swim and a 112-mile bike ride like he'd have to do in an IRONMAN triathlon.

Then again, I remember daring to think, *this is one tough cookie.*

And here he was just a year later, back at Lake Placid with his bike, his friends and family, and an official wristband that said "ATHLETE" on it. Was it possible that he could pull this off?

I saw him often during race week. He wasn't unrealistic about his prospects, knowing the extreme difficulty he was facing. The training had been excruciating at times, but he'd been buoyed by his marathon finish the year before. He had no delusions about turning in a great time; he just wanted to beat the cutoff clock. And, as he was all too well aware, it was going to be all about the run.

We spotted each other a few minutes before the start. "Promise me one thing, Mike," he said. "You'll call me across yourself."

Like there was any other possibility. Normally, hearing that from an athlete gets me anxious and gnaws at me a little during the day, because it's impossible for me to call everybody, but I sure don't want to disappoint anybody. And there was no way in the world I was going to disappoint this guy.

Matt had a good swim, 1:27, not surprising because his upper body had been the least injured and he'd built it up to where he was actually more muscular than he'd been before the accident.

The bike was more of a problem. It took him more than 7-1/2 hours. We didn't have sophisticated, real-time tracking systems back then, just a handful of timing mats and spotters with walkie-talkies calling information in. All of them were keeping an eye out for Matt and I was getting reports throughout the day. I also got calls from Matt's friends and family who'd driven out onto the course to follow him on the bike. He was struggling here and there, but didn't look like he was in trouble.

I was at the finish line calling in the pros when I got word that Matt had racked his bike and headed out on the 26.2-mile marathon. "How does he look?" I asked.

"Eh…" came the reply after a moment's hesitation. I wasn't very surprised because it was normal for people, especially those with physical challenges, to be sore and unsteady after so many hours on the bike. But I also knew that Matt was entering what was sure to be the worst part of the day. The marathon leg of an IRONMAN tri eats healthy people alive. How bad was it going to be for a guy who could barely walk a year ago?

As it turned out, pretty bad. The spotters, who were experienced race watchers, were nearly universal in their appraisal of Matt's chances. "No way this guy makes the cutoff," was the most optimistic report. The pessimistic ones were that he'd have to be carried off the course. The medical vans were notified to be on alert.

Matt's Mom and Dad were waiting for him at the finish line. They were anxious for any information, but all I told them was where on the course he'd been seen. I didn't say anything about how he looked. Every time I got a report I glanced at the race clock and did a rough mental calculation. I remember thinking that he'd have to be slowing his pace at some point, but somehow he was keeping it up. Still, it was obvious that it was going to be a very tight race against the clock. If he faltered, even for a few minutes, he wasn't going to make it.

An IRONMAN staffer known as JD was with Matt for the last five or so miles of the race. Knowing it was going to be close, and being ex-military, JD didn't mince words. "You better get your ***** ***** moving or you're not going to be a ****** IRONMAN!" is a close enough approximation of his exact words. He then asked Matt if he needed anything to help him through the last couple of miles.

Matt said, "If you get Heather Fuhr to come out here and run with me, I'll make it!"

Well, 1997 IRONMAN world champion and future Hall of Famer Heather Fuhr, who'd won this race five times, was standing next to me when JD's call came in over the radio. As soon as he finished speaking, she didn't hesitate for a second. "I'm gonna go get him," she said, and took off out onto the course.

Matt wasn't hard to spot despite the darkness; he was one of a very small handful of athletes still out there. When Heather ran up to him, JD would later tell us, Matt nearly went into shock before breaking into a mile-wide grin. Heather then ran alongside him—if you could call it running; Matt was moving so slowly it was barely a brisk walk for her—veering off only when they got to the last turn on the Oval and the finish line lay directly ahead.

The Oval is a magical spot in Lake Placid. It was the outdoor skating rink for the 1980 Winter Olympic Games. The US won six medals that year; five of them were by Eric Heiden, skating on this very Oval that now served as the last 200 meters of the IRONMAN race.

I heard the noise from the spectators before I spotted Matt. I was already down from the tower and ran toward the finish line in time to see him rounding the last curve before the final straightaway. Just before I crossed over the line and into the finishing chute, I looked up at the clock: Four minutes left. A lifetime, even at Matt's slow, jerking pace. I heard in my earpiece that he was going to be the last finisher. But he was going to make it.

Barely able to control my voice, I told the crowd a highly summarized version of Matt's saga. Nobody heard me finish, because as Matt came into the glare of the lights, they sent up a roar that drowned out even the powerful PA system. Energized, Matt picked up the pace, but when he spotted the clock and knew he had it made, he slowed down, waved to the crowd and high-fived me. As he reached the line, he paused momentarily to tap the finish arch overhead, then stepped across to even wilder applause.

I gave him his moment, then grabbed him to try to get a few words. I started by reminding him what he'd said to me a year ago, that he was going to come back and do this race.

"I'm an IRONMAN again," he told the crowd when I turned the mic towards him. But he didn't get very far because a new noise arose down at the last curve. Another finisher was coming in. Matt wasn't last!

He and I both looked up at the clock. There were only 28 seconds left before the cutoff.

Matt pushed the mic away. "Go get him!" he shouted.

I ran back to the finish line and made as much noise as I could along with the crowd, trying to get some adrenaline into the guy, whose name was Paul Goldstone. He hit the mat at precisely the 17:00:00 mark and no one greeted him more enthusiastically than Matt himself, who would go on to befriend him and call him "Last Place Paul" ever after.

James Cooper Photography

The celebration as the race officially ended was epic. It was after the midnight cutoff and nobody wanted to leave. It was like hearing the last song at a concert and the crowd wants more, an encore of some kind. I so badly wanted to say something to the crowd to satisfy that yearning. *My* yearning.

Those of you who have been with me at a finish line or an awards banquet know that, at the very end of the evening my sign-off is, "I only have one more thing to say. You are an IRONMAN!"

That night in Lake Placid was the first time I did that. It was the only thing I could think of to give everybody just a little bit more, like the band coming out for one last song. I think it worked for the crowd. It sure worked for me.

And for Matt. You can see the whole thing on my website, along with a link to his wonderful book, *The Long Run: A New York City Firefighter's Triumphant Comeback from Crash Victim to Elite Athlete.*

ALL TOO OFTEN WE HEAR DISMAYING STORIES about people who courageously battled ravaging diseases or terrible trauma, only to lose in the end and pass from us before their time.

We also occasionally hear about healing that seems to come from nowhere: a patient in a vegetative state suddenly wakes up; a supposedly lethal cancer goes into spontaneous remission.

As you know by now, I've seen an awful lot of profoundly inspirational things in my thirty years of being in this sport. But Brian Boyle, Jim Howley and Matt Long go well beyond the inspirational and into the downright *miraculous*. I used that word purposely because, absent any scientific explanation, we're apt to reach for a spiritual one, which is not only comforting but acknowledges that there's more at work than what we can perceive or understand.

Yet I think there's more to it than that, something far more down to earth. Although it's beyond speculation that attitude plays a role in healing, very little is known about the hard science behind the mind-body connection. It's difficult to pin down, because who's to say what brought about the healing?

I can't tell you the science—nobody can—but I know for a dead certainty that there is real healing power in undertaking something as mentally and physically demanding as an IRONMAN triathlon. I don't for a second believe that Brian, Jim or Matt could have come half as far as they did without taking on that challenge in addition to the ones they already faced. In Jim's case, it's not even clear that he'd be alive today. And I've told you only a fraction of the stories like theirs that I've been witness to over the years.

Someday, somehow, science is going to figure out the mechanisms that underlie the role of intense physical activity in the healing process. It won't be about just the activity itself, but the mental discipline required to engage in it fully.

When that happens, it won't surprise me to see "Rx: Start training for IRONMAN" on a prescription pad.

CHAPTER 5

I didn't intend for this book to be autobiographical, but a little background on how I got started might help to illuminate something of this world I now inhabit, especially for those of you who haven't had the unique pleasure of experiencing IRONMAN for yourselves, as either an athlete or a spectator.

I grew up in Toledo, Ohio, and was living there when I got my degree in special education. My brother Don had mustered out of the Navy fifteen years earlier and was living in San Diego. He and my other brother, Pat, had some pull in the school district there and got me an interview for a job teaching kids with learning and physical disabilities.

It was a tough job in a very tough school. I took to running in Balboa Park, not just to stay fit but to work off some stress. I'd wrestled in college and was in pretty good shape, so it wasn't long before I met up with people I could run with. At that point I'd never even heard of triathlon—it was 1978 and hardly anybody had— but some of the people I ran with told me about some athletes who were doing this weird three-sport thing on Fiesta Island. The names didn't mean anything to me at the time, but some would turn out to be pretty big deals in the tri arena, like brothers Scott and Jeff Tinley.

My first tri was SUPERFROG on Coronado Island in 1980. The year before, the inaugural of the event, my wife Rose and I supported a friend as he raced it. There were only nineteen entrants, half of them Navy SEALS, and it was the very first IRONMAN 70.3 distance event, although it was called a Half IRONMAN at the time. It was a brutal race: freezing cold water and no wetsuits, a meandering bike course that cyclists had to navigate themselves using paper maps, and a run that included miles in the sand. By the time I did it the following year, I'd quit teaching to open up some running stores with my brother Don. I could run a marathon under

2:50, so my goal was to pass a few SEALS on the run after they killed me on the swim and bike, and I did.

Later that year I was signed up for a 10K but got a minor injury and couldn't run. I went, just to watch. As the horn sounded and the runners took off, race director Lynn Flanagan asked me why I wasn't running. I started to tell her that my hamstring was acting up, but as soon she got the gist she cut me off and told me there was a small sound system set up at the finish line. "You know most of the runners," she said. "Why don't you grab the mic and call them in?" Then she handed me a dot-matrix printout (remember those?) of all the entrants.

I was kind of apprehensive, but I had a lot of buddies in this race and couldn't resist the opportunity to razz them a little. It was a bit nerve-wracking because I wasn't well-prepared, but it was also fun. I especially liked the connection I seemed to develop with the spectators. Regardless, the next time Lynn called I turned her down. I'd already signed up for the race and wanted to run, not announce.

The next time, she offered me $150. That wasn't bad money in those days so I took it. I did some homework this time, learning who the top runners were, what the course looked like, and some history of the race. That made things much more enjoyable for the spectators and a lot more fun for me. Word got around and I started getting other announcing gigs.

Meanwhile, Don and I sold the running stores and I went to work as the West Coast sales rep for a number of vendors who used to call on me as a customer when we were selling their products. The biggest was Saucony, but I had ten others as well, including PowerBar. By that time, I was also calling about two races a month and had expanded into marathons.

And triathlons. That sport had exploded in popularity, partially fueled by Julie Moss's famous crawl to the finish line of the 1982 IRONMAN. I loved calling triathlons because of their richness and complexity. There was so much more going on than in a pure running race: three different sports, two transitions, varying levels of strength and weakness in each discipline and a lot of strategy: Should the strongest cyclist pour it all into that part of the race and hope for a big enough lead to fend off the best runners? Should a good runner be worried about lagging in the swim? And how did things like that change depending on the race distances?

It was exhilarating and unpredictable, and I considered it part of my job to convey

T1 on the pier in Kona, 1989

Lois Schwartz

all of that to spectators who were still learning about triathlon. A lot of people weren't even spelling it correctly in those days. (It's not "triath*a*lon.") The more they understood, the more exciting it would be for them to watch how a race unfolded.

I somehow came to the attention of Valerie Silk, who owned the IRONMAN race in Hawai'i at the time. Mike Plant was the race announcer and, as the event grew, Valerie felt he could use some help. In 1989, she asked him to give me a call. I jumped at the chance.

I WAS PLANT'S ASSISTANT THAT YEAR, but he was generous in letting me share some of the fun stuff. Not being the lead guy, I had a little more time on my hands than I would after taking over the reins in 1991, which is why I happened to be climbing the announcing tower during the swim start while Plant was down on the pier.

Because of the way the start-finish area was constructed, the tower was higher than it is now. When I got to the top I had a commanding view of the swim start, and the first thing I noticed was some guy tying a rope to a kind of harness around his chest. The other end of the rope was connected to a small boat. Lying in the boat was a person, a spindly looking kid who seemed to have some difficulty controlling his arms. What were they doing in the middle of a chaotic swim start?

Then the guy started swimming. And he was pulling the little boat behind him,

African Queen style. I'm wondering if this is some kind of stunt and are the officials going to do something about it. But everybody nearby seemed calm about the whole thing, including the safety people on surfboards, and then I noticed that every camera in the vicinity was pointed at the guy and the little boat.

I had absolutely no idea what was going on. There was a race official at the base of the tower so I yelled down to him, "What's with those guys and that boat?"

Turned out the official was very familiar with them. He motioned to his walkie-talkie so I picked mine up, and he explained that the guy doing the Humphrey Bogart imitation was Dick Hoyt, a Lt. Colonel in the Massachusetts Air National Guard, and the kid in the boat was his 27-year-old son, Rick. The reason Rick's arms were moving around was that he was a "spastic quadriplegic with cerebral palsy," the result of his umbilical cord having gotten wrapped around his neck during birth and nearly strangling him. The damage was so severe that Dick and his wife Judy were urged to institutionalize their son because he was never going to walk, never going to speak, and had no hope of a normal life.

"So what are they doing here?" I asked when he'd finished explaining.

"They're doing the race," he said.

What on earth was he talking about? "All of it?"

Yes, all of it. Dick intended to pull his son around the 2.4-mile swim, carry him out of the water and load him onto a seat mounted to the front his bike, pedal him for 112 miles, then transfer him into a custom-designed running chair and push him over a full marathon.

"There's no way," I said. This race has brought some of the fittest athletes on earth to their knees—literally—and this guy was going to do it while dragging an extra 200 pounds of bike and son around with him?

"Probably not," the official said. "They tried last year and didn't make it."

Later during the day, I pieced together the rest of the story. The Hoyts had not institutionalized their son, and early in his life they got some strong indications that, while Rick's motor functions had been badly compromised, his intellect might not have been. With the aid of some clever computer technology, they found a way for him to communicate. Rick's first words weren't "Mama" or "Papa." They were "Go Bruins!" Now they knew for sure that Rick was acutely aware of what was going on around him, and he was a sports fan to boot: The Boston Bruins were in the Stanley Cup finals that year.

Rick's mental capacities weren't just intact; he was one smart dude. When finally admitted to public school at the age of 13, he excelled, and now he was on his way to Boston University. That's a pretty amazing story right there, but "Team Hoyt" was about far more than "normalcy."

When Rick was 15 he asked his father to push his wheelchair through a 5-mile race to benefit a Lacrosse player who'd been paralyzed in an accident. Dick was no runner, but he agreed. They came in next to last, but it was what Rick said when they'd finished that changed their lives forever. "Dad, when we run, it feels like I'm not handicapped."

They began doing every kind of race they could find: 5Ks, 10Ks, marathons, duathlons and triathlons. As Dick got fitter and Rick got happier, they kept looking for new challenges.

Their moonshot was going to be the 1988 IRONMAN World Championship, but it didn't happen. The seas were rough and Dick became so nauseated they couldn't finish. So here they were, back for a second try.

This time they came out of the water with plenty of time before the cutoff. We got a lot of reports from the course because a camera crew was covering them for ABC's *Wide World of Sports*. I'd been hoping that they'd make it before the 17-hour cutoff, and as the day wore on it became apparent that they were well ahead of that pace. They made it in the ridiculous time of 14:26:04, and the delirium that greeted them at the finish line was like nothing I'd seen before. Rick was so excited that his arms were flapping all over the place and I thought he might fling himself out of the chair; Dick could barely get fluids into him. (That was when I realized that Dick not only has to pull and push his son for hours during a triathlon, he also has to feed him and make sure he stays hydrated.)

After the ABC show that November, Dick found a message on his answering machine from Ronald Reagan. The president said that he and Nancy had been so stirred by Dick and Rick that they'd watched the entire show just to catch glimpses of them.

The Hoyts went on to do six more IRONMAN races. They'd also gotten their marathon times down in the 2:40's. They'd go on to do over 1,100 races, including the Boston Marathon 32 times. On April 8, 2013, they attended the dedication of a bronze statue of themselves just a few hundred yards from the start line of the Boston race, and came back a week later to run it. With one mile to go, two bombs exploded at the finish line. Like everyone else, Dick and Rick were hustled off the course. They came back and did it in 2014, announcing that it would be their last.

Being down at the finish line when they came across in 1989 was one of the most profoundly moving experiences of my life. After it became clear that they were going to finish and I wasn't worried about it anymore, all I kept thinking about was the depth of that extraordinary bond between father and son. A doctor had told the Hoyts that their kid was going to be a vegetable—in those words—and now they were able to joke about trying to figure out what kind of vegetable their son was. When Rick finally went off to college, Dick kept up his training by loading cement bags into the chairs normally occupied by Rick and pushed them all over town, ignoring some pretty odd stares along the way.

It can't have been an easy life, but in all the years I've known them I've never heard a single complaint out of Dick. In 2008, Team Hoyt was inducted into the IRONMAN Hall of Fame. Bringing them on stage to a standing ovation in Kona was absolutely glorious.

As DAY TURNED INTO EVENING during this, my first IRONMAN experience, I had a very powerful feeling that this was where I belonged. I'd heard actors and musicians talk about making a connection with an audience, and I'd gotten a fairly good idea of what that meant during the ten years I'd been announcing, but none of that prepared me for talking to the spectators at an IRONMAN finish line. I had this unmistakable feeling that I was linked in some way to everyone there, like I was whispering in their ears instead of shouting over a PA. I felt keenly what the crowd's mood was, and I was anticipating what their reaction would be to what I was saying even before I finished the sentence. Those reactions shaped what I was saying and how I said it, and at some point I had a realization that shook me and hasn't left to this day: I wasn't talking *to* these spectators; we were having a *conversation*, a dialogue every bit as real as two people chatting over a cup of coffee. I used words, and the response came back as emotions. I was listening to them as attentively as they were to me.

I want to end a race feeling like every athlete who came across the line got the full measure of attention he or she deserved. And I want everybody watching to feel like they're a part of that and helped make it happen. So what I try to do is set up a self-perpetuating cycle in which the spectators pour their hearts out to the finishers, who in turn throw their arms in the air and flash bright smiles in gratitude, energizing the crowd even further and letting them know their cheers and shouts are appreciated, which motivates them to do the same for the next finisher, and on and on.

I take it personally if the energy ever flags, like it's my fault, because it is. I don't care if it's raining or burning hot or there's a typhoon underway. All that means is that the athletes were out racing in awful conditions, and even if we at the finish line are uncomfortable and feeling sorry for ourselves, we still need to bring the racers home in a way that honors their accomplishment.

I don't get tired as the night wears on, at least not that I'm aware of. Later I might crash like a burned-out meteor, but as the hours and minutes wind down, my energy level actually increases. I try to remember something that the Olympic marathoner Frank Shorter once said that stuck with me. I'm paraphrasing, but it was something like, *Don't clap for me because I ran 2:20. Save your applause for the people who finish in five hours. I don't know how they do it; I could never keep going that long!*

In 2018, Germany's Patrick Lange set a World Championship record of 7:52:39, breaking the previous mark (which was his) by over nine minutes. It was a thrilling achievement and, when he finished, there were hundreds of athletes who hadn't even gotten off their bikes yet. Some of them would still be out there for nine more hours, including 86-year-old Hiromu Inada, who would come in with only six minutes left on the clock.

Those people deserved some serious props. And I aimed to see that they got them.

YEAR 1 IN KONA WAS A DREAM. My first year in Australia…not such a dream. "Oz" is arguably more adoring of triathlon than any other country in the world, including the U.S. To non-practitioners here in the States, triathlon is still a novelty; down under it's a major sport. Top level triathletes are well-known even among the general populace, and their age groupers are some of the fittest I've ever seen. Spectators tend to be very knowledgeable and man, do they know how to party at a finish line.

IRONMAN Australia is the fourth oldest IRONMAN event in the world, and the third to be staged outside of the U.S. It had a very rocky start, but when the reins were handed to a local shoe store owner named Ken Baggs, a member of the Great Lakes International Triathlon Association (GLITA), his iron-fisted "my way or the highway" approach brought some much-needed discipline to the event. Under his leadership, it became one of the most popular races on the international circuit.

My tenure there had an equally rocky start.

While the event had become one of the best known in the world since its debut in 1985, it was having trouble drawing international athletes. Graeme Hannan, a good friend of mine from Sydney, worked for IMG, the company that held the license for the event and contracted with GLITA to produce it. Graeme felt the race atmosphere needed perking up and thought I might be able to help. He began quietly talking me up to GLITA in 1993. Some of the members had been to Kona and were already familiar with me, and two years later a deal was struck to have me come to Australia.

I was incredibly excited about the challenge of breathing a little more life into a premier event, and thought everyone down there would be, too, since both IMG and GLITA were parties to the deal and discussions had been going on for two years. I was as yet unaware of the "old boys' club" inside GLITA.

I went straight from the airport to the start-finish area to get a feel for the venue. I hadn't been in town for even an hour when a guy walked up to me and said, "You Reilly?"

He was wearing a GLITA shirt so I flashed a big smile and said, "Yes! And you are…?"

"I don't know why the hell we had to bring in a bloody Yank to announce this race!"

That was pretty funny—Aussies are notorious for their good-natured ribbing—so I laughed and held out my hand.

He didn't take it. "We were doing fine just the way we had it."

This guy wasn't kidding; he was dead serious. It was one of the few times in my life that I was struck speechless, which is just as well because I wouldn't have gotten a word in edgewise anyway as he freely shared his opinions without benefit of diplomatic nicety. The diatribe included an assurance that other members of the committee shared his feelings about this unnecessary intrusion by know-it-all Yanks.

Now I knew why the discussions had gone on for two years. It didn't take much insight to realize that reasoned debate had eventually given way to emotional squabbling and bad feeling all around. The final decision hadn't resulted from consensus but from a vote, which left the losing faction, of which this guy was clearly a member, bitter and resentful.

And not at all shy about letting me know, as he was doing now with undisguised hostility. Only twenty or so seconds had passed before he turned on his heel and walked away, but it felt like twenty minutes, and I don't mind telling you I was badly shaken. I'm in a strange country over 7,000 miles from home and just got told by someone I was supposed to be working with that I wasn't welcome.

My first urge was to turn right around and head back to the airport. That not being a practical option, I went to look for Graeme. By the time I found him, sitting with his business partner and the event's communications director, Nick Munting, my shock had turned to anger.

"What the *(bleep)* am I doing here?" I said. "GLITA doesn't want me so why was this deal even done!"

Graeme held up a hand and said, "Whoa, what happened, mate?"

I told him who'd come up to me and what he'd said. Word for word.

He nodded knowingly. "Not surprising," he said. Nick was nodding his agreement.

Now I was puzzled in addition to angry. "You knew about this? So why am I here if they don't want me!" By now I was thinking that Graeme, representing the owner of the race license, had in fact exercised his authority and forced GLITA to bring me in.

"Forget what they want," Graeme said. "This race has to change and you're the guy to start making it happen."

I was skeptical.

"You can win them over," he went on. "The athletes want you here calling them home. We've done the research and that's a fact. They're already on your side so your job is to win the organizers over."

I told him that sounded way too simple.

"It *is* simple, mate," Graeme said. "Just do what you do in Kona and they'll come 'round."

I don't know if he was reading into my soul or just winging it, but what he said struck a deep chord. He'd gotten my Irish up and framed it as a challenge. No way was I limping home with my tail between my legs. I was going to prove that it was the right decision to bring me in. Then I'd go home and they could get somebody else to kick around next year.

As I left to go back to the finish area, I didn't get half a block before it was *me* doing the kicking, and it was myself I was kicking. I couldn't believe I'd entertained for even a few seconds such a nasty, self-absorbed thought as the one that had popped into my head. Prove something? Strut my stuff to feed my ego and then take off?

I'd forgotten the "prime directive" that was at the heart of my announcing philosophy: It's all about the athletes. They are all that matters. They're the ones who have been training and struggling and sacrificing all year and would be pushing themselves to the brink to make that finish line on Sunday. My job was to honor them and make sure they had the experience of a lifetime, and to ensure that everyone watching would have the same. And I wasn't about to let some cantankerous and territorial committee members get to me and goad me into messing this up for the athletes.

I instantly felt calmer and could feel my self-confidence coming back. By the time I returned to the start-finish area I was already visualizing how the day would go, where the crowds would be positioned, what options I had for moving around with a portable mic, how much time I'd have to talk about each athlete, given the distance between the finish line and the exit behind the stands.

During the week, I went to every planning and production meeting, even the ones I didn't need to attend. I got the cold shoulder from some of the GLITA people at every one, but I kept going. It helped that Ken Baggs, who was the overall director of IRONMAN Australia, was also at every meeting and was one of the people who'd wanted me involved. I found myself gravitating towards him and he treated me well. Ken introduced me to Peter Beckaleg, a well-established figure in the Australian multi-sport scene. Peter and I would be working together and we hit it off right away.

I was so anxious for Sunday I could hardly sleep.

IT TURNED OUT TO BE ONE OF THE BEST events and finish lines I've ever worked. Kona was the only IRONMAN race I'd ever announced—it would be four more years before I called the inaugural North American championship in Lake Placid, NY—so I didn't have much basis for comparison. But I had the time of my life interacting with the boisterous Aussie crowds that were enthusiastic, energized and loud. They treated every finishing athlete like a world champ, and as I yelled "You are an IRONMAN!" over and over and watched finishers throw their arms in the air, many of them would point at me and clap or blow a kiss and I'd point, clap or blow a kiss right back. Like I said, Aussies know how to party, and this was one great day-long bash.

Yet, for some reason I felt a little let down the next day. I'm always somewhat blue after an IRONMAN event, just because it was so much fun and now it's over, but this was different, like something was missing. The awards ceremony went beautifully, and a lot of athletes came up talking about how much fun it was at the finish line, but still…

I got busy packing. I was going to travel to Sydney with some of the American pros who'd raced. About 30 minutes before we were due to be picked up in front of the hotel, who comes walking up to me but my old GLITA friend from the first day, the guy with all the kind words. Did I really have to stand there and listen to another outpouring of invective?

But this time he looked different. Almost sheepish. "Got a minute, mate?" he said, calling me over with a tilt of his head.

Sure, why not? I'll never have to see him again. He turned around as I approached so we were both facing the same way. "Listen," he said softly after clearing his throat, "I won't be putting this around, but…"

He then proceeded to shock me for a second time, but now it was with grudging but sincere praise for how the day had gone. Modesty demands that I spare you the details, but it ended with him saying, "So, um, if you're willing, we'd like to have you, er, come back next year."

I knew it couldn't have been easy for this fiercely proud man to have gotten that out, and it touched me. Nevertheless, I'd already resigned myself to never coming back.

"It'd be my pleasure," I said, and stuck out my hand.

This time he took it and grasped it in both of his. "Thanks, mate," he said, with what seemed like great relief. I almost laughed, thinking that maybe the rest of the committee had tasked my most vocal opponent to be the one to invite me back.

I learned a couple of important lessons from this experience. One was to listen closely to advice from friends you've come to trust, especially the stuff you'd rather not hear. True friends will tell you the truth, so if you don't like the way it sounds, think about what it's taking for them to give you the straight scoop and listen twice as hard. You might not end up agreeing, but don't dismiss it out of hand.

The second lesson is to trust your instincts, but only if there's a basis for that trust. If you don't know a thing about cars but think that funny rattle is coming from the carburetor, go see a mechanic and let him figure it out. If you *are* a mechanic, don't let anybody plant doubt about the abilities you've come to rely on. I know how to be an IRONMAN race announcer, and when that guy got in my face, the right reaction would have been to think, *No worries, I've got this*, and then politely thank him for his opinion. It wouldn't have been a conceited thought, just a confident one. But I let him get in my head and make me worry about whether I was the right guy for this job and was I going to make the people who believed in me look bad. Thankfully, the first lesson above kicked in shortly after, and I trusted my friends.

That was 1995. I did go back, and my love affair with Australia deepened in 1999. At the awards ceremony I quoted one of my favorite lines, from a book by Bryce Courtenay, to the athletes in the audience: "What you are speaks so loud that what you say cannot be heard."

After the banquet my dear friends (and many time IRONMAN finishers) Alex and Brenda Hamel came up to me. Alex, who runs one of the largest ad agencies in Australia, said, "Mike, do you read Bryce Courtenay?"

I told him that Courtenay's book *The Power of One* was one of my favorite books of all time and had been my motivational bible for fifteen years. I also knew that, although born in South Africa, he lived in Australia and was one of the country's most well-known and respected authors.

"I work with Bryce in Sydney," Alex said. "Longtime mate of mine."

I could hardly believe it. Alex was a fan, too, of course and we spent some time talking about Courtenay's books.

The following year Alex called me the day I arrived in Forster and invited me to dinner. When I arrived, there was a gentleman with Alex and Brenda. I didn't recognize him at first, then it hit me just as Alex said, "Mike, say hello to Bryce Courtenay."

I almost fainted. Alex seated me next to Courtenay and I had a magical evening talking to this enormously talented man I'd admired for so long. He stayed to watch the event, and sometime in the middle of the day when I was announcing at the busy "hot corner" of the bike leg, I spotted him in the crowd. He was looking at me, and as soon as he saw me looking back, he shot me a big smile and a thumbs up. What a boost of self-confidence that gave me: One of the most celebrated writers in the world liked what I was doing!

When I got back home the following week, there was a book waiting for me, a special combined edition of *The Power of One* and *Tandia*, his searing novel of a brutalized child growing up in Africa. Courtenay had written a heartfelt and very complimentary inscription that affected me deeply. We stayed in close touch right up until he passed away in 2012, and that book became one of my most cherished possessions.

I'VE BEEN BACK TO CALL IRONMAN AUSTRALIA over twenty times, and race director Ken Baggs became one of my dearest friends in the sport. I described him earlier as "iron-fisted" but that didn't mean he didn't have a healthy dollop of Aussie fun in him. One of his great innovations was bringing a woman named Karen Pini to the finish line in 1987 to help drape medals over finishers' heads as they came over the line. Already an IRONMAN fan, she was an actress in an Australian soap opera as well as *The Paul Hogan* ("Crocodile Dundee") *Show*, had appeared on the cover of *Penthouse* magazine, was the centerfold model in the first Australian issue of *Playboy*, and hosted the weekly televised New South Wales

Lotto draw. Karen kept appearing at finish lines even when the race moved to a more distant location. Over the years she presented over 20,000 medals, along with becoming a race commentator and hosting at awards ceremonies. In 2008 she became the 14th inductee into the Australian IRONMAN Hall of Fame.

Ken retired as race director in 2015 after thirty years, and was inducted into the IRONMAN Hall of Fame three years later.

I RONMAN is one of the most daunting mainstream sporting events in the world.

By "mainstream" I mean that it's well-established and respected and has many thousands of participants, unlike any of a number of one-off, crazy things like rowing solo across the Atlantic or climbing Everest without oxygen or skydiving from 90,000 feet.

Racing IRONMAN is difficult primarily because of the distances, which are not arbitrary but have history behind them. The swim is 2.4 miles long because that was the distance of the Waikiki Rough Water Swim, a competition for lifeguards. The bike covers 112 miles because that was roughly the distance of a famous bike race that went around the island of Oahu, which is where the original IRONMAN was staged. And 26.2 miles was the distance of the Honolulu Marathon.

Each of those races was considered the toughest in their respective sports, so when Navy Commander John Collins (who would retire as a Captain), his wife Judy and a couple of their friends decided to see who was *the* toughest—swimmer, cyclist or runner—they combined the three into a single event, all in one day, with no breaks.

I said IRONMAN racing is hard primarily because of the distances, but there are other factors that increase the difficulty. Rarely is this more in evidence than at the World Championship in Kona.

It's hot, windy and humid. The bike course cuts across lava fields where the dark rocks absorb and re-radiate heat from the fierce tropical sun. Temperatures a few inches off the pavement can easily top 130 degrees. The hills in the middle third of the course, between the port area of Kawaihae and the bike turnaround in the little town of Hawi, are not the steepest or longest on the IRONMAN circuit, but howling winds can make even the flat stretches feel like a 20-degree climb. On a bad day, it's not unusual to see strong cyclists standing on their pedals and pumping furiously to hit ten mph on a stretch of the Queen K Highway, where they could ride well over 35 mph on a calm day. One hundred twelve miles in those conditions can trash even the fittest athletes, and that's before they start the marathon.

So try to imagine what it's like for someone missing an arm or a leg, or who is confined to a wheelchair because her legs are paralyzed. Or who is blind.

Nils Nilsen

Not too long ago, attempting an IRONMAN triathlon with those kinds of disabilities would have been considered unthinkable. But it's been done, a remarkable number of times, and there are few examples of the strength of the human spirit that are more inspirational than the stories of the challenged athletes who pulled off these almost inconceivable feats.

I'm going to tell you about just three of them that I know well and whose heroics I had the privilege of witnessing personally.

S ARAH REINERTSEN IS A PRETTY GOOD ATHLETE. She ran seven half marathons on seven continents in seven days and placed seventh in *The Amazing Race* (40,000 miles across 13 countries). She's been featured on the cover of *Runner's World* and was named one of that magazine's Heroes of Running.

Now, this is the point where you're probably expecting me to tell you about something terrible that happened to this terrific athlete. Okay, here it is: Owing to a congenital abnormality, Sarah had her left leg amputated.

When she was seven years old. Those feats of running I just told you about were accomplished with one flesh and bone leg she was born with and one titanium and aluminum leg she had to buy.

In retrospect, it's not surprising that Sarah would be the one to break new ground in the world of challenged athletics. The decision to amputate the leg was her own; she saw a prosthetic replacement for her own useless limb as liberating, giving her mobility that she could only dream about before the surgery.

A word about leg amputations: There are two basic types, known as above-the-knee (AK) and below-the-knee (BK). BKs are the less radical of the two, obviously. Most prosthetics for BKs have no moving parts. The main problem is that the ankle, or where the ankle would be if there was an ankle, doesn't bend. But people who use these devices adapt pretty quickly to that lack, and if a BK amputee is wearing long pants, it's often impossible to tell she's walking on a replacement limb. BKs routinely run marathons and compete in triathlons.

I'm not trying to minimize the difficulty of running with an artificial foot. There's nothing easy about it. But an above-the-knee amputee like Sarah faces an additional set of problems. There's no direct, brain-initiated control over any of the hardware hanging below the hip, nor any muscle to generate motive power. Until relatively recent advances in prosthetic engineering, the only way to walk was with crutches.

Even now, walking is not easy for Sarah. It's a matter of lifting and swinging her hip to get the hinges to (sort of) mimic natural articulation. And that's to get from the bedroom to the kitchen. Running is an entirely different kettle of fish, and running a marathon? I still find it hard to believe that's possible.

And then there's cycling. Simple, repetitive motion, right? There's just one small problem: Sarah has no quads on her left side. Those are the muscles you use to pedal. When her good right leg goes down and the left pedal comes up, she has to shift her weight to the left and press down with her hip, not her leg, then quickly shift back to the right so the pedal can come back up.

In other words, one leg does all the work. After weeks of crashing and falling, you finally learn how it all works and can bike down the block, and that's a major achievement. But Sarah was looking beyond a hundred yards of cycling.

She was looking at IRONMAN. Not just any IRONMAN, either, but The Beast in Kona, with its potentially vicious winds that have knocked able-bodied athletes clean off the road.

As of 2004 no female AK amputee had ever finished an IRONMAN race. *Any* IRONMAN race, let alone the toughest one of all. Telling that to Sarah was like tossing a sirloin in front of a starving lion. The 29-year-old qualified for the 2004 World Championship at IRONMAN 70.3 Lubbock in Texas, trained hard, then went to Kona fully prepared to crush the course and become the first female AK to cross an IRONMAN finish line.

Didn't quite work out that way. The World Championship is not a Lifetime Channel special. It's a great white shark bent on devouring anything in its path incapable of outrunning it. And on this day, the little blonde fireball with one leg and a big heart couldn't outrun it. After struggling in rough surf, Sarah got slammed with high winds on the bike that were not only head-on but occasionally sideways. It was as much of a battle to stay upright as it was to make forward progress. On the way back from Hawi the effort made her ill and she started vomiting, which cost her even more time.

Still she kept going, and covered the entire hundred and twelve miles. But as she approached T2, the bike-to-run transition, the readout on her bike computer confirmed what she'd feared: She wasn't going to get to transition before the cutoff time. Her race was over.

I'd been getting reports all day. I thought the world of Sarah and had already planned some of the things I would say when she crossed the line. I was up in the tower when I heard cheering and applauding. Turning, I saw that Sarah had come in so I lifted the mic to let everyone know of the milestone.

But it was curious that she wasn't moving quickly into transition. Then I glanced at the race clock, and elation turned to disbelief as I realized she'd missed the cutoff. Now all I could think about was how devastated she would be. I was close enough to see her try to maintain her composure, but it wasn't working.

DNF'ing (short for "did not finish") is bad enough after training for and visualizing your finish for a year. Now try to imagine it when your family is there, the entire Challenged Athletes Foundation is watching and cheering for you and, worst of all, an NBC television crew has been following you all day. Even as you limp in, they've got a camera pointed at you. Watching her just tore me up. For a second I thought about running down there to try to be of some comfort.

I felt a tap on my shoulder. "Someone's coming!" a voice said. I turned to see a finisher approaching the line. How could I make this call when I felt so bad?

I just did, that's all. Sarah's race was over but this finisher deserved a rousing cheer. I forced myself back into the right frame of mind and made an enthusiastic call. Sarah ate some food, drank some water, gathered with her family and headed straight to a folding chair at the finish line to help celebrate the athletes as they finished. I looked down just in time to see Sarah's armor crack. Once the first tears came she broke down and began sobbing.

What I didn't know until I spoke with her later was that I'd caused it.

"The sharpest pain I felt was hearing you call someone an IRONMAN," she told me, "That's when I really lost it."

If you think that's the end of the story, you don't know Sarah Reinertsen. I came down out of the tower and gave her a big hug. She didn't say a word, but when she pulled back and looked at me, it was like she was shooting me a telepathic message.

"Seriously?" I said, reading the message clearly.

She nodded. "I got unfinished business."

She'd given herself about twenty minutes to feel sorry for herself, then she'd turned to her mother and said, "I'm doing this next year."

I would never dream of discouraging an athlete from pursuing a difficult goal, but I have to admit to a moment of doubt. I knew how hard she'd trained, and couldn't imagine her stepping it up. Was she going to hope for more forgiving weather? She'd only missed the cutoff by about fourteen minutes, and might have made it had the winds been more gentle.

I kept those thoughts to myself, and it's a good thing I did because Sarah didn't know at that moment how she was going to do it. But, having made the decision, she'd morphed back into her old cheerful self and was the hit of the finish-line party.

The answer to "how" came from the good people at the Cannondale bike company. They'd gotten wind of what had happened, saw the problem immediately, then contacted Sarah and told her what had gone wrong. "You rode a bike built for a six-foot male with two good legs," they said. It was 112 miles through heavy winds with all the efficiency of a chicken on roller skates.

They put her in the lab, measured her from head to toe and built, from scratch, a bike tailor-made for a half-pint monopod who was one quarter bionic.

Sarah wasn't about to rely on the new bike alone, though. "I was so sure I would

finish Kona that I never considered the possibility that I could fail," she said. She considered it now, and it gave her the motivation to increase the intensity of her training. Anytime she was tempted to back off a little she reminded herself of what it was like to disappoint her friends, her family, her fellow challenged athletes, her sponsors, the employer who'd cut her a little slack so she could train, the packs of reporters who'd followed her around all day...she felt like she'd disappointed the whole world, and that wasn't going to happen again.

And the idea of simply finishing was out the window. She set a "dream time" of 16:05. If she was going to do this, she was going to do it with gusto. The whole endeavor took on the trappings of a project, and it even had a name: "Unfinished Business." That was Sarah's mantra. There was a logo, and t-shirts, and for all I know there was theme music, too.

It's difficult to describe what it was like at the finish line when Sarah sprinted – yes, you read that right—*sprinted* across the finish line. I'd been telling the crowd her story all day, and once I knew she was safely on her way in, I told them about her 16:05 goal. When she came across nearly *an hour* faster than that, the sound that rose up from the crowd was like an F-15 fighter jet in full afterburner.

Another thing I can't describe is what it was like for me to be the one who got the privilege of telling this mini-Amazon warrior that she was, at last, an IRONMAN. I had to fight to keep my throat from catching so she'd hear it loud and clear.

At the awards banquet the next night Sarah got up and gave an emotional speech about her odyssey, and officially declared resolved the "unfinished business" she'd been carrying around for a year. Had there been a roof over the banquet area, the crowd would have blown it off when she was done.

Sarah was the very first female AK amputee to finish an IRONMAN triathlon, and the only one ever to do it in Kona. She was also the second to do it there, because thirteen years later she came back and did it again.

What makes pioneers so special is that they don't know in advance if what they're attempting is possible. It's one thing to climb Mt. Everest now, when hundreds of people have done it. Not easy, of course, but you already know it's possible. When Tenzing Norgay and Edmund Hillary tried it, all they were sure of was that everyone else who'd made the attempt had either turned back or died.

Plenty of people had told Sarah Reinertsen that doing an IRONMAN race on one leg was impossible, especially for (oh my!) a *girl*. And to try it in Kona? Madness.

What they didn't know was that they weren't dampening her enthusiasm; they were stoking her fires. The more impossible it seemed, the sweeter the feeling of accomplishment would be when she demonstrated what was truly possible.

Another thing about pioneers is that they pave the way for others, and motivate them to even loftier heights. If Sarah could do it on one leg, was it possible to do it on *no* legs?

That was the question that haunted a man named Scott Rigsby.

What a beast of a man. How is he going to do this race?

That was my first impression of Scott when he showed up at IRONMAN Coeur d'Alene in 2007. The guy was huge, like an NFL linebacker. I don't know if he was the biggest ever to tackle IRONMAN but he had to be high up on the list. How was it possible for someone to drag that much tonnage over 140.6 miles?

And that's before I noticed that he was missing two legs.

Doing an IRONMAN triathlon on an artificial leg had been done, but this was new. A double amputee had never accomplished that feat. And if someone was going to make the attempt, you'd think it would be someone smaller than a Buick. But here he was, full of the kind of swaggering bravado that was probably necessary to get past the nervousness of venturing into the unknown and willingly subjecting himself to a day of pretty serious pain. With metal legs banging right up against his stumps and supporting all that weight, it had to be uncomfortable just standing there, never mind biking and running.

The crew and I followed Scott's progress, but there comes a day when even an aggressive attitude and the kind of will that got you this far are just not enough. He crashed on the bike, fracturing a vertebra. Even then he wouldn't quit, and somehow made it through twelve miles of the marathon before the pain and exhaustion overwhelmed him.

I felt so bad for him. I was really rooting for him to write history that day, to join groundbreaking challenged athletes like John Maclean, Jim MacLaren, David Bailey, Carlos Moleda, Marc Herremans and Sarah Reinertsen. They'd all led the way not just by overcoming seemingly insurmountable obstacles, but by believing so completely that they could. That's the way of IRONMAN, to do the unbelievable and so inspire others that they're willing to jump into the same fires. And I think it's a positive thing that so many of the pioneers failed the first time out and then came back and got it done. It lets the others know that stumbling is a beginning, not an end. To me, failed attempts don't make you a failure. Not learning from your mistakes and not trying again is what does.

A guy I know named Brian Aubuchon missed IRONMAN cutoffs *six times* before he finally did it in Mont-Tremblant. Thomas Edison's response when asked about the thousands of substances he tried before hitting on tungsten to make his electric light? "I have not failed; I just found several thousand ways that won't work!"

I didn't know what was next for Scott. I had doubts that he could pull off an IRONMAN race. But, having witnessed his resolve, I was pretty sure he was going to try.

Scott was eighteen the summer after graduating high school. He'd taken a job as a landscaper in rural Georgia so he could put together some money before heading off to college. After a hard day on the job one Friday, he and some friends were riding home in the back of a pickup truck towing a 3-ton trailer when it got slammed by an 18-wheeler. Scott got thrown under the trailer and was dragged the length of a football field before it finally stopped. His right leg was severed, and the left hung barely attached.

What followed was an agonizing period of endless doctor and hospital visits. Scott battled at first, but after 26 surgeries, and the eventual loss of his left leg in addition to the right, he just couldn't take it anymore. He sank into depression and alcohol abuse, alienating people around him and causing financial hardships that only pushed him deeper into an abyss.

But he had enough sense of self to know he couldn't live like that. He said a prayer, asked for a way out, and found it. I'm compressing an incredible story here, but Scott discovered the world of endurance sports and dove into it head first. He ran, he did marathons, he did triathlons. And he did them really, really well. In one year he set records for a double amputee in the marathon, the international distance triathlon and IRONMAN 70.3.

Of course he was going to go for the granddaddy of them all, a full-distance IRONMAN race. And of course he was going to go for it again if it didn't work the first time.

Someone up there must have been listening to his prayers, because a month after Coeur d'Alene he got a call from one of the sponsors of the 2007 IRONMAN World Championship. They were giving Scott their Everyday Hero award, and it came with (drum roll, please) a trip to the race in Kona.

Experience is a cruel teacher; it gives the test before it gives the lesson. Scott learned the lesson and, at 39, was going to take the test again. There was never a question about that. But the World Championship is a harder race than the one he'd just bonked in. Sure, he'd had a crash and that's what did him in, but there was nothing to say he could have finished even had he stayed upright. So Kona wasn't going to be like re-taking a mid-term; it would be like taking the bar exam.

I saw Scott several times in Hawai'i during race week. He was a much different person than he'd been back in June. He was calmer and had lost some of the earlier swagger. He was still nervous, though, especially about the bike. I was surprised at first, because he'd ridden a decent 8:20 in Coeur d'Alene, but the notorious Kohala Coast winds were on his mind.

For those of you unfamiliar with the World Championship course: It's the winds that can make or break a racer. When the air is calm, records fall like dominos, as they did in 2018. In 2014, the winds were so fierce that only one age group record was broken out of the twenty-four divisions racing. Former medical director Dr. Bob Laird used to say that he could accurately predict the number of IV bottles he'd need in the medical tent based on nothing but the wind speed. It was the wind that had tripped up Sarah Reinertsen on her first attempt, and Scott was well aware of that.

The winds that year weren't bad at all. It was the heat that was awful. Scott looked great coming out of the water. His arms had gotten pumped during the swim and he looked like a weightlifter as he headed to transition. The bike was tough, but he rode it well. He finished a minute faster than he had in Coeur d'Alene so I figured he'd gotten stronger since then, given how much harder this course was.

Now he had to deal with the run. People running with prostheses have some special problems beyond the obvious ones. Their stumps get beaten up badly, and they need to plan for how to dump perspiration that collects between the artificial limb and their skin. Modern prostheses have combinations of wicking and valves, but they don't always work. Sometimes the athlete has to stop, take off the limb and pour out the perspiration the old fashioned way. And it isn't comforting to see blood mixed in with the sweat, which is not at all unusual.

For some reason I didn't get a report on Scott until he hit Mile 20, which was roughly at the exit of the Energy Lab, a looped section that ends with a half-mile climb. It's a gentle slope, but after 134 miles of swimming, biking and running, it can feel like scaling the side of a building. That Scott had made it up was a good sign, and a quick calculation showed that he'd make it in even if he slowed his pace slightly.

Soon after, my assistant Robe (pronounced "Robby") Whittemore rode out on a moped to survey the final stretch of the course to get an idea of who was still out there and who among them would be likely to finish. He found Scott and radioed to me that he was holding steady and would make it. Robe was a very good judge of such things so I felt comfortable getting on the horn and filling the crowd in on Scott's background, his experience at Coeur d'Alene and the fact that he was going to enter the history books very shortly.

I was down at the finish line to welcome him in. It's one of the few times I couldn't hear my voice coming through the speakers because of the roar rising up from the spectators. But Scott could hear it; he'd been waiting for it for a long time. As soon as I called him an IRONMAN, his arms came up into a biceps-flexing pose, one of the coolest finishes of the night. A lot of guys go into a muscle pose at the finish line but Scott's flex was *immense.*

University of Central Oklahoma Endeavor Games

I remember my thoughts at that moment, because I'd had them before. *I sure wish the rest of the world could see finishes like this, not just the people in our sport. Accomplishments of this magnitude are inspiring and need to be shared.*

The scene before me also reminded me of one of my favorite posters, of a little kid named Cody McCasland. (In case you can't see the photo in your edition, it shows Cody running on two prosthetic legs. He's got a big grin and the caption says, "Your excuse is invalid.")

Scott Rigsby and Sarah Reinertsen were the Roger Bannisters of the challenged athlete world. And, in much the same way that the four-minute mile would eventually be eclipsed (ten American *high schoolers* have broken that fabled mark, and famed American miler Steve Scott did it 136 times), there was still room for more amazing accomplishments.

There was already a way for people without any use of their legs to compete in an IRONMAN race, using specially designed recumbent bicycles that were pedaled with hands and arms instead of feet and legs, and racing wheelchairs that were also arm- and hand-powered. Try to imagine pumping and pushing your way around 140.6 miles using only your arms. It's no wonder that these PC (physically challenged) athletes all look like Schwarzenegger from the waist up.

And they're way past just trying to finish. The PC division is hotly contested, with thrilling battles and longstanding rivalries. The best known of these took place in 2000, when the ever-gracious Carlos Moleda waited for his rival, David Bailey, who'd had a mechanical problem, to catch up and get the race going again.

Scott Rigsby was the first double amputee to complete an IRONMAN triathlon. It was a stupendous, much celebrated feat, as we've seen. But there was an even harder challenge out there.

Which brings us to a young man named Rudy Garcia-Tolson. His story parallels Sarah's in several ways, and veers away altogether in others. He was born with enough physical calamities to challenge half a dozen lives, but the worst were abnormalities that affected his legs. After fifteen surgeries to try to correct the defects, Rudy pointed to his scarred, twisted limbs and asked his doctors if he was ever going to be able to run around on them with the other kids.

"Well, no," was the reply. "You're going to be in a wheelchair for the rest your life."

They told the family that his best bet was a set of prosthetic legs. Which, of course, meant cutting off his real ones. But how do you convince a little kid of that?

So they explained the situation, and it took about three seconds for Rudy to say, "Fine. Get rid of 'em."

Which tells you something about Rudy. The rest, as they say, is history. It didn't take long for Rudy to push his new metal limbs to their limit, and sometimes beyond: No one kept count of how many of them he broke trying to do all the sports the other kids were doing. And every time they broke, the manufacturers came up with new ways to make them more resilient and responsive.

His favorite sport was swimming. Most swimmers get little propulsion from kicking, which primarily serves the purpose of keeping the drag-inducing legs high in the water. This is why the best swimmers in the world have short legs and long torsos. Without legs, Rudy was a torpedo in the water, and routinely came out on top in swim meets. Six years after ridding himself of his useless legs, he became the youngest challenged athlete to earn a medal at the USA Swimming National Disability Championships, setting the U.S. record in the 200m breaststroke.

It wasn't enough. So he tried running. The following year he set a national record in a half marathon, then broke it himself the year after that.

But that still wasn't enough, so he also cycled, and it was inevitable that he would discover triathlon. At first he competed on relay teams, but it wasn't long before he did all three disciplines by himself. He became the poster boy of the Challenged Athletes Foundation, a remarkable organization co-founded by my good friends Bob Babbitt, Jeffrey Essakow and Rick Kozlowski. Rudy was an inspiration and mentor to dozens of kids with serious physical challenges, who looked at him and saw possibilities for themselves.

It was a good life. He became a many-time medal winner at the Paralympic Games, competed in races all over the world, and gave motivational talks to rapt audiences. And yet...

A lot of the people he hung around with, including Babbitt, were deeply involved in IRONMAN. Always in the back of Rudy's mind was the question, "What if...?" It didn't help that his friend Sarah Reinertsen was unable to finish in her first attempt. When she triumphed in her second, that got him thinking more seriously. And when Scott Rigsby crossed the line? That sealed it altogether.

Wait: I may have forgotten to mention something: Rudy's double amputation was AK; above the knee. Rudy doesn't exist from the mid-thigh down. He ends at the same place Bermuda shorts do. He'd watched his friend Sarah, with one intact leg, struggle mightily and fail to finish an IRONMAN race her first time out. Even the second time, it was no picnic. Did someone with no knees and no quad muscles have any business even contemplating the attempt? A lot of very knowledgeable people, even those who'd devoted their lives to helping people with physical disabilities become competitive athletes, thought he was crazy to try.

They weren't worried about the swim. Rudy was *fast* in the water, and had two Paralympic gold medals to prove it. They were concerned about the run. Rudy uses a special pair of legs that make him look like he's standing atop two letter C's. The little bit of spring action in those half-circles of fiberglass substitutes for the natural springiness of ankles and calves under a hinge-like knee. What they don't do is retract the trailing foot upward as it's brought forward so that it clears the ground before being planted in front again. So instead of bringing the back foot straight forward under him, he has to swing it outward in a wide arc. (Athletes who run with Rudy have learned to treat him like they would one of those chariots with the spiked wheels in *Ben Hur* or the armored trucks in *Mad Max*: You give him a wide berth.) He'd run half marathons, but his stumps had taken a terrible beating; how much worse would it be after 112 miles of cycling?

Hard to predict, but that still wasn't the main concern. It was the bike that gave everyone pause. Without quad muscles or knees, Rudy has to cycle with his hips and glutes. He can't stand up on the pedals when ascending hills. He can't stand up *ever*, which means there's no way to give his butt or his back a break.

But he'd already done IRONMAN 70.3 races, the half distance. And one of them was Wildflower, proving he could handle hills.

Even so, IRONMAN would be exponentially harder. And he'd chosen Kona (of course), which would up the difficulty even further.

Rudy took in all the warnings from his friends and advisors, then threw it all away. "I'm doing this," he declared.

Two weeks before the race, one of his stumps swelled up alarmingly after a training run. It was also warm to the touch, so he was put on antibiotics. He didn't run another step until race day.

Didn't matter. He was going for it. And it wasn't all about him, either. Rudy was keenly aware of the impact he'd had on other challenged kids.

"If I finish an IRONMAN?" he mused. Then he shook his head, answering his own question. "Those kids are going to believe there's nothing they can't do."

Try talking him out of that.

What a great story, right? I narrated it for the crowd as NBC filmed him stepping up to the start line. I sang his praises as they got him coming out of the water after a terrific swim, and again as they ran alongside as he mounted his bike and got underway to waves of emotional cheering from the spectators.

Remembering back to Sarah, it was, as Yogi Berra once said, déjà vu all over again, right down to Rudy failing to make the bike cutoff. I got the word unofficially, from someone coming into the booth, and at first I discounted it. I knew that Rudy would have to get off his bike a few times, maybe sit by the side of the road or lie down to relieve the ache in his back. That might look like he was quitting, right?

But it was true; he couldn't finish. It was hard to tell by looking at him how he felt about it, but he showed up at the finish line and was greeted warmly. Déjà vu, sure, but with one exception: Rudy wasn't going to try again the following year; he was going to try again in *six weeks*, at IRONMAN Arizona.

This time it wasn't just a few people telling him he was crazy; it was pretty much everybody. He'd just beaten himself up badly and should be taking time to recover. Instead, he was going to step up his training?

I worried that another defeat might crack Rudy's storied resolve. Again, I'm not about to discourage anyone's ambitions, but I did ask a couple of pointed questions.

I didn't get very far. Rudy waved them all away. "If I can just get off the bike," he said, "I know I can handle the run."

Arizona made sense. It's a very flat bike course, and I remember thinking that, if he couldn't do it there, he probably couldn't do it at all, anywhere. But why so soon?

Because he didn't want to sit around and worry about it for thirteen months. Besides, he was trained up right now and hadn't run a step.

"I just need to get through the bike," he repeated.

It seemed a reasonable plan, and it seemed reasonable through his training and it seemed to still make sense as the weeks went on. Right up until about the fourteen-hour mark of the race.

As I high-fived Rudy into the water in Arizona, I noticed that he didn't have his goggles on. When I asked him why, he held them up and I saw that the strap was broken.

"What're you going to do?"

He shrugged and threw them aside. "Swim without 'em," he said, and jumped into the water.

Damn, he's tough. I was starting to feel pretty excited about the day.

I was still excited when he came out of the water with 1:01 on the clock. That was only two minutes slower than his goal, a pretty amazing feat without goggles. It put him in 141st place out of 2,400 competitors. I was even more excited when he came through the first lap of the three-loop bike course, as were the many spectators who'd come to Arizona to follow him.

Until he got closer and I saw his face. The bike wasn't going well. Nobody had expected that it would, and Rudy knew it was going to be a bear, but it was worse than he'd anticipated, as I found out from support people out on the course. Unable to stand on the pedals, pain settled into his lower back and kept getting worse. Pedaling into a headwind for the second loop didn't help, but the tailwind on the way back did. He hammered the last ninety minutes and looked pretty good coming into T2. It might not have been pleasant, and it took him nearly nine hours (for you IRONMAN newbies, that's a very, very long bike ride; some top athletes had already finished the whole race by then) but he was a half hour ahead of his goal.

Those of us watching him come into transition agreed: It looked like the weight of the world had been lifted off his shoulders. The dreaded bike ride was behind him, and he had a comfortable seven hours to get through the marathon. He took his time in the changing tent, and knocked back a sandwich and some chips. When he finally got going, he came out so fast he passed a dozen startled runners within the first 200 meters.

The Arizona course at the time was shaped like a figure-8, with one short and one long loop. He covered the first short loop, 3.5 miles, in an average of 9:15 per mile, a great pace for an amateur, greased lightning for a double amputee. The buzz about this miracle man was starting to spread through the crowd scattered around the course.

The next nine miles didn't go as well. His pace dropped to 13:24. He began walking periodically, stopping occasionally to stretch. Still, no real surprise there. He'd practically killed himself on the bike and had shot out too fast on the run because he was so excited to have gotten to that part of the race. He still had five hours to cover the last 17 miles and, as he himself had put it, "Once off the bike I could probably walk twenty-six miles and still get there in time."

By the third segment, the wheels were coming off. It was more walking than running now, and Rudy wasn't looking good doing either of them. His run cadence tends to remain constant because of that need to swing his legs in a wide arc. If he can't maintain that tempo, he can't run, and transitioning from walk to run involves a serious decision about whether he has the strength to get his legs swinging. If his form breaks down, one leg or the other doesn't go wide enough and he has to lean to compensate. All that leaning strains his back, which saps his strength, which compromises his form, which strains his back…it's a vicious cycle that's hard to break.

It got worse. At several points he had to lie down to relieve the awful pain in his back. A volunteer who was riding a bike nearby had started calling in to the finish line to let us know what was going on. Rudy had stopped for massages twice, once taking off his legs to get his stumps worked on. After the first session he'd shot off like a man reborn, jaunty and rejuvenated and making great time. It lasted about a quarter of a mile, then he got back on the ground, took off his legs and rubbed the stumps himself.

Up to this point, Rudy had tried to remain upbeat, slapping hands with other runners and smiling at shouted encouragement. Now he'd gone glassy-eyed and uncommunicative, at some points not even responding when the volunteer tried to speak with him. By Mile 22 he was in a deep hole. His average pace for the previous segment had been 16:25, and during one stretch it had taken him over half an hour to cover a mile.

I answered another phone call. "I don't see how he can finish," the volunteer said. "I'm not even sure how he's going to manage to stand back up."

Dejected, I turned to Cherie Gruenfeld, who was standing next to me at the finish line. "Doesn't look good," I said.

She pointed to my phone and I handed it over. Cherie is a 27-time IRONMAN finisher and 13-time age group world champion, but she's also an IRONMAN U certified coach. She asked the volunteer a few questions, including where exactly they were, then said, "Get him to the next aid station and put two cups of chicken broth into him. Don't ask him if he wants it; pour it down his throat if you have to!"

She looked at the race clock as she handed back the phone. "He's got ninety minutes to cover four miles."

"Can he do it?" I asked.

She nodded. "Yes."

And he did. We wouldn't know the full story until afterwards but something clicked in Rudy's head. He thought about failing again, he thought about all the CAF (Challenged Athletes Foundation) kids who were following his every move, and he thought that there wasn't anything he couldn't endure for another ninety minutes. He'd come there to *represent*, and he had a statement to make. There were no options here.

Once he'd made up his mind, the fog cleared and he got back into his earlier groove. He was barreling along so smoothly that even a short but steep uphill didn't faze him. By the time he crossed the last bridge he was moving at an insane sub-nine-minute pace.

About two hundred meters before the finish he yanked off the sweater the volunteer had given him, so everyone could see his CAF uniform, then he made the final turn and ran into a sea of photographers and race officials, along with spectators so loud they drowned out the low-flying jets descending into the nearby airport.

I had to wait until some of the noise died down before I could interview him. I was amazed at how lucid and happy he was, and I didn't even know the half of what he'd gone through out there. It was a towering accomplishment, a "double above" finishing an IRONMAN triathlon, and to this day it's never been duplicated.

By Tuesday Rudy was still aching everywhere and had developed a case of pinkeye from the ungoggled swim. As he mentally replayed the experience, he found most of his thoughts centered around the support he'd received and the effect it had had on letting him succeed. Coaches, family, friends, the Challenged Athletes Foundation, untold numbers of spectators and fellow competitors along the course...if there was a way for him to thank each of them personally, he would have. But at this moment he had to force himself to refocus.

The next morning he was heading down to Rio de Janeiro to compete in the world short course swimming championships.

As I said earlier, I believe that we are the cause of our own experiences. There are things in life we can't control, but many of those things can be overcome if we're determined enough.

I find inspiration at every IRONMAN event I cover, but I don't think there's anything that touches me more deeply than the stories of athletes like Sarah, Scott and Rudy. They were dealt hands that would have floored even the strongest among us, and not only survived but conquered their disabilities. We build the best in ourselves when no one is watching, and while their triumphs were public, their struggles to get there were private. Like every endurance athlete, their races weren't won on the race course; they were won out on the practice fields, swimming, running and biking lonely and painful mile after mile. Sure, they had loads of support from friends, family, physical therapists and the like. But nobody turned the pedals for them and nobody took those hundreds of thousands of steps for them.

Truly, they were causing their own experiences.

What makes it even more wondrous for me is that each of them failed the first time out. I can't imagine what a crushing feeling it must have been. All that work, all that pain, and all of it only after first struggling back from the initial trauma of losing their limbs. They visualized their races a thousand times, seeing every inch in their minds, watching themselves on a mental big-screen cross the finish line. Then it didn't happen.

That it might never happen didn't enter their minds. People like these don't think that way. That's not the attitude that got them as far as they'd managed to go. Each had failed dozens of times, whether it was taking that first step on a prosthetic leg and falling into a clumsy heap or crashing awkwardly on the bike because they couldn't snap a shoe out of the pedal fast enough. If adversity is what introduces you to yourself, these three were discovering themselves anew on a daily basis, and every day they got stronger. All failure meant was that they weren't strong enough yet but would get there soon. Blowing it the first time is not how any of them had planned it. But my bet is that they wouldn't rewrite it even if they could.

CHAPTER 7

1989 was a watershed year for me, the start of my IRONMAN career. It was also one of the more extraordinary years for IRONMAN itself, as you'll soon see. What I didn't know when I accepted the offer to co-announce the World Championship was that the very first IRONMAN athlete I would ever greet across a finish line was one of the best who ever lived. Not only that, but he would be winning what was arguably the greatest head-to-head competition not just in IRONMAN, but in any sport, ever.

My very first day on the job, I ran smack into the legendary race that would go down in history as Iron War. You may have heard about it, but I want to tell you about it from my perspective.

IT WAS THE CLASH OF THE TITANS, a *battle royale* between the irresistible force known as Mark Allen and the immovable object called Dave Scott. If a Hollywood screenwriter had dreamed up the lead-in to the race, his script would have been rejected as too far-fetched.

Dave had raced the World Championship seven times. Six of those times, he won.

Five of those times, the second place finisher was Mark. He was the Phil Mickelson of IRONMAN, at that time the best in the sport never to have won a major. He could beat Dave anywhere on Earth—and he had—except in Kona.

The big showdown came in 1988…or at least it was supposed to. Dave had an injury and couldn't race. Mark did, but he had two flat tires and came in fifth. I think it's just as well, because if he had won, it would have been like Evander Holyfield winning the world heavyweight championship, knowing that everyone was thinking only one thing: Nice belt, but it doesn't mean a thing until you beat Mike Tyson.

Great champions aren't defined by being the best; they're defined by *beating* the best. Winning puts them on the podium. Rivalries put them in the history books.

Which brings us to 1989.

Mark lived and trained in San Diego, so he was the favorite of everyone in the endurance crowd I ran with there. Each year when he went off to Kona we cheered for him, then we were pained at how he'd gotten beaten up by Dave. It was mystifying how he'd win everything he entered the rest of the year but the World Championship still eluded him.

So in 1989 we were hopeful again. We couldn't help wondering if we were being like Charlie Brown trying to kick the football that Lucy kept yanking away, but this time it was different, and if that screenwriter might have had a plausibility problem before, the road to Kona in '89 would have gotten him laughed off the studio lot altogether. Disney teaming up with the Lifetime Channel couldn't have thought up anything this sappy, but it happened for real.

Mark ran races around the world nine times that year. He won them all. In two of them, the second place finisher was Dave. So that was it, game over, time for Dave to step aside, Kona in October was a foregone conclusion.

Then Dave goes to Japan and rips the IRONMAN world record to shreds with a mind-blowing 8:01:32. So much for the foregone conclusion.

That these were the two best triathletes in the world was inarguable. Which one was *the* best in 1989 no one could say, and there was only way to settle the question: By winning the Big One, the one that counts, in head-to-head competition. That, of course, was the IRONMAN World Championship in Kona, where Dave and Mark would meet for the sixth time.

This time, both men were healthy. There weren't going to be any injuries or mechanical problems. Everybody knew that, barring an alien abduction of one of them, they were the only two men in contention. The rest of the field was competing for third place.

Everyone knew it was going to be epic. What they didn't know was what an understatement that was going to turn out to be.

And this time, I was going to be right in the thick of it. What a debut for me as a newbie announcer.

I had a moment of anxiety and hesitancy when the invitation came. As it happened, I'd been training to race an IRONMAN triathlon myself. I was a good marathoner and my swimming and cycling were improving all the time. Then I got the call to come and help announce the World Championship, and I couldn't do that and also race, so...

That moment of hesitancy actually lasted about 20 nanoseconds. Calling the World Championship was an irresistible opportunity. That it was going to be Mark vs. Dave was just the icing on the cake. (As it turns out, I never did do an IRONMAN race. Were I to do it, I'd want it to be Kona, but I'm not about to forgo announcing it, which means everything to me.)

One of the first things that occurred to me when I accepted the invitation was that I'd need to set aside any favoritism I might feel toward Mark in this rivalry. It would be disrespectful and unfair to Dave, and just plain unprofessional. It had also always rankled me a little to see sports play-by-play specialists showing bias, even when it seemed justified. I remember on-air broadcasters more favorably covering John McEnroe's opponents than John, because they disapproved of his personality. Same thing with Reggie Jackson, who treated the media with something less than graciousness and was sometimes paid back with less than objective coverage.

I wasn't going to fall into that trap. I feel it compromises the announcer's ability to convey to his audience a fair assessment of how a contest is going. Judgments about performance are perfectly acceptable: "That was a terrible return," or "I can't believe he let that one drop out of his glove." Subjective, of course, but good play-by-play is always subjective. It's the subtle or overt favoritism shown toward one athlete that is troublesome, and it's the reason that, while I'm happy to make observations about the strengths and track records of athletes I'm familiar with, I never make predictions about who's going to get to the podium.

In any event, making predictions was a moot point on October 14, race day. Dave and Mark had been the talk of the town in Kona all that week, and although much of that talk was about who was going to win, nobody had any idea, me included. I was just happy to have a ringside seat.

Dave knew that he was going to have to work harder than he ever had in a race to beat Mark again. He'd actually been surprised that Mark hadn't won before. Although he would never admit this out loud, he was in awe of Mark's running abilities, and he didn't know what it was about Kona that seemed to stop those abilities from pulling out a win. Was it a nutritional thing, or something about hot weather? Whatever it was, Dave had a premonition that this year the stars might align for Mark.

For five years Mark had tried everything to win, and nothing had worked. He didn't know why, but one thing he knew for sure and had resigned himself to was that Dave knew how to win in Kona and he didn't. Trying to figure out why was pointless, so he came up with a plan that might work without knowing why: He was going to shadow Dave for the entire 140.6 miles of the course. That meant staying right with him, no matter what. He wasn't going to surge if he felt good, he wasn't going to hang back to regroup if things got tough, he wasn't going to make any decisions of any kind. Only at the very end would he make his move and try to pull ahead.

There's a well-respected mantra in endurance sports: Run your own race, not someone else's. Mark was going to do the exact opposite.

At the time, of course, nobody knew what was going on in either of their heads, which was why it was so thrilling to watch the race and not truly realize what was happening until it unfolded in front of our eyes. Even then, because of the lack of modern technology, only the people who were right there on the course got the true picture. The rest of us relied on intermittent reports and wouldn't grasp the full impact until much later.

The first hint that this was going to be really different was when Dave and Mark climbed out of the water together. That was unusual because Dave was the stronger swimmer and had always gotten out well ahead of Mark. A little later, when the water safety people started coming in, they told me that Mark's fingertips were literally brushing the bottom of Dave's feet the entire length of the swim.

But they were not the leaders out of the water. They were second and third. #1 was Wolfgang Dittrich, who smashed the swim course record and came out with a 3-minute lead. It was pretty normal for stronger swimmers to jump out and then get reeled back in on the bike, and it was likely that Dave would be the first to catch Wolfgang. But there was no guarantee: Wolfgang wasn't the best runner in the field but he was one of the best cyclists. Mark and Dave had their work cut out to try to trim that huge lead before the marathon started. And surely the two of them would separate once they got on their bikes and tried to run Wolfgang down.

But they didn't separate. And while they trimmed Wolfgang's lead down to one minute, they never caught him on the bike.

The only race communications we had back then were walkie-talkies of limited range and standard, land-line telephones. Volunteer spotters out on the course would radio position information to each other, then the first guy to hit a pay phone would call it in if they were out of radio range. One of my jobs early in the day was to field those calls in the tower and relay the information to lead announcer Mike Plant, who was keeping the spectators informed of progress. Even back then there weren't a lot of pay phones out on the course, so those calls could come in 10 or 15 minutes apart, and sometimes we wouldn't hear from anybody for nearly an hour.

The reports, when they did come in, were a little odd: I hadn't heard one word about Wolfgang since they'd all come out of T1 to start the bike. I was aware that nobody was seriously thinking that anyone but Dave and Mark had a chance in this race but still, Wolfgang was the leader. Shouldn't somebody at least be figuring out how far ahead he was? Apparently not, because all eyes were on the reigning world champion and his challenger.

At one point when I was filling Plant in, he handed me the mic and said, "*You* might as well tell them." I thought I'd died and gone to heaven. This crowd was aching for information and I got to give it to them.

Except that I had nothing new to tell them. Plant had been saying "They're together," and "They're *still* together," almost since the bike leg began. Not much information there, and none on Wolfgang, but IRONMAN spectators are a sophisticated lot; they realized the significance right away, and it was being reinforced with every new update.

Still, I wanted to provide a little something more. I remembered a story about Ronald Reagan when he was broadcasting baseball games over the radio. He'd get the play-by-play via telegraph, which had a tendency to fail periodically, and he'd fill the dead spots by announcing what he thought might be happening, keeping his fingers crossed that it would make sense when he was back online.

I wasn't about to do anything that blatant, but I took a look at the last bunch of race reports, did a quick mental calculation, and said over the PA, "Mark Allen and Dave Scott are gaining on Wolfgang Dittrich. They're so far ahead, fourth place isn't even in sight behind them." Turns out that was sort of true, depending on how good the spotter's eyesight was.

We had other people in town to catch the riders as they rode in with six miles left to get to T2, the bike-to-run transition area where they'd jump off their bikes, put on running shoes and start the marathon. T2 is right in town now, in the same physical area as T1, on the pier, but back then it was six miles down Ali'i Drive. The spotters told us Mark and Dave were still together. Some of the spectators had left the finish area to go watch them as they passed by and confirmed that it was so.

Interesting and exciting, for sure, but still not that big a deal. One of them was bound to push the pace on the run. It would probably be Dave, unless Mark had hit on some magic formula and was about to confound expectations.

What *was* a big deal was how far ahead of the rest of the pack they were. Wolfgang was one minute ahead, and fourth place was six minutes behind Dave and Mark, an eternity, like a six-lap lead on AJ Foyt halfway through the Indy 500. Chatter around the booth had it that Dave and Mark had goaded each other into burning themselves out trying to catch Wolfgang, leaving nothing for the run, and what a shame that would be.

We had a spotter stationed at T2. By my estimate, Dave and Mark should have gotten there already but we'd received no call. I tried the radio but there was no response. The crowd was getting itchy because we'd told them about the astonishing lead off the bike, so I tried again.

Nothing. By this time Plant was shouting, "What's wrong!" so I tried yet again, this time yelling stupidly into the radio, like that was going to make the signal stronger or something. We were out of touch and helpless.

Then the phone rang. My hand was already on it so I picked it before the first ring finished. "What's going on!" I barked.

"They came in together," the spotter said. "They got off their bikes together, and they ran out of T2 side by side."

"Hang on, I'm going to announce it," I said.

"Wait!" the spotter shouted. *Wait for what?* I thought. "The thing is…well…they just passed Mile One."

"And…?"

"Well, I'm timing them by hand. And I'm pretty sure they went under 5:45."

For those of you not familiar with running numbers, let me tell you: That's a fast pace. And that's if you're running a standalone marathon. If you just swam 2.4 miles and biked 112 and *then* you run a marathon, it's a blistering pace. I wasn't sure I even believed it.

Then I remembered something else. In 1989 runners came out of T2 on a steep uphill and almost immediately ran down a big hill into what was called The Pit, then back up it. They had to do it on legs still wobbly from over four hours of biking. Now I was certain that the spotter had gotten it wrong. So I updated the crowd, but didn't tell them Mark's and Dave's time at Mile One, only that they'd already blown past Wolfgang, and then I added that the guy in fourth place still hadn't even gotten his running shoes on.

The spotter was on a bike, so I told him to get to Mile Two as fast as he could. It seemed like no time at all had passed when he called me. "Under eleven," he said.

Now I knew he was off his rocker. Maybe they'd worked the adrenaline for the first mile but I just couldn't believe that they'd actually speeded up. They would have to have gone under 5:15 that second mile and I simply wasn't buying it. But the show that we'd been eagerly anticipating was definitely underway now.

I don't remember the exact numbers at Mile Three but Mark and Dave were clearly laying waste to every notion we had about what was possible in an IRONMAN marathon.

I decided to keep holding off on announcing numbers and focus on color commentary. I asked the next spotter what was going on.

"Their shoulders are practically touching," came the answer.

I felt something electric run up my spine. "Are they talking to each other? Is one in front? Are they trying any surges?"

"No," he said, "None of that. They're just...they're not looking at each other, not saying anything. They're just running. It's really weird..."

I hung up and picked up the mic. "Folks, we have an update. Dave and Mark are running side by side, step for step. You could tie them together with a short string and it wouldn't break, they're that close."

Just then a spotter from the bike course came into the booth. He had a kind of dazed look as he took off his motorcycle helmet. He was a veteran who'd been working IRONMAN races almost since the beginning.

"Never seen anything like it," he said, shaking his head. "You couldn't have driven a Volkswagen between those two guys the entire way." The *entire way* was 112 miles.

Lois Schwartz

"Do you have the official times?" Plant asked him.

The spotter nodded and fished a piece of paper out of his pocket. Plant read it, then handed it to me. Mark's time was 4:37:52. Dave's was one second behind that.

Out on the run, neither of them was willing to slow down, even for a second. Dave was onto Mark's plan, of course, and knew that if he took a break, Mark would take one, too, and he wasn't about to give him a break. And Mark wasn't going to let Dave get even a body length ahead of him. They were so close that they kept bumping into each other.

Somewhere out by the airport, with about seven miles left in the race, Dave decided to see what would happen if he tried to push the already insane pace even further. He managed to open a gap of about six feet. Normally in a marathon, that wouldn't even be worth mentioning, but on this day it mattered.

Unbeknownst to Dave, he couldn't have tried this tactic at a worse time for Mark, who was in agony and trying not to show it. His legs hurt so bad it was difficult to even put one foot in front of the other, much less maintain this pace. He'd developed blisters, and they were starting to burst, bloodying his shoes and causing even more pain. He felt his energy start to drain away, and here was Dave speeding up?

Mark tried to put his mind on autopilot, conjuring up comforting images to take his conscious mind away. He didn't need a lot of mental energy to focus on his running, because his only task was to keep up with Dave. No need to look at a clock or check his turnover rate. Just watch Dave...

Except Dave was pulling away. Now Mark had to reach way down inside to find something that let him slowly work his way back.

What Mark didn't know was that the little surge was a last ditch effort by Dave to drop him. Dave was close to his limit also, and when he felt Mark closing the gap he knew that he had no moves left. He just had to hang on.

By now both of them were entertaining destructive doubts, but still they held the pace. They knew they were in the lead, but they didn't know by how much, and they didn't know how fast they were running, and neither of them cared about any of that.

But back at the finish line, we were getting reports, and we knew. At one point on the way back into town they were *three miles* ahead of the next group of athletes. I can't even find the words to tell you how preposterous that is in an IRONMAN triathlon, where gaps among the lead racers are usually measured in yards. And the guys in that second group were no slouches: In addition to Greg Welch, there was Ken Glah, Pauli Kiuru, Wolfgang Dittrich and multi-time world champion Scott Tinley.

Just under two miles before the turn from the Queen K Highway onto Palani Road was the last aid station, the last opportunity for an athlete to grab some fluids before the final push. Dave had been setting the pace all day long, but at each aid station up until this one, it was Mark who'd taken a few fast steps to be the first in. Dave had to drop back momentarily or risk not getting what he needed, which was a real possibility when runners were too close. If there was only one volunteer when both athletes reached for something, the guy behind might lose out, with no way to recover without slowing down. So Mark's moves at the aid stations weren't tactical, just practical.

But Dave had been having some trouble catching back up to Mark after the last few aid stations. At Mile 23 it had taken an uncomfortably long time. He couldn't afford that at the last station, because he knew that if he was behind before the turn onto Palani, he'd be in some serious trouble. A long downhill was coming up, and while Dave was better at downhills than Mark, he wasn't a whole lot better. So he had to get into the aid station first.

Mark felt the same way about being first before the turn. And that's why he had a plan: No matter what it took, he was going to surge before the turn and make sure he was ahead. It would be the only time all day that he would stop shadowing Dave and run his own race.

Dave was successful in reaching the aid station volunteers first. But a second later Mark arrived. And as soon as he did a voice in his head cried, "Go!" Just that one word.

And he took off without stopping for any fluids. Dave, who'd slowed to grab some water, stared in shock as Mark accelerated past him, opening a ten-foot gap, the longest of the day. Dave dropped the water and sped up.

Or tried to. The gap became fifteen feet. They were still on a slight uphill, which was Mark's strong suit, and he pressed it with everything he had before they reached the downhill.

Twenty feet. Mark threw caution to the wind and accelerated again as he made the turn. When Dave got there himself, one of two women looking at their watches said to him, "He's got thirty-three seconds on you." Dave knew that information from bystanders could be notoriously inaccurate, but when he turned onto Palani he couldn't even see Mark. Dave's plan was to go a sub-five-minute pace down the hill, but he calculated that Mark was rocketing near 4:30. As soon as he started the downhill, he knew it was over.

At the bottom of Palani there's a left-hand turn. As Mark took it, he looked back and didn't see Dave. He stopped, right in the middle of the road, bent over and clenched his fists and hissed "Yes-s-s-!" before taking off again.

I was waiting at the finish line. It was pure delirium as Mark turned onto Ali'i Drive and came into view of the crowd. Someone had handed him a little American flag, and he was waving it and gesticulating wildly as he ran. By the time he reached the finish line, tears were streaming down his face.

I didn't have a prayer of getting to him to try to get a few quick words. Catchers and friends were swarming all over him and he was far too overcome and drained to say anything anyway. Fifty-eight seconds later Dave crossed, and the crowd's appreciation for his part in a once-in-a-lifetime performance was as heartfelt and loud as it had been for Mark.

There was no smile on his face, just a look of confused disbelief. He fell into the arms of his wife and I heard him say, as more of a question than a statement, "I didn't win?"

"No, Dave," she answered. "You were second."

He had to know, of course, but what I was seeing was the mind of a champion at work, a mind that had so conditioned itself to winning that it could barely comprehend losing. He needed some external confirmation that it had actually happened before it could fully sink in. "I didn't win?" really meant, "Is this possible?"

Neither Mark nor Dave had any idea what they'd accomplished that day in relation to past IRONMAN performances. Dave had been the World Championship record holder coming into the race, and had demolished that record time by a jaw-dropping eighteen minutes. Mark, of course, demolished it better, by nearly a minute more, and his time was a full *thirty minutes* faster than his previous best in Kona.

Australian Greg Welch, who would finish third, didn't cross the line until more than 22 minutes after Dave. And he'd had a terrific race. He'd gotten off the bike somewhere around fifteenth and picked off runners one by one until passing Ken Glah on Palani and moving into third.

Mark would go on to win the World Championship five more times, making him, along with Dave, one of the greatest champions in history. Dave wouldn't win again, but five years later he managed second place at the age of forty, a stunning achievement that he believes was the best race of his illustrious IRONMAN career. (The winner that day? Greg Welch, the first non-American to win the World Championship. Welchie broke the American stranglehold on the title and gave hope to contenders from all over the world.)

Thirty years later, people still talk about the day that two men pushed themselves to the outer limit of their abilities. Witnessing it was one of the most memorable moments in my life. Later in the day I remembered that (slight) hesitation I'd had about whether to race or announce. I was so glad about the decision, and elated to have been a part of this day.

A week later, a Nike store in Chicago changed its closing time from 8:00 pm to 8:09:15, which was Mark's record-breaking finish time.

Postscript: Mark also broke the IRONMAN marathon record that day, with a time of 2:40:04. It would stand for the next 27 years. The man who broke it was Patrick Lange, at the 2016 race. Interestingly, despite that amazing run, Lange came in third. After he crossed the line and I announced the new record, I said to him, "Come on: You have to come talk to Mark Allen." He held back, shy and embarrassed. "No, no!" he said, his eyes wide. "I can't do that!" I pulled him along and when he came up to Mark, the only thing he could think of to say was, "I'm sorry!" Mark threw back his head and laughed, as did Dave Scott, who was standing next to him. "Don't worry about it," Mark said, ever the gracious gentleman. "It's about time someone broke it. It's been around too long." He held out his hand. Patrick, smiling now, took it…and wouldn't let go. He was at a loss for words but didn't want to stop shaking his idol's hand.

CHAPTER 8

Doing It for a Living

L ike marathoners, the vast majority of IRONMAN athletes are amateurs. And, like marathoners, amateur triathletes get to run right alongside the pros. Well, figuratively, anyway: There are not that many amateurs who have the stuff to run alongside professionals. If they could, they'd be professionals, too.

That's one of the best things about triathlon, and endurance sports in general. In how many sports can Joe Sixpack mix it up with the top competitors, toeing the same start line, getting the same assistance during the contest, crossing the same finish line? You don't see a lot of guys from the neighborhood shagging balls in left field at Dodger Stadium or running downfield in the Superdome. But when you cross the finish line in Kona or South Africa or New Zealand, you're apt to get a high-five from the man or woman who just won the race.

I just love these guys and gals, but my respect and admiration are based less on their amazing athletic abilities and accomplishments than on how they live their lives, conduct themselves as people, interact with age groupers and represent the sport. There's no formal obligation to do any of that, but the ones who make it a point to honor the sport like that build a much stronger legacy than just winning races.

Part of the reason for how much humility there is among pro endurance triathletes is that the sport tends to draw good people. I know that's simplistic, and I have no formal study to prove it, but I've been at this for a very long time and have brushed shoulders with more triathletes than I could possibly count. I'm constantly amazed at how humble these people are, and that's a little surprising, because this is not an inexpensive sport to pursue and few pros come from especially humble backgrounds. There *have* been studies about IRONMAN athletes, primarily as part of a city's economic justification for hosting an event, and they are way up high on the socioeconomic scale. Your typical IRONMAN athlete is college educated, financially secure and very driven. That is often a combination that spells a sense of entitlement and self-importance, but somehow those people tend to get weeded out. Or maybe they started out that way but got humbled in a hurry by the demands of the sport and the fact that their fellow competitors—trust me on this one—do not suffer self-obsessed snobs lightly. Yes, there have been one or two jerks here and there, but it's very rare and they don't last long.

The other reason that pros tend to be so well-grounded as people is that it's an incredibly tough way to make a living. So tough, in fact that very few pros are able to sustain themselves solely through racing. Prize money has gotten better over the years but, even if you consistently finish near the top, you can only do so many races in a year. The expenses of travel and equipment and coaches and physical therapists come due whether you win money or not, and endorsement revenue is available only to a rare few. Many have "day jobs" so they can pay the bills while still pursuing the sport they love. And if you get injured, there's no contract or other guarantees to fall back on.

So there are not a lot of pros who can put their noses in the air. They're jes' plain folks and it's a pleasure to be around them. Which is one of the reasons why, despite IRONMAN not getting the kind of media attention the "major leagues" attract, fans adore their pro heroes and have plenty of opportunities to get up close and personal with them.

One of those adoring fans was my son, Andy. I once pulled him out of school to come to the 1997 IRONMAN Australia with me, which resulted in a very memorable experience for him, albeit it with a harrowing beginning. Graeme Hannan, the IRONMAN license holder I told you about earlier, had arranged

Cody Beals

Sachin Shrestha/IRONMAN

for the top pros and Andy and me to be driven from the airport in Sydney to the race site in Forster, NSW, in a van hauling a trailer holding everyone's bikes. Most of us were on the same flight, so we collected our luggage and, as per Graeme's instructions, trudged over to the transportation pickup site.

There were two enormous vans, with equally enormous trailers, waiting at the curb. Graeme pointed to one and said, "I'm driving that one." Then he pointed to the other and said to me, "You're driving that one."

Wait. What? I'd never driven anything that heavy and ungainly, and certainly not with the driver's seat on the right!

"No worries, mate," Graeme said in a way that wasn't at all reassuring. "Besides, there's no one else here that's driven in Oz before."

So I climb in and put my hands on the wheel and, of course, we're on the left side of the road. Then I look in the rearview and see Paula Newby-Fraser, Canadians Peter Reid and Lori Bowden, and a few others piled in behind me. And I think, *Okay: I've got the best IRONMAN triathletes in the world in here along with my 11-year-old son. No worries, mate.*

I was hoping for a few words of encouragement but got only the kinds of stares you might see if the cabin door suddenly popped open at 35,000 feet. Then, as

I swung out into traffic, Peter said, "Don't worry; Mike has this. We're in good hands." To this day I don't know if that was supposed to be cynical or not.

Anyway, I got us all there safe and sound. Peter won the first of his three IRONMAN Australia titles, and on the way back I was driving again. Andy was in seventh heaven, sitting smack in the middle of IRONMAN royalty and lapping it all up. Peter, not normally known for being especially gregarious, struck up a conversation with him, and seemed to be genuinely enjoying it.

Then he did something remarkable. Peter was sponsored by a running shoe company that made custom, one-of-a-kind racing flats for him with his name embroidered on the back. He pulled a pair out of his bag and said to Andy, "I just won the race in these. Y'want 'em?"

Andy's eyes grew wide as saucers as Pete handed the shoes over. They were smelly and dirty and my son handled them like they were made out of solid gold. I was so happy I'd pulled him out of school to make this trip. What an object lesson he'd received about graciousness and generosity.

ONE OF MY FAVORITE IRONMAN TRADITIONS is the male and female winners coming back to the finish line to hand out medals to age groupers. I don't think that happens in many other endurance sports. Every time I think about that I remember one pro in particular, Jordan Rapp, at IRONMAN Arizona in 2014.

It was just before 10:30 at night and athletes were streaming in. It would be another half hour before the stream was reduced to a trickle, which was when I usually climbed down from the announcing booth to head to the finish line and greet finishers face to face. At that time of night my stomach is always grumbling for real food. Gels, carbo bars, pretzels and sports drinks only go so far.

The reason I remember the time so well is because it was when a smell hit me like a strong gust of wind. It was an aroma I knew all too well but I'd never smelled it at a finish line before. It made my mouth water, as I'm sure the "founders" had intended. I had just called in a finisher and looked out toward the beginning of the chute. No athlete in sight so I had a few seconds to investigate the source of the smell. I looked down toward where the timers were stationed and saw Jordan, who'd won the race hours earlier. That wasn't all that unusual, as Jordan always came back to the finish line after getting showered up and changing, to greet age groupers in the final hours.

But at that moment it wasn't Jordan I cared about. I took one more look down the chute—still no athletes—and scrambled down the ladder to grab one of the four dozen In-N-Out "Double Double" cheeseburgers he was holding in two large boxes. If you're not from the U.S. Southwest, you might not have heard of In-N-Out, an iconic chain of burger joints that, in my opinion, makes one of the best burgers in all the land.

Puzzled, I asked Jordan (but only after taking a first blissful bite) where all these burgers had come from.

"I bought 'em," he told me. "For the volunteers and workers, to thank them for being here."

Understand, Jordan had not only won the race, he'd broken the course record and cracked his own bike record as well. He should have been giving interviews and reaping all kinds of ego-feeding glory. Instead, he'd driven away from the race site and bought food for everyone. Burger in hand, I climbed back up the tower thinking that this was one of the nicest things I'd ever seen a pro, or anyone, do at a finish line.

Another pro I came to admire tremendously was three-time world champion Craig Alexander of Australia. "Crowie," as he was first called in Oz but now everywhere, was one of the best runners in the sport. (The nickname, by the way, has an obscure origin: His friends started calling him that because of his resemblance to well-known Australian surfer and lifeguard Jonathan Crowe.) The first time I saw him start out from T2 at a mad pace, I said to someone nearby, "He's going to burn himself out." The response was, "He's going to look exactly like that when he finishes."

And he did. His running form was beautiful, a textbook example of the right way to do it. Watching him put me in mind of another of the truly great runners, Mirinda "Rinny" Carfrae, who's won three IRONMAN World Championships. Coaches all over the world try to get their clients to emulate their form. Watching Crowie and Rinny run is like watching a bolt of silk unfurl.

I first met Craig at the Chicago Triathlon, which he'd won a few times, but didn't really get a glimpse into the man until the inaugural IRONMAN 70.3 World

Championship in Clearwater, Florida in 2006. We had a few interview sessions
during the week with the top pros. Craig struck me at first as quiet and somewhat
somber. I put it down to shyness or nerves being at a World Championship event.
But it wasn't long before I discovered how quick-witted he was, with a dry sense
of humor that crept up on you before you knew it was happening. There was no
nervousness, just a calm confidence and a distinct lack of bravado or swagger. In
other words, a normal guy you'd like to have as a next-door-neighbor.

The "normal guy" won the race with a two-minute margin over Simon Lessing,
himself no slouch, making Craig the first IRONMAN 70.3 World Champion. The
question that swirled around immediately afterward was whether Crowie would
become the first Australian to win in Kona since Greg Welch in 1994. He wouldn't;
that distinction went to Chris McCormack, in 2007, ending a long drought for the
triathlon-crazed Aussies. Crowie came in second that year.

In 2008, he was still talked about as a possible winner, but without quite the same
conviction as the year before.

One of the questions I'm asked most often at a race is who I think will win. I
never make predictions, and people probably think it's because I'm being discreet.
But the fact is, I try to avoid even thinking about that, because I don't want to
subconsciously put a favorite in my head. My job is to talk about each pro as though
he or she has a real shot to win. They all get equal billing from me and I don't want
to have a pick in mind that might cloud my objectivity.

Which is not to say that I wasn't thrilled when Crowie took the 2008 title, much
of it owing to a blistering 2:45 marathon. As exciting as his finish was, though,
it's not the part I remembered most fondly. That was the next day, at a party at a
restaurant following the awards ceremony. It was a boisterous affair, athletes and
race workers blowing off steam. I didn't see Craig, so I wandered around until I
finally found him, and his beautiful wife, Neri, standing by themselves at the end
of a bar connected to the restaurant.

Now that was odd, the newly-crowned world champion just standing off to the
side having a private conversation with his wife while everyone else was celebrating.
Was something wrong?

I approached cautiously. "Hey, congrats again, Craig," I said. "But what are you
two doing off by yourselves away from all the action? Most of it's for you!"

Craig shook his head in wonder. "Mike," he said quietly, "we're just so overwhelmed. We can't believe this has happened and we're just so humbled by it all!"

As I said, just like your next-door neighbors. They could have been mixing it up with everyone else and lapping up some well-deserved glory, but instead they were enjoying a moment together to reflect on this awesome experience. I thought, *this* is the standard for a world champion.

Craig would go on to win the world title twice more, his last coming in 2011 at the age of 38. He set a new world's best time of 8:03:56 in that race, cementing his reputation as, the way none other than Dave Scott put it, "the first true men's champion the sport has seen in years." That same year he won the IRONMAN 70.3 World Championship, becoming the first man ever to achieve the "double," winning both World Championships in the same year.

And the hits just kept on coming. The following year, at the inaugural IRONMAN Melbourne, Craig cemented his reputation as "Alexander the Great" by cracking the 8-hour mark.

And it was in 2014 back in Melbourne where we had the third encounter I want to tell you about. He was 41 by then but far from a novelty act; when he toes the start line, he's there to win, even at his ripe old age and against a very strong field like he was facing that morning. It wasn't a great day, beginning with a slower than normal swim. His efforts to make up the time were heroic but futile. His 8:05:46 time was certainly respectable, and even downright amazing for someone his age, but it put him in fifth place.

Despite that, the spectators greeted him as though he'd won. Crowd favorite that he is, I brought him over to the mic for an on-the-spot interview. I started it out with, "It looked like a pretty tough day out there for you."

By now there were dozens of video and still TV cameras pressing in all around us. Which made it all the more awkward when Craig didn't respond right away. He's usually an easy interviewee, articulate and quick, but now something was up, and as the seconds ticked by it was clear there were a lot of emotions at play. We let him have his time.

"This is it," he finally said, his voice quavering. "I'm done and need to retire."

His next words were captured verbatim by a publicist standing nearby. "I feel like my body is a rental car and I've been racing with the handbrake on for a while now.

I don't want to be fifth. I want to be the guy on the podium spraying everyone with champagne."

All of us who heard him and knew him were deeply touched by that public admission. Here was one of the best ever declaring that, unless he could play at the highest levels in a game he so loved, it was time to hang it up.

Robbie Little/FinisherPix

There are a lot of such "I'm never doing this again" declarations made in the immediate aftermath of an event as grueling as an IRONMAN triathlon. It's a standing joke among age groupers that most of them who "retire on the spot" are right back in line at the sign-up desk the next morning. Craig gave it one last shot, later that year at the World Championship in Kona, finishing just off the podium, and that was it. There would be no second-guessing himself for Crowie. We'd just seen his last IRONMAN competition.

As he walked away, graciously granting a few words along the way to any reporter who asked, I thought back to that shy guy in Clearwater, and to that devoted couple off to the side in Kona trying to process what had just happened, all the way to the end of a brilliant career. The way he'd chosen to go out, firmly and with no regrets, affirmed for me his stature as one of the greatest champions of all.

As it turned out, Craig was hanging up only his full-distance spurs. A year later he attacked the IRONMAN 70.3 circuit with full vigor. He's still racing it to podium finishes all over the world.

THERE HAVE BEEN DOZENS OF WONDERFUL, memorable moments involving pros, and most have been well-documented. One that is less well-known took place in Kona and involved the great Cameron Brown, one of the nicest guys in the sport. I once stayed at his house with him and his family when I was in New Zealand. Cam won the IRONMAN there, his "hometown" race, an unbelievable *twelve* times, which is a record number of wins for any single IRONMAN event, anywhere. Nobody could touch the guy.

Except in Kona. He never took the title there. The first time he tried was 2001, the year of his first victory in New Zealand, and it was an epic race. He was way behind but somehow found a new gear and began mowing his competitors down one by one, including 1997 champion Thomas Hellriegel. But American Tim DeBoom, pouring it on in the first of his two World Championship victories, had built an insurmountable 15-minute lead and Cam couldn't catch him.

The crowd by then was up to full steam. Tim was the first American male since Mark Allen to win in Kona. It couldn't have happened at a more poignant time, either: The nation was still reeling from 9/11, which had happened just the month before, and here comes an American across the line. You could practically hear "Don't Back Down" playing in the background.

After Tim took his bows, the spectators turned their attention and their energy to Cam. By then they knew what was going on, how he'd muscled his way through the front-runners, and they were revving up to give him a rip-roaring welcome. As he came down Hualalai Road and prepared to turn onto Ali'i Drive, the final stretch, I told them he was on the way in and they went crazy-loud, giving him everything they had for his amazing second-place finish.

I was down at the finish line, out of the tower, and someone got my attention and pointed behind me. I turned to see IRONMAN New Zealand race director Jane Patterson screaming at me, veins standing out on her neck. I couldn't hear a word over the crowd noise but she was holding her cell phone out towards me and shaking it. I'm thinking, *What the heck is she doing? It's going bonkers at the finish, race officials are moving in, and I don't want to miss Cam coming in!*

I held my arms out to my sides, like *What in the world are you doing!* But she only got more frantic and was now waving the phone back and forth in wide arcs, pausing only to stab at the buttons, hold the phone to her ear, then thrust it forward again. I figured I had about a minute before Cam hit the line so I ran over.

"Jennifer's on the phone!" she yelled as I got closer.

"Cameron's wife?" I asked.

She nodded and handed me the phone. "I just thought I'd set up a call between them. Can you give the phone to Cam?"

Now that was a first. I knew Jennifer was back in New Zealand, because she'd just had their first child barely two weeks before. "Is anything wrong?"

"No. She just wants to talk to him."

Well, okay. I took the phone and tried to talk to her but could barely hear anything over the noise. I finally made out, "How is he doing?"

"He's going to come in second!" I shouted, then added that I'd try to get him on as soon as I could.

Cam came in and looked like he was about to collapse. Then he collapsed. He'd given it everything he had and there was nothing left, so he just sat down about fifteen yards past the finish line.

I knelt down and put my arm around him, giving him my congratulations, and said, "Jenny's on the line."

He looked at me as though he couldn't have heard that right. Remember that this was 2001 and cell phone technology wasn't quite what it is today. I hoped that the connection from New Zealand hadn't been broken. (I found out later that the line had dropped four times while Jane was holding the phone, which is why she kept punching buttons, trying to get Jennifer back on the line.)

Then his look turned to one of alarm but I smiled and assured him everything was all right. "She just wants to say hello."

It all sounds normal, right? But if you've ever been to an IRONMAN finish line you know there was nothing normal about this. There are thousands of people watching this all going on, an athlete sitting on his bum in the middle of the finish area, music blaring, a dozen photographers behind Cam snapping away, the race announcer squatting down holding out a cell phone.

And I figure, what the heck: As long as this guy is going to chat on the phone in full view of the crowd, they might as well hear it. So I stick the mic in his face.

"Hi, hon! What? I did good today. Yes! I came in second!"

The crowd is laughing now. "Tell her how much you won," I say to Cam.

"How much did I win?" he asks me.

"Twenty thousand dollars!"

He paused for less than a second, then said into the phone, "Honey, we won $68,000 Kiwi!"

Bakke-Svensson/IRONMAN

The crowd roared, realizing that he'd done the calculation in his head almost instantly, and—I'm pretty sure—thinking that Cam hasn't figured out that everybody can hear him.

"Love you, honey. See you soon!"

By now the crowd is in hysterics. The whole thing took about a minute, and wrapped up just in time for me to get back up and greet Thomas Hellriegel as he came across in third place.

What a great moment for this tremendous athlete and wonderful mate. In 2016, Cam became the oldest male ever to win an IRONMAN race when he captured the title in New Zealand at an incredible 43 years old. I was there to call him across, just as I'd been for his eleven other titles there.

THE GREATEST IRONMAN CHAMPION EVER was Paula Newby-Fraser, the "Queen of Kona," with eight world titles. In my opinion, that record is right up there with Joe DiMaggio's 56-game hitting streak. One is reluctant to ever say never, but Paula's record will be the toughest in the sport to equal.

Which is not to say that someone won't come close. The closest female is Switzerland's Natascha Badmann, with six wins. The "Swiss Miss" was an overweight, chain-smoking secretary when a co-worker (and future husband) entered the picture and got her into endurance sports. Natascha's first go in Kona was in 1996. She might have won, but finished an impressive second because she happened to be up against Paula and her eighth and final victory.

Natascha was easy to spot out on the course: She was the one with a nonstop grin on her face the entire 140.6 miles. Some people racing IRONMAN look like they're on a forced march through an Amazonian rain forest. Natascha looks like she's at Disneyland. Which isn't to say she wasn't tough as nails. At the World Championship in 2007 she was rocketing along the Queen K Highway at 37 mph when the wind pushed her into a traffic cone. The crash shattered her bike and also shattered Natascha. She had a broken rib, torn tendons in her shoulder and "road rash" all over the place.

All of which she tried to ignore. She jumped on a replacement bike and got about another thirty miles before her husband-coach convinced her to stop. Smart call: It took several surgeries and a lot of rehab to put her back together.

Eighteen months later she set a course record at IRONMAN 70.3 New Orleans. In 2012 she won IRONMAN South Africa at the age of 45, making her the oldest IRONMAN winner ever, male or female.

But her oddest victory had come in 2004 in Kona. She'd already won the world title four times and was favored to do it again, but she finished in a surprising second place. As it turned out, the woman who came in first was later disqualified, so Natascha was the real winner.

Great victory, right?

Wrong. I remembered when American swimmers were awarded Olympic medals many years after their events, when the East Germans were finally disqualified for systematic, state-run doping. At the time I, like most other people, thought how great that must have been for the Americans, how exciting and fulfilling.

Boy, was I wrong. Winning an Olympic medal is about music playing, crowds cheering, your fellow athletes going nuts with admiration and happiness, your national flag being draped around your shoulders, then marching in glorious victory at the closing ceremonies while your parents piled all their neighbors into the house to watch on television with them.

The American swimmers got none of that. They got a medal in the mail with a note that said "Congratulations." It might as well have said, "…and don't forget to take out the garbage." No pomp, no ceremony. For many, it was just depressing, opening old wounds with very little to make up for them.

That kind of explains Natascha's reaction when she got the news that she was the actual victor. "The most hurting thing was not getting flowers," she said. People would say things to her like, "Come on, you got the paycheck, right?"

They just didn't get it. "That's not what I race for," Natascha said. "Coming down Ali'i Drive, *that's* the paycheck."

Bob Babbitt and I used to emcee a major event in San Diego called the Endurance Sports Awards, where we recognized the greatest performances of the year in triathlon, cycling, marathon running, long-distance swimming, etc. In 2004 it was scheduled to take place a few months after the IRONMAN World Championship. Bob and I cooked up an idea to help Natascha get the moment in the spotlight she'd missed out on the previous October. We set up a little finish line, stretched out an IRONMAN finishing banner, and brought Natascha up on stage to run across the line and grab the banner. When she did it, I called out, "Natascha Badmann… you are an IRONMAN world champion!" The sold-out crowd got to its feet and cheered themselves hoarse as Natascha, tears streaming down her (smiling) face, waved the victory banner.

The next year Natascha went back to Kona to claim her sixth and last title.

THESE ARE JUST A FEW OF THE MANY GREAT STORIES surrounding these giants of the sport. IRONMAN fans around the world are always hungry for news from the finish lines, and the pros have provided reporters with an endless stream of material. In 2018 Daniela Ryf of Switzerland got stung by a jellyfish in Kailua Bay, which cost her time in the swim, but she still managed to break the course record.

Chrissie Wellington, who won the IRONMAN World Championship in 2007 as a virtual unknown, came back the next year to defend her title. That's when we found out what this amazing Brit was made of. She got a flat tire at the 50-mile mark of the bike and watched her competitors fly by as she struggled to change it. We've seen athletes completely melt down when something like that happened, but Chrissie was unfazed. She fixed the flat after fellow pro Rebekah Keat generously tossed her a CO_2 cartridge (assistance no longer allowed under today's rules), got back on her bike and had the ride of her life. She claimed the second of her eventual four victories, and was unknown no longer.

Greg Welch, one of the best all-around triathletes ever, tripped and broke his collarbone hours after winning the 1994 World Championship, then spent the whole flight home fighting the pain of passengers coming up to shake his hand, because he didn't want to disappoint them.

One of the best episodes occurred at the awards ceremony in Kona in 1992. No recording exists, to the everlasting regret of everyone present, and I can't possibly do it justice in a written description, but here goes: Mark Allen had just won his fifth World Championship and, as is tradition, was called up to say a few words to the crowd of about 4,500. Now, understand that Mark is a very reserved guy, known for the spiritual approach he brings to racing and living. He could be spotted just before every race, off by himself in the finish line bleachers, eyes closed in a meditative state, wanting nothing to do with anybody at that moment. This is not a guy given to yuks as he accepts the crown of world champ.

Also understand that this was a few nights before Halloween.

So here comes Mark to the podium…wearing a wig. As he arrived at the lectern and I shook his hand, he had a deadpan expression, like, "What? Is there something wrong?" The crowd watched in confused silence, with no idea what was happening, until Mark started to speak.

In a thick, comical Italian accent. That's when everyone in the audience realized that Mark was playing Father Guido Sarducci, the fictional gossip columnist and rock critic for the Vatican newspaper made famous on *Saturday Night Live*. Mark's imitation was dead-on and eerily flawless. He skewered everything in sight, including himself ("Hey, Mark: Say something spiritual so they know it's you!"). Unfortunately, he didn't tell anybody what he was going to do, and there were no cell phone cameras in existence then. His performance is lost to the ages, so you'll have to trust me that it brought the house down. Everybody was laughing so hard I think I missed half his lines, and people talked about it for years afterwards.

You gotta love our pros.

CHAPTER 9

Better, Not Older

Paul Phillips/IRONMAN

I n Japanese culture, young people are taught to revere their elders, and to address them with perfect manners and all the respect they can conjure up.

My parents, Don and Mary Alice, gave my five siblings and me a great foundation of how to work hard and always have respect for our elders. Because I had such respect for them, I obediently showed it to other adults, even though some of the senior citizens I grew up with had few respect-worthy traits other than their age. They smoked too much, drank too much, they were overweight and cranky and unhappy and made everyone around them miserable. Sure, I was nice to them because I had to be, but even at a young age I knew that these weren't going to be my examples of how I wanted my life to go.

As I got older and stepped out into the world a little more, I started to encounter better role models. When I was 19 and a college wrestler, I worked in the health club that my brother Pat used to train and work in. Like him, I found my first mentor there.

He was an ancient 45 but in terrific shape. A wrestler as well as a weightlifter, he routinely mixed it up on the mat with guys half his age. There were also plenty of 50- and 60-year-olds who came in and worked out religiously and had positive attitudes about life. Now these were the adults I had real respect for, not because I was told to pretend that I did but because they deserved it.

Years later when IRONMAN came into my life, from the very first older racers I brought across the line it was love at first sight. The oldest female in Kona in 1989 was Joanita Reed, from Texas, and the oldest male was Norton Davey from California. These were not your typical grandfather and grandmother. They both looked like they could turn right around and do another 140.6 miles.

Funny story about Norton: He had a tendency to get surly at the award ceremonies in shorter races in which the medals are given out right after the race. It was surprising, because Norton is normally one of the nicest guys you could ever hope to meet. Somebody finally figured out that he never drank enough in the latter stages of a race and it was dehydration that was altering his mood. Getting some fluids into him as soon as he crossed the line solved the problem.

Joanita was 62 and Norton 71, which seemed miraculous back then. Now, the female 70-74 category is a fiercely contested age division, and in 2018 I brought Hiromu Inada of Japan across the line a month shy of his 86th birthday. The senior age divisions are immensely popular with finish line crowds, and a lot of spectators are aware of the exciting rivalries that go back many years.

Understand that, in triathlon, everybody battles on the exact same course that the pros are racing on, and the cutoff clock isn't adjusted for age. This isn't adult league soccer or half-court basketball; it's Wembley Stadium and Madison Square Garden.

Over the years I've had the pleasure of calling in standout athletes like 78-year-old Harriet Anderson, a grandmother of four whom I impulsively (and uncharacteristically) called the most beautiful IRONMAN ever when she finished the last of her 21 Kona races in 2013. And she was! What made that finish especially remarkable wasn't so much that she was the oldest female finisher ever, but that she'd had a bad bike crash out on the Queen K that sent her flying over a guardrail.

She was bruised, but nothing was broken, unlike the year before. In that race, she got cut off by another cyclist and went down, breaking her collarbone. She finished the ride, got fitted with a sling in T2, and was released only when she promised the medics that she'd walk the entire marathon and not run. Of course, she was only 77 that year!

One tough granny. A month after her last World Championship I received a hand-written card from Harriet. She told me that in 1989 she'd decided to do one IRONMAN race, but fell so in love with it that "…you called me an IRONMAN 22 times."

One of my favorite race week events in Kona is the IronGents and IronLadies Reception. It's a chance for athletes 60 and over to have dinner, talk about the upcoming race and swap stories. I stop by every year, along with IRONMAN CEO Andrew Messick and Senior VP of World Championship Events Diana Bertsch, just for the chance to hang out with these extraordinary people.

Tony Svensson/IRONMAN

One of the IronGents is physicist Lew Hollander. When Lew came across the line in Kona in 2012 at age 82 he still looked like someone you'd want on your side in a bar fight. He was the oldest ever finisher at the time— it was Lew's record that Hiromu Inada broke in 2018— and three years later he was still at it. His philosophy is to keep moving; he takes "Move it or lose it" very seriously and goes anaerobic every day, and never lets a day go by without his name being on at least one upcoming race list. That attitude has gotten him through 58 IRONMAN finishes.

A similar attitude got Mike Greer through 400 triathlons. A Harley-driving Texan, retired Lt. Colonel and former president of USA Triathlon, Greer (nobody calls him Mike, not even his wife, Marti) is the founder of IRONMAN 70.3 Buffalo Springs Lake, just outside of Lubbock, Texas. (It has since morphed into "IRONMAN 70.3 Lubbock.") I loved calling Buffalo Springs, which Greer and

Marti still direct, because of the down-home, country-style intimacy of the race, complete with on-site barbecue smokers at the awards banquet. Greer's 400th race, at the age of 79, is all the more remarkable because he did it thirteen months after a stroke he suffered while cycling. Races 393-399 had also taken place after that incident, which threw him over the handlebars of his bike.

Think you know tough? A few minutes after this photo was taken at the 2013 Memorial Hermann IRONMAN Texas, Fred Hemsath was carted off to the hospital for a major surgical repair of the collarbone he splintered in a fall at Mile 24. Now 77, Fred has done 461 triathlons in his 39 years of racing.

Nils Nilsen

One of the more memorable seniors is Bob Southwell, patriarch of a well-known family of triathletes from Australia. The first of the clan to do an IRONMAN race was son Tony in 1985, the inaugural year of IRONMAN Australia. It took Dad a few years to get the bug, but he did the same race in 1993, at the age of 64. One of the most amazing experiences I ever had as an announcer was calling seven Southwells across the line in 2004: Bob, all five of his sons, and a daughter-in-law. In the entire 33-year history of IRONMAN Australia as of this writing, with the exception of one year, at least one Southwell has raced, with plenty of podium finishes in their respective age groups. Son Chris was the fastest, with a personal best time of 8:47.

It was nonstop laughter around this good-natured bunch. This was a very colorful family, and saying that about people in the Aussie tri scene is saying something indeed, since there are some legendarily wild and crazy personalities from Down Under. But I think a few of the Southwells probably taught even wild and crazy Greg Welch some lessons in pranksterism.

I still remember the sight of one of the boys (I'll never say which!) at the hot corner in Australia entertaining passing athletes with a gesture it would be charitable to call "rude." Race director Ken Baggs was so amused he sent security out there to shoo him away.

Bob was the most reserved of the lot, with never a cross word for anybody, and I loved watching his face light up with pride whenever he talked about his family. They were from Cronulla, a beach-side suburb of Sydney. Cronulla was like the Boulder or San Diego of Australia, the training ground for such great IRONMAN world champions as Craig Alexander, Michellie Jones, Chris McCormack and Welchie himself. Bob was an icon in those parts, and it made me feel like a million bucks when this IRONMAN Australia Hall of Famer told me that I'd done a good job.

Bob came to Kona in 1994 and broke the 65-69 course record on his way to winning first place. His record stood for eight years. Ten years later he came back and broke the 75-79 record, one of the longest-standing age group records. It had been set by Jim Ward twelve years earlier. (When I was inducted into the USA Triathlon Hall of Fame, Jim—posthumously— was one of my fellow inductees.) The Southwell family, led by this humble, unassuming giant of a man, are legends in the Australian tri world.

The annual IronGents and IronLadies dinner was started by Bill Bell, one of the true pioneers of late-age IRONMAN racing. During one of his races, IRONMAN California in Oceanside, we got a little worried because he hadn't arrived at the finish line at the expected time. Then-president of IRONMAN North America Graham Fraser and a group of Marines went out on the course, found him, and practically dragged him in. After he crossed, he said, "Sorry I was so late, Mike. Thanks for waiting." The crowd heard it and laughed so loud that it became a running gag with Bill, who said it again in every race thereafter. It was especially apt once in Kona when he came in around 1:30 in the morning, long after the cutoff. There were still people waiting for him, though, and he said it again. (Sorry, Bill…I was long asleep by then!)

Sadly, but inevitably, we lose these wonderful people occasionally. A couple from Florida, Katie and Ralph Perry, used to race side by side the entire distance and hold hands across the finish line. The first time they did it in Kona was the first time I called out, "You are an IRONMAN couple!" After Ralph passed, Katie came back to do it one last time. The sight of her running alone down Ali'i drive was absolutely heart-wrenching, and she got an especially warm welcome at the finish from people who had watched and admired her and Ralph over the years.

One of the older athletes I was especially close to was John Cook from Connecticut. I met him on my way to an IRONMAN race in the mid-1990's. He was the pilot of the plane I was about to fly on and caught sight of my IRONMAN gear as I boarded. He asked if I was doing the race, and when I told him I was the announcer, he said that he was on his way to do it. I'm a bit of an airplane buff and here was a pilot flying to a race, so that was pretty cool. We got to talking at the race site but I didn't think much about it, other than that I might run into him at another event.

But over the next few years John was the pilot on four more flights I took to races. It got so I always peeked into the cockpit whenever I used that airline. They had over 14,000 pilots at the time so you can do the math yourself. The odds against my running into John like that were overwhelming.

He retired in 1998 after more than 30 years of commercial flying as well as a stint as a US Navy pilot. He still did IRONMAN races and I enjoyed getting to spend time with him when we met. I loved introducing him to friends as "my pilot." When I was preparing for the 2004 World Championship I noticed his name in the list of athletes. I was looking forward to seeing him again but he wasn't going to be my pilot because he'd retired. But when I got on the plane, there he was in the cabin as a passenger. When we caught sight of each other, we laughed and shrugged. "Well, this is normal," John said.

He didn't do well in Kona, though. It was a brutally windy year and quite a few of our older athletes had to drop out. He was back in 2006 and attended the

IronGents and IronLadies Reception the Monday before race day. I had the honor of addressing them. I've done this twenty years running now, and I always have the same thought: This is reversed. They're the ones who should be doing the talking. The knowledge and experience this audience has is far beyond whatever I can tell them. Their collective life experience could fill Kailua Bay.

I had nothing practical to tell them so I just told them what I felt, that they are our leaders, shining examples of the good that's possible in the world. The pros, the age groupers and the race organizers all look up to them, and they have truly earned our respect. I was looking at John as I said that and I thought about his DNF ("did not finish") two years prior. He was now two years older, and I hoped fervently that things would be different this time around.

They were. John came in with nearly an hour to spare, 10th in the 70-74 division. Calling him across was one of the highlight calls I made that day.

John ran his last triathlon in September, 2016, at the age of 81. By then he was a nine-time IRONMAN and also a USA Triathlon All American. Shortly thereafter I found out he had been diagnosed with brain cancer. I called him and we talked for a long time, about his radiation treatments, his seven Kona finishes, and how much fun it was to find ourselves on the same flights.

Toward the end of the conversation, I raised my voice and said "Hey, John: You know you're an IRONMAN!" He thanked me for that, we wished each other a Merry Christmas, and that was it.

The IRONMAN *ohana* lost John the following April. It didn't surprise me to learn that he'd donated his brain to science to help further understanding of his disease.

Now you understand why there's often a little catch in my voice when I welcome one of these amazing people at the finish. It's about respect, and my respect for these marvelous athletes knows no bounds.

CHAPTER 10

Racing for a Reason

Everybody who races does it for a "reason." What I'm talking about here is doing it for a cause outside oneself, whether it's to raise money or heighten awareness or to honor a memory.

I'll never forget the sight of Robert "Fireman Rob" Verhelst coming across the line in Kona in 2012. A 31-year-old firefighter from Madison, Wisconsin, Rob spent eight days at Ground Zero in the aftermath of 9/11, as part of the Search, Rescue and Recovery team. It was a life-changing experience for him, and exactly ten years after that unspeakable tragedy, on 9/11/2011, he raced IRONMAN Wisconsin to help raise money for the Code 3 for a Cure Foundation, to honor the 343 firefighters who were lost at the World Trade Center.

The following year he did nine more full-distance races. That's mighty impressive but to see why it was off-the-charts awe-inspiring, check out this photo:

In every one of those races, Rob ran the 26.2-mile marathon in full fire-fighting gear, including a full length fireproof suit and a metal oxygen tank on his back.

And one of those races was the World Championship in Kona. The heat and humidity on that course has felled the fittest of athletes over the years—I've known *spectators* who have fainted in that weather—and here comes this guy wearing fifty pounds of equipment (did I mention the helmet?) in tribute to his fallen brethren. No wonder that was IRONMAN's Performance of the Year.

It's also why Rob had been such a hit in the IRONMAN Wisconsin race. When he came in wearing all that gear, the crowd wouldn't stop roaring even after he'd left the finish area, so he had to step back for a curtain call.

Another Rob, Rob Ladewig, is a former Air Force officer whose brother fought in the Vietnam War and was killed there. His body was never recovered, and Rob decided to race IRONMAN as a way of bringing attention to his efforts to bring his brother's remains home. When I asked him how long he planned to keep doing IRONMAN races he said, "I'll keep doing them until they bring my brother home." Rob is seventy now and has raced in over forty IRONMAN events, including Kona in 2018. For all I know he'll keep going until he's 100. But I hope his brother comes home before that.

Which brings us to a man named Jon Blais. Jon was one of the toughest, most determined guys I'd ever met.

And he stayed that way the whole time he was dying.

Up until the spring of 2005 things were going really well for Jon. Massachusetts-born, he'd moved to San Diego in order to pursue his passion for triathlon and the multisport lifestyle. A dedicated teacher, he also had a personal mission to work with at-risk, learning-disabled children. He was on the staff of a school that shared his goal of transforming troubled young people into productive citizens. This was the source of one of my strongest connections with him: My degree was in special education and, like Jon, I'd taught troubled kids in San Diego.

Then came May 2, 2005.

A word about amyotrophic lateral sclerosis, better known as ALS or "Lou Gehrig's disease." There's no positive spin you can put on anything to do with ALS. It's a disease in which the nerves controlling voluntary muscles degenerate and eventually die. There's no heroic fighting, there are no miracles. There's no cure. It's progressive, which means you get steadily worse, slowly losing your ability to eat, to stand or walk and, eventually, to breathe on your own. It's insidious and it's evil, striking otherwise healthy people in the prime of their lives. I've said it elsewhere in this book, that there are few things worse than parents losing a child, but watching it happen over a period of two years, and knowing how it's going to end and there's nothing you can do about it, is the very worst of all.

ALS leaves your mental functions unimpaired, a special cruelty in itself. "No one is beating ALS," Jon said. "No one has done anything but walk away and die."

But Jon didn't walk away from his May 2 diagnosis. He wasn't going to kid himself into thinking he could beat ALS, but he was absolutely determined to outwit it at least once before his time was up. I found out about it just before I interviewed him at a function in San Diego in 2005 right after his life changed forever.

John was going to race IRONMAN. In Kona.

I was incredulous. "Do your doctors think this is a good idea?"

He laughed. "One of them said that the only way I was going to make it across that finish line is if they rolled me across."

During the interview I asked, "How do you feel about finishing?"

"Mike," Jon responded, "even if I have to be rolled across the finish line, I'm finishing."

By then the idea of racing for a cause had taken hold. Jon was going to do as much as he possibly could in the time he had left to raise awareness and money in pursuit of a cure. He dubbed himself the "Blazeman Poet," wrote poetry, and talked to as many people as he could about the dire need to find a way to rid the world of this disease. He had no illusions about being able to save himself but wanted the rest of his life to mean something. The mantra of the Blazeman Foundation, an organization created at his urging, was "So that others may live."

By the time the World Championship rolled around that October, Jon was ailing and out of shape. His doctors had resigned themselves to him doing the race, but they were steadfast in their insistence that intense training would shorten the time he had left. Nevertheless, there he was, stepping into the waters of Kailua Bay.

"It was the longest day of our lives," Jon's mother Mary Ann remembers. "He carried the weight of so many PALS ("persons with ALS") that day."

Thirty-one minutes before the midnight cutoff, Jon appeared at the finish line.

And then he stopped. He got down on the ground, stretched his arms above his head…

And rolled across the line, sticking it to the beast, if only for a moment, and creating one of the purest moments of inspiration I'd ever seen. I won't even try to describe how the huge crowd in the finish area reacted.

The next year Jon was in a wheelchair but he came back to Kona, this time as a spectator. He was positioned at the swim exit, and it was incredible to watch swimmer after swimmer emerge from the water and veer off to the side to give Jon a hug or a hand slap before moving on. We saw a lot of each other during race week, and he'd lost none of his sense of humor. He kidded me endlessly about running in my skivvies during the annual Underpants Run charity event, and laughed 'til his face reddened when I shot back that at least I didn't have hairy legs like his.

One of the highest honors I ever had was at the IRONMAN 70.3 World Championship in Clearwater, Florida that November. It had only been five weeks since Kona but further deterioration was evident in Jon. He had difficulty speaking so, with him next to me on stage and his parents standing behind his chair, I read aloud a letter Jon had written. It was poetic, uplifting, and contained not a hint of

Blais Family

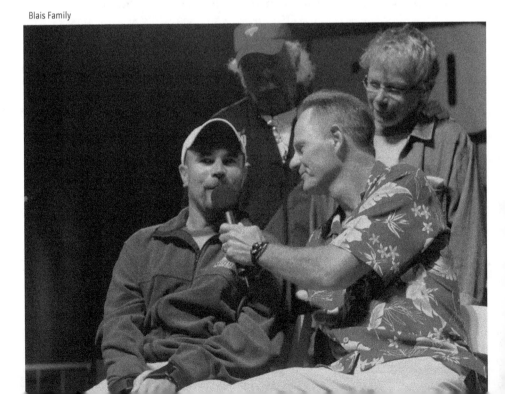

self-pity. He talked about his foundation and toward the end challenged the crowd with this: "They say hope is a good thing, maybe the best of things, and good things never die. It is my hope tonight, as I become a part of your past, you never let go of the competitor who lives within you."

Reading that letter was one of the hardest things I've ever done, but I viewed it as a sacred trust, and did what I could to make sure every word was clear so that Jon's message could come through.

The following May, we lost the Warrior Poet. He was 36. We all knew it was going to happen, but it didn't lessen the sadness. I announced IRONMAN Coeur d'Alene shortly after, and out of nowhere Jon popped into my mind and I found myself on the PA dedicating the day to him. I wasn't looking for a response but was touched when all the athletes raised their arms in the air and cheered. That winter Jon's parents Mary Ann and Bob came to San Diego and we spread some of Jon's ashes near Mission Bay, close to the site of the first-ever triathlon.

Jon's legacy is in full force. His parents have dedicated themselves to the Blazeman Foundation, which urges research into ALS and raises money to support the efforts of researchers. Supporters include such IRONMAN luminaries as Leanda Cave, Andy Potts, Mirinda Carfrae, Chrissie Wellington, Matt Russell and Scott Tinley.

The Foundation was intentional. But Jon also started a tradition without realizing it. I can't swear as to who did it first, but those pros I mentioned began rolling themselves across finish lines in imitative tribute to the first—and so far only—person with ALS to finish an IRONMAN triathlon. It came to be called the Blazeman Roll, and before long triathletes the world over were doing it to bring attention to the cause of finding a cure.

Four-time world champion and former world record holder Chrissie Wellington saw Leanda Cave roll across the Kona finish line in 2007. "I met Jon's parents, Bob and Mary Ann, later in the evening of my first World Championship," Chrissie told me, "and was so moved by his story that I followed Leanda and a few other professionals in becoming a patron of the Blazeman Foundation." Chrissie has rolled across the finish line of every triathlon she's done since that day.

The World Triathlon Corporation also began a tradition of allowing selected athletes to wear bib number 179 in IRONMAN events. It was the number Jon wore in 2005.

Like I said, there's no positive spin to put on ALS itself. But there's a lot we can say about one special man's extraordinary effort to not cede total defeat. Jon's race in 2005 wasn't just a personal victory but a spark that ignited awareness and a more concentrated search for a cure. IRONMAN competitors who knew Jon or knew of him evoke the memory of his superhuman effort to keep themselves going when their bodies threaten to surrender.

A few years ago I opened a package from Bob and Mary Ann Blais to find a beautiful piece of art. It's a swirl of color and, if you look carefully, the number "179" emerges. I keep it on my office wall as a constant reminder that, as Jon and forty years of IRONMAN have shown us, we are often at our very best when things are at their very worst.

CHAPTER 11

I t's become half cliché, half joke to ask, "Are these people crazy?" It's not an unreasonable question for "outsiders" to ask. After all, an IRONMAN triathlon is no 5K. It's not the kind of race you can run every weekend and train for by putting in five or six hours a week. IRONMAN athletes put in as much as five or six hours a *day*, and often more. It's about getting up before dawn to get in a swim in time to start running or cycling by the time the sun is up. Imagine a year of doing that if you have a job and a family.

And if you do have a job and a family, IRONMAN is not a solo endeavor. It takes cooperation from your boss and colleagues, and a full commitment from your significant other and your kids. They're going to see a whole lot less of you than they're used to, and when they do see you, you're likely to be exhausted, not just from training but from the effort of juggling your life to make it all fit.

It's a pretty expensive sport, too. The average bike costs twice as much as my first car (which, by the way, is still parked in my garage). There are very few IRONMAN events down the block from where you live, so you're going to be traveling, by air, and not just to your primary race but to all the training and warmup events. And if your goal is to get to the Big One in Kona, you're going to have to qualify by finishing high up on the podium at an earlier IRONMAN competition.

All of that just to spend a full day of agony dragging yourself across 140.6 miles under your own power. And for what? Bragging rights? Because unless you're one of a very small handful of elite racers, there's no money in it.

Is this the very definition of obsession?

Good question. To try to answer it, let me introduce you to The Club.

T HE CLUB IS AMONG THE MOST EXCLUSIVE in the world, but there are no dues, no newsletter, no officers, no assets, not even a website. (They do have shirts, though.)

The Club only has five members. That's not because they want to keep others out. Quite the opposite. They'd be thrilled to have more and, as a matter of fact, if you qualify, there's no interview or other admissions process. There's just a single, simple criterion for admittance, and if you meet it, you're in, no more questions asked.

That simple criterion is this: You have to have done every single IRONMAN race currently in existence at least once.

The unwritten rules include one small codicil: If a race changes cities, it's a new race. Which is why all five members had to show up in November 2018 to participate in IRONMAN Florida, which had moved to Haines City.

What, you may ask, happens if someone misses a new race but does it the following year? Do they get thrown out and readmitted? Is their membership put on suspension? Philosophers will undoubtedly debate this for years, but for now it's moot, because they all showed up in Haines City, as evidenced in this photo:

From left to right:

- John Wragg, Canada (68, retired schoolteacher): IRONMAN Florida was his 248th. Yes, you read that right. With a tendency to go to the extreme no matter what he does, he channeled it toward a pursuit ("exercise addiction") that will never get him into trouble. He'll tell you that the camaraderie of the Club is the best thing he's ever had in his life.

- Elizabeth Model, Canada (59, CEO): IRONMAN Florida was her 92nd. She's head of the 1500-member Downtown Surrey Business Improvement Association. Surrey is the second largest city in British Columbia, Canada, and her job entails economic development, government advocacy and marketing.

- Luis Alvarez, Mexico (56, industrialist): In addition to his 161 IRONMAN finishes, he's climbed the seven highest peaks in the world, including Mt. Everest. He also guided a blind athlete through an IRONMAN race. Twice.

- Holger Mueller, Germany (45, software developer): 59 races. He's the newest member, having been inducted (i.e., "Here's a beer…you're in") after finishing the race on Pescadores Island in Taiwan in 2018. Back in 2002 his longest swim had been 20 meters. He didn't do his first official IRONMAN race until 2005, in Austria. He's never had a trainer, never trained with a group, but he finished 59 IRONMAN events in fourteen years.

- Jeff Jonas, USA (54, data scientist): Became a quadriplegic after a car accident. He recovered, and is the only member of The Club to have done every IRONMAN race just once. (61 altogether, which is more than the current count of races, because a couple of them moved to different cities.) After his recovery, Jeff decided to simplify his life. And, since nobody in this little family ever does anything halfway, he took "simplify" to its limit. His goal (which he reached) was to never have more than 200 pounds of possessions. He sold his houses, his cars, and nearly all his clothes. He took a picture of all his IRONMAN medals and gave them away. He lives in hotels 365 days a year and rents bikes.

If you're someone who thinks that only an obsessive would undertake an IRONMAN triathlon, what do you think about five people who, collectively, have done over 600?

Before you answer, let me add a little fuel to the debate fire: In 2016, Jeff and Luis decided they wanted to do IRONMAN races in both Mallorca and Chattanooga. Given their considerable fitness and sturdiness, it doesn't seem unreasonable, offhand. Except that Chattanooga was one day after Mallorca. Nevertheless, they both finished both races.

Unbelievable, right?

Oh, wait…I forgot one little tidbit of information. Mallorca is in Spain. For those of you without a globe handy, that's 4,600 miles from Chattanooga. So they chartered a Gulfstream G4 to fly them back to the U.S., along with their "Sherpa," Dave Orlowski, one of the original IRONMAN finishers in 1978. They got to Tennessee at 4:00 am, just in time to start setting up their bikes at 5:00 am.

So now I think we're ready to start talking about obsession. The medical definition is, "a persistent, disturbing preoccupation with an often unreasonable idea or feeling."

The bottom line for me? IRONMAN athletes might be driven, goal-oriented, highly-motivated, focused, determined and obviously preoccupied, but that doesn't constitute "obsession" because there's nothing disturbing or unreasonable about what they do.

And that goes for The Club, too. The key line above is, "They chartered a Gulfstream." It takes a lot of money to charter a Gulfstream, and they could afford it because these are very successful people. Jeff started and sold a bunch of businesses, and recently started a new one. Luis is a hugely successful businessman based in Tlalpan, Mexico. He owns a string of factories and manages to keep a tight hand on the tiller even while training and racing. He's also got a beautiful family that loves—and shares—his preoccupation.

The only thing abnormal about this group is their off-the-charts levels of achievement. "Halfway" isn't in their vocabulary. So when they got into IRONMAN, it was only natural for them to find a way to take it to the limit. They didn't start out with that ambition, but when they each discovered that there were others out there with the same record of having done every IRONMAN event, they gravitated towards each other and became a family.

Why do they do it? For the same reason someone climbs mountains or swims the English Channel (which, incidentally, Luis is planning to do in 2019). It's difficult, it's fun, it gives you something to shoot for that very few people have accomplished.

In the case of The Club, it's also about bonding with others who "get" what you're doing and are committed to helping each other keep going. I had dinner with all of them the night before they did the inaugural IRONMAN Florida Haines City in 2018 and I got a pretty good feel for what this bunch is all about. It's not the streak itself that's important; that's just the vehicle that lets them be with other IRONMAN people, grow tight over a common pursuit and travel around the world to do more than lie on a beach. They get excited at the prospect of a new event (like the one they were doing the next morning) because they'll all go and have a chance to race together and keep the chain going. How cool is that?

Is there some ego and bragging rights in there? Of course there is. What's wrong with that? Everyone who's accomplished something extraordinary has ego wrapped up in it, whether it's winning an Olympic medal or the presidency, getting a PhD or becoming a surgeon, being promoted to manager of the receivables department or getting that last petal on your Good Manners Clover in kindergarten. Ego is what drives us to achieve, and that's as true of Gandhi as it was for Muhammed Ali. As long as you're doing it toward a worthwhile purpose, whether it's for your own self-betterment or that of others or both, I say go for it. But the members of The Club are not publicity-seeking chest thumpers. Most people in the IRONMAN world don't even know the Club exists. It's more of an inward thing, an ongoing sense of satisfaction and camaraderie. "No way any of us could do this alone," Elizabeth said to me at dinner. "If any of us stopped, we'd be done."

Which is not to say that an unhealthy obsession with IRONMAN is unheard of. It isn't. People occasionally overdo it and behave selfishly, putting their own dreams and aspirations ahead of concern for their families. I met a guy in Lake Placid who lost his home, his family and almost his life because what he really lost was his balance. He became pathologically fixated on his training to the exclusion of everything else. But there's no doubt in my mind that, had he not gotten into endurance sports, his addictive personality would have found another way for him to self-destruct. (Thankfully, he recognized the problem and got himself straightened out, without giving up long-distance racing.)

IRONMAN has a way of worming itself into your life. A lot of people who plan to do just one for the bucket list and be done with it find themselves drawn in, because IRONMAN isn't just a race; it's a lifestyle. My co-author loves to tell the story of his wife, Cherie, who took a 6-month leave of absence from an enviable executive position in the artificial intelligence industry to try just one IRONMAN triathlon. It happened to be the World Championship, and when she came across the line, he took one look at her face, turned to her brother and said (his words, verbatim), "That broad ain't never going back to work!" (He was right; she went on to do 26 more and rack up 13 world titles to boot.)

I've heard it a thousand times, that doing this race gives people purpose and makes them focus. They love being part of the IRONMAN *'ohana*, and they love being trim and fit and full of stamina.

I've announced at more marathons than I can count, and run over a dozen myself, and can tell you that endurance runners are one fit bunch of people. It's pretty impressive to see those bodies massed at the start line, but a lot of them, especially the elite runners, look a little on the thin side.

But if you're ever at the start of an IRONMAN event, your eyes will bug right out of your head. Imagine a marathoner who did body-building for a year and that's what your typical long-distance triathlete looks like. These are the fittest people on earth; who wouldn't want to be like that?

I've met thousands of IRONMAN athletes, from the top pros to do-it-once amateurs to The Club, who've made IRONMAN their hobby. I've listened to their stories and I'm not buying this crazy obsession business, not on any level. To the contrary, in addition to being a healthy and rewarding pursuit, it's one of the most successful non-pharmaceutical antidotes to a troubled or aimless life you're ever likely to see.

And speaking of The Club: I've never met a happier, more successful and tightly-knit group of friends in my life. Five minutes with them and you'd feel the same. What they do might sound obsessive on paper but they're challenging themselves—and having an absolute blast doing it—while leading balanced lives. (At the dinner I attended, newest member Holger had been welcomed in only a month before and beamed the entire evening like a kid who'd just moved to Disneyland.)

I have to confess that I get a little apprehensive when I call one of The Club across the line, or other streak legends like Ken Glah, a former pro who's done Kona 35 times in a row, in case there's a rookie running in at the same time. I try to make everyone feel special, as though they're the only ones who have ever heard, "You are an IRONMAN!" I can't help wondering what one of them would feel like if, a few seconds later they heard, "Here comes Luis Alvarez finishing his 161st IRONMAN!" as though their own accomplishment was something lesser. Fortunately, the "Fab Five" don't give a hoot whether I provide that information to the crowd or not, so I do whatever works at the moment.

By the way: John and Elizabeth met at the post-race food tent at IRONMAN Arizona in 2006 and hit it off right away. John lives in Toronto and Elizabeth in Vancouver, on the other side of the continent, but John did a running event in Vancouver just to race with her. That was their first date. They're an item now, and they've decided that Elizabeth should try to qualify for the World Championship in Kona again as her 100th IRONMAN race, and the next day they'll get married.

I'll put the photos on my website.

CHAPTER 12

P eople race IRONMAN for a lot of reasons, many of which I talk about throughout this book. Pushing yourself that hard can bring healing, serenity, transformation and discovery.

It can also help people cope. Whenever I think about that, several people pop into my mind, especially two different Kristins. One of them is Kristin Jarrett. Her story, although terribly sad, brings a smile to my face every time I think about it.

Kristin was an experienced IRONMAN triathlete and also very close to her mother, who was a source of great inspiration to her. During Kristin's training for the 2016 IRONMAN Texas, which she planned to do with her husband Chad, Mom was diagnosed with bile duct cancer. It quickly became a terrible struggle, and Kristin, 31 at the time, decided she wasn't going to do the race. But Mom was adamant that she not abandon her training. During the next six months, Kristin would spend a week at home, then drive three hours to spend a week with her Mom while she underwent chemo. Inspired by her daughter's training, Mom was determined to fight back as hard as she could. She'd walk twice a day and, when the effects of chemo were too debilitating, she'd ride her recumbent bike inside.

Mom and her courageous battle were all Kristin could think about while swimming, biking and running. She told her mother that it was all for her, and promised that any medal she won would be hers. When Mom passed away before the race, Kristin was devastated and found herself unable to even think about getting into a pool or riding her bike or hitting the pavement.

But she'd made a promise, and considered it sacred. So she resumed her training, with renewed purpose, and tried to fight back the way her mother had.

The race did not go well. She somehow ingested water and had trouble breathing, unable to take more than two strokes at a time.

She called to one of the safety kayakers, knowing that she could still continue the race so long as she didn't make any forward motion while grabbing on.

But the medical team pulled her out of the water and took her to the ER. She was spitting mad, but it turned out the medics had made a great call: Kristin's oxygen saturation level was a dangerously low 90% and a chest x-ray revealed a pulmonary inflammation. By then she was sobbing uncontrollably, stabbed by the pain of having failed to keep her promise.

Her husband had no idea any of this was going on, and had a terrific race. When he learned what had happened to his wife, he felt awful for her. On the way home she told him that, given that terrible experience, planning a baby and the demands of work, she wasn't going to do an IRONMAN race again.

Chad was having none of it. "You're in shape," he said, "and you promised your mother. So let's try it at home."

And thus did he engineer the best part of this story. Chad set up a private, full-distance IRONMAN Texas II right in their neighborhood. As Kristin told me afterward, "He was my race director, lifeguard, volunteer coordinator, aid station captain, traffic controller and substitute Mike Reilly."

It started in Joe Pool Lake near Dallas, where Chad had measured out a swim course. Her bike was set up in the parking lot, and Chad rode with her, carrying nutrition in a backpack. Bathroom breaks came at a Porta Potty at a construction site. "T2" was inside the house, and her transition bags were the ones from IRONMAN Texas.

The run consisted of loops through nearby neighborhoods. Each loop ended at the house, where Chad stayed to man the aid station. Each time Kristin showed up, he was playing different music and wearing different clothes, and even different sunglasses, to heighten the illusion that she was running through different aid stations.

At the end she was greeted with finish line music ("Don't Stop Believing") and the front door wide open. As she ran through the "arch," she saw her dining room chairs lined up on two sides, draped with blankets and banners. It was her finishing chute.

I often call out "Welcome home!" to athletes as they end their races, but this may have been the only time in triathlon history that it's ever been literally true. And, you guessed it: She got a big, loud, "Kristen Jarrett...you are an IRONMAN!" from Chad (she told me he totally nailed it), and then he hung the medal he'd won the week before around her neck.

Her time, according to the race clock on Chad's wrist, was 12:52:07. First place in her age group that day! (In the interest of historical accuracy: The bike course at IRONMAN Texas had been reduced to 95 miles because of flooding, so that's how far she rode.)

Kirstin found that race incredibly satisfying. Mom had always told her to work hard, even when there was nobody watching. At this finish there was no fame or glory, no audience, no after party and no big celebration. It was perfect.

Kristin panicked when she got into the water at the start of IRONMAN Chattanooga later that year, remembering her disastrous first race in Texas, but she thought about her mother and got over it as soon as the cannon went off, and ended up with her best finish time ever. Six weeks later she and Chad raced IRONMAN Florida, a year later Chad realized his dream and competed in Kona, and a year after that they had their baby boy, Eli.

"IRONMAN isn't about winning a race or even winning a medal," Kristin told me. "It's about working hard, not giving up and fighting. It's about pushing even when someone else says we don't stand a chance. I will never be the fastest athlete out there, but I'll continue to be inspired by my mom, and will draw strength from the one who taught me what real strength is. My mom deserves the title more than anyone. She is my IRONMAN."

So that was the first Kristin.

IRONMAN *Santa Rosa, 2017*

My son Andy and I had just videotaped an interview with a 38-year-old age group competitor named Kristin McQueen. She was thin and fragile-looking and, as she walked away after the taping, Andy said, "Dad, do you think she's going to make it?"

One of the most gratifying things about being a parent is earning enough respect from your children that they value your opinions. What a joy when they ask for your advice, especially when they're grown and are making their own way in the world. That they still seek your counsel makes you feel like you did something right. They might not always follow your guidance — and who's to say your guidance is always sound? — but having an adult back-and-forth with the kid whose diapers you used to change is a blessing beyond description.

So here's my strapping 32-year-old boy, a boy no longer, settled into a beautiful family of his own and running a successful business, asking me what I think about this woman we just spent some time with.

Except, he doesn't sound like a grown man. He sounds like a little kid, a scared one, in fact, with a bit of a tremor in his voice. Because he's not asking me if I think Kristin McQueen is going to make it to the finish line tomorrow.

He's asking me if I think she's going to live.

WHEN WE FIRST MEET SOMEONE, all we see is the physical aspect. That's only natural, but sometimes it leads to snap judgments that blind us to the far more important inner being.

That interview was my first meeting with Kristin. I knew that she'd already completed 17 IRONMAN races, including the World Championship in 2015, but as she walked up to me that day in Santa Rosa I would have bet half my life savings that she'd never make the swim cutoff the next day.

That began to change as soon as she hugged me, greeting me like an old friend based on the email relationship we'd struck up. Weird as it might sound, I felt something powerful emanating from her, something that transcended the surprising physical strength of her embrace. It seemed to come from within, from a place that no infirmity could touch.

So let's get to that infirmity. Fourteen years prior, at the age of 24, Kristin had been training as a physical therapist. The objective of the day's class was to feel parts of the body and become familiar with the placement and role of muscles, bones and tendons. Running her hand upward from her shoulder, she felt a soft, pea-sized lump on the side of her neck. It wasn't painful or especially noticeable, so she ignored it and continued on with the assignment.

Three months later the little pea had grown and solidified into a hard marble, and now she was worried. Three doctors told her she shouldn't be. But Kristin was an active marathon runner typically full of boundless energy, and she'd begun to feel run down and sluggish. When she mentioned this to a fourth doctor, he thought it might be a good idea to run some tests.

It was metastatic cancer. It had started in her thyroid but had spread to the soft tissues of her neck and lymph nodes. It's a mean, nasty disease that not only wants to kill you but causes terrible pain while it's trying. Kristin's cancer gave her trigeminal neuralgia, a condition that affects the largest of the cranial nerves. I'll spare you the details but just tell you that the pain is so excruciating and chronic that often even powerful opioids don't help. Its intensity can impact both physical and mental capacity; another name for trigeminal neuralgia is the "suicide disease." Kristin told me it sometimes feels like going through five root canals at once.

The prognosis for victims of metastatic thyroid cancer is not good, but Kristin tried to push negativity out of her mind. She continued competing in marathons in between neck surgeries and radiation therapy. She had no desire to be pitied as that poor girl with cancer. She wanted to be respected and appreciated for her work and her accomplishments, and to maintain normal friendships that weren't centered around her illness.

For about three years, it seemed to be working. The radiation was shrinking her thyroid cancer. Then she got thrown the nastiest curve ball yet, when the cure turned out to be worse than the disease: All of that radiation to treat her thyroid had given her brain cancer. And multiple surgeries were going to be required.

As if surgery on her neck hadn't been daunting enough. How would you have reacted upon hearing that news? Me, I would have been tempted to just curl up into a ball and roll into a dark corner.

But Kristin took it very personally. Cancer was no longer some mindless "thing" that was happening to her. Now it was the enemy, and you don't just resist and defend against an enemy: You attack.

Up until now, her "fight" had been largely passive. She took the medications, she underwent surgeries, she absorbed whatever radiation the doctors threw at her. What else can a patient do but let things happen to her? She had tried valiantly to maintain a normal life but that had only gotten her so far. Wasn't there a more forceful way to stick it to cancer?

Maybe. Kristin decided she was going to tackle an IRONMAN triathlon, and she was going to do it in parallel with the brain surgeries. Both journeys would start together and proceed together. It was her way to tell cancer to "Suck it!"

(Side note: To my mind, there's no situation where it's appropriate for an announcer to utter a profanity over a PA system. Over 40 years I can count only twice when I let little mild ones slip. But it sure does feel good to yell, "Suck it, cancer!" every time Kristin steps over a finish line.)

Alan Ramirez

Her brain surgeries and IRONMAN journey began in 2008. When her problems were limited to the thyroid cancer, she raced marathons to help her get through it. When the surgeries got tougher and moved to her brain, she moved to IRONMAN to make the races tougher. Every start line was a victory, every finish her way to tell cancer where to go. She raced with purpose, too, having become an advocate for the American Cancer Society six years prior. Every race she does is for the cause, and so far she's raised over $185,000 to help in the fight against this most universally dreaded of all diseases. She carries an "angel list" containing the names of cancer patients she's racing for, including the ones who are no longer with us. When she finished the World Championship in Kona, she held it up high for all to see.

Cancer has wreaked havoc on her life and taken many things from her, but it can never steal her smile, or sense of humor, or that energy I felt within her.

Which is not to paint too rosy a picture of her situation. She's had a number of debilitating complications, starting with her second brain surgery in 2008. Trying to work his way through a complicated part of the procedure, the surgeon nicked the nerve responsible for balance and hearing. She awoke with the room spinning crazily and the only thing she could hear out of her right ear was something that sounded like a train horn blowing straight into it. She couldn't open her eyes without throwing up, so a few days later when she asked a resident when she could start training for IRONMAN racing, he laughed out loud and told her to find a new hobby.

Struggling with vertigo, she had to re-learn how to sit, stand and walk without falling over. Wearing a "fall risk bracelet" on the bike and run, she pressed on.

And all those physical challenges were compounded by the financial ones. Her insurance didn't come close to covering her costs and, although she wanted desperately to have a steady job and felt she could handle one, her medical history wasn't something potential employers looked on kindly.

Let me cut to the chase, because it's so incredible there's no dramatic lead-up necessary. Kristin has a simple goal: to keep the number of her IRONMAN races higher than the number of her surgeries. Ten years after waking up in that spinning hospital room, she'd completed 20 IRONMAN races and 6 IRONMAN 70.3 events, with not a single DNF. She'd also fought through 24 total surgeries, 16 of them on her brain. So it's IRONMAN 26, Surgery 24.

Suck it, cancer!

The incredulous and disbelieving resident who dismissed her ambition with a laugh has faded into memory. Kristin found a doctor who cares deeply about her and arranged for advanced treatments to deal with the cranial pain, which still attacks her with depressing frequency. It means more surgeries but, based on the race schedule she recently sent me, she has every intention of gaining ground on her competition with cancer. And, her new surgeon is so supportive of her ambition, he schedules her operations around her IRONMAN calendar!

Andy, here's the answer to your question: Kirstin has already made it, and she's still making it. The title of this chapter is "Coping," but that's far too limp and reductive to describe what Kristin is doing. She's thriving, and doing it gloriously.

As I write this, I'm staring at her name on the competitor list for the 2019 IRONMAN Wisconsin.

CHAPTER 13

"You don't throw away a whole life just 'cause it's banged up a little."

A great movie line, spoken by trainer Tom Smith (played by Chris Cooper) about a feisty, undersized, injured horse about to be put down by its owner. Smith stops the shooting and takes the horse for his own. Its name was Seabiscuit, and you know the rest of that story.

Every life has value, but sometimes it's difficult to know just what the right formula is for bringing that value into the light. I've often wondered if each of us is born to do a particular something, and whether a good life is about finding out what that something is.

Sometimes, it's obvious. Shaquille O'Neal was six-foot-six by the time he was 13, so it wasn't a great leap of imagination to think he might try his hand at basketball someday.

Sometimes, it's not so obvious. Scott Kelly was a troubled, troublesome teen headed nowhere until he got bitten by the space bug. Fascinated by the idea of going "out there," he straightened himself out, knuckled down in school, and was relentless in pursuit of his goal, which was to enter the astronaut program. Eventually, Kelly spent a year on the International Space Station.

A destitute country boy trying to open a general store in the 1840s bought a barrel of books from an equally poor farmer, not for the books but because he wanted the barrel for his store. It turned out it was full of law books. The young man read one, devoured the rest, and decided to become a lawyer. His name was Abraham Lincoln.

Stories of transformations like these fascinate me. How do people, especially those in difficulty, manage to latch onto something that gives them hope and direction? And what are those *somethings* that have such power to bring about significant and lasting changes?

For many people, IRONMAN fills that bill. And over the years I've been blessed to witness some of those transformations up close and personal.

Some are very visible and obvious. In 2015, Marcus Cook weighed 489 pounds and was one steak dinner away from a heart attack. His mentor in business took him aside one day to reveal a diagnosis he'd just received. "Marcus," he said, "I've got cancer." Then he said something that would change Marcus' life. "I'm dying of cancer; you're dying by choice." Scared straight—his friend would be dead within a year—Marcus, then 43, dropped half his body weight over the next three years and I was overjoyed to call him over the line in Kona. Which was pretty cool right there, but then he picked up a (giant) picture of his old (giant) self and ran it into the finish area.

Jason Reinhardt

What a trip to see pro triathlete Andrew Starykowicz place a Hawaiian lei around Marcus' neck in honor of his splendid achievement.

That transformation was right out there for all the world to see. But they're not all as visible as his.

*L*YNNE *M*ILLS [A PSEUDONYM] was born to two people whose idea of a perfect family was one boy and one girl who could effectively raise themselves while the parents pursued their private ambitions. Lynne, being the second daughter instead of a son, managed to ruin those plans at the moment of her birth, and things only went downhill from there. Mom was a striving politician who amazed the community by being able to juggle family and career, without anybody realizing that she'd long ago dropped the family ball. Dad was raised with such brutality that he was frightened of raising kids of his own. So Lynne was a virtual orphan left to the care of her resentful older sister, who solved the problem of having to drag her little sister everywhere by locking her in a closet and thereby not having to drag her anywhere.

Lynne spent a chunk of junior high in a psychiatric facility, where "family therapy" consisted of her mother wondering what the big deal was, her father cracking endless jokes while insisting that the problem wasn't his but Lynne's, her sister unhappy that Lynne was even born, and everybody demanding that the psychiatrist "fix" her to avoid the humiliation of a family member being institutionalized. Meanwhile, to her astonishment, her parents had had another child, this time a boy, and they doted on him.

Lynne's solution was to run to the roof of the five-story psychiatric facility and try to throw herself off. She was caught by the staff and put into restraints. That resulted in her being sent to a residential treatment school, which is where she decided that ending her life was her best option.

After somewhat of a therapeutic breakthrough, there was a reprieve. Lynne got a job with the Second City Theatre in Chicago where she was treated as family. She got a bachelor's degree from the University of Illinois as well as a master's on a full ride from Northwestern. She even got married, and now things were really looking up, but her husband turned out to be a sociopath who, after smashing up her house, chased her, caught her and put a loaded gun to her head. She had 911 on the line and when her husband demanded the phone, she heaved it through a closed window and escaped while he was distracted by the breaking glass.

That happened the same weekend her brother was getting married. Her family's reaction? *Don't ruin your brother's special day with your little problems.*

She pulled herself together enough to go to L.A., where she got a second master's degree, found a job teaching disabled children, and started doing triathlons despite bouts of severe depression. She was good at it, too, never finishing lower than fourth in her age group, which typically had a field of over a hundred competitors. A club she was part of signed her up for the 2012 IRONMAN Arizona. She resisted at first, then relented because she thought having a tough goal would help her. She'd be 45 on race day.

But she couldn't find a way to stop the downward mental spiral. During spring break, the darkness deepened, and there was nothing she could do about it. She made the decision to end her life. Not at some vague sometime, but Friday of that very week.

She made lists of final wishes, and she wrote some goodbyes in which she tried to explain why she was doing this. She didn't want her friends to trot out the standard simplicities about selfishness or weakness but to understand that there was no understanding among the uninitiated about how deep and lightless the abyss of depression was. Her awful childhood might have played a part, but it didn't explain everything. Nothing could.

A close friend discovered her plan and somehow managed to extract a solemn vow from her. "Promise me you'll make it to the finish line on November 18," he said. "You'll hear a guy named Mike Reilly say, 'Lynne Mills…you are an IRONMAN!' and then if you still want to die, I'll help you do it myself, that very night."

It was six months away, a seemingly unendurable eternity, but she agreed. The thought of finishing the race kept her going, but this is no fairy tale story: The thought that her life would finally be over in six months is also what kept her going. By the way, she had no idea who I was back then. But her friend told her I'd call her over the line whether she came in first or last.

I know the rest of the story from a long letter Lynne wrote to me. It's very heartfelt and emotional, and I was tempted to include it verbatim, but the letter is mostly about me. While that's certainly flattering, Lynne missed the point. What happened to her in that race and afterward wasn't about me, despite what she thinks and how she makes it sound. It was about having a goal and latching onto a symbol of that goal. The symbol happened to be me, and I was glad to play that role, but that's what I was: a symbol, not a savior.

The run portion of the race was three loops. In her letter she told me that she could hear me calling racers over the line when the first two loops got close to the finish area.

The third time, as she headed in towards her own finish, a song came on over the PA system and right into Lynne's brain.

Let me take a minute to tell you a little about the role of music at an IRONMAN event. It's one of the most critical elements of making the race day experience as rich as possible for athletes and spectators alike, as important as anything we announcers have to say. Music sets the mood, hails the champions, rocks the crowd and welcomes home the athletes. Music fills the air with life and provides a continuous soundtrack to everything that's going on.

Back in the day, I carried folders full of CDs, including both straight commercial recordings and mixes I made myself. When the iPod came out I thought it was a genuine miracle, every song I could ever dream of right there in my hand. At one World Championship I actually did hold it in my hand, microphone in the other, and was able to play the perfect song for the moment all day long. It was the best "atmosphere tuning" tool I ever had.

Many athletes can tell you what was playing at that moment they crossed the line. I would love to be able to play a custom-selected song for each finisher, but that's impossible when you have as many as 3,000 athletes to take care of and a hundred of them can come down the chute within a minute of each other.

Which makes all the more remarkable what happened to Lynne. She was expecting to hear me call her an IRONMAN, of course. Her friends had prepared her for it. And she heard me doing it for others all throughout her run in Arizona. But as she came towards the finish and reached the point where she could hear the speakers, an electric shock ran up her spine when a song ended and was replaced by Elton John's "Someone Saved My Life Tonight."

To this day Lynne is dead convinced that the cosmos had conspired to make her hear that song. She decided then and there not to take her life that night, but to live it a day at a time and see how it goes. She also thinks the "someone" in the song was me, but it wasn't.

Lynne sent a message to me a few days later. I called her and we spoke for a while. I learned something about her struggles, but didn't get the details until she sent the letter afterwards. I also didn't appreciate how much that call meant to her. She introduced herself to me at IRONMAN Arizona in 2013, where she'd come to volunteer and support friends who were racing. I saw her again at IRONMAN Oceanside 70.3, and I brought her in at the inaugural IRONMAN Boulder where she was a volunteer handler for a CAF athlete. Lynne kept doing races, and also volunteered as often as she could to support people who, as she had, needed some help.

In 2016 Lynne went into surgery to have a medium risk procedure performed. Things went south very quickly, and when the surgeon lost her blood pressure and pulse, he cracked her chest to release the blood that had flooded her pericardium and caused her heart to stop beating, then stitched a hole in her atrium. She awoke the next day, confused, in pain and unsure of what had happened. While in the ICU she was aware that people were concerned and trying to keep her alive, and she remembers having a horrible thought: Why were they bothering? Was she really worth all that fuss?

Those thoughts were automatic, like the ones she was used to having all her life. Then she remembered her racing, and what it meant to have goals and to accomplish them, and to have friends who cared about her.

By the time she told me of this frightening episode, she'd had time to think. She vowed to be back at the starting line someday. I told her that getting better wasn't about everything being perfect, that life is like a game of Frogger: Sometimes it's easy to cross the street and some days there are many obstacles, but with the right mindset we can all make it to the other side.

As I said, Lynne thinks I saved her life, but I didn't. I have no magical powers (in case you were wondering). I'm not a healer nor do I claim any special insight into the human psyche and I have no training in how to talk to troubled people. When Lynne called me the first time I didn't scramble to find the right words or strain not to upset her or walk on eggshells thinking that if I said the wrong thing she'd leap off a cliff.

But I was mindful that, to her, I was the representation of the difficult goal she'd set for herself. She now had something new and powerful in her life, and I was its human face. I didn't need to embellish what she'd built up in her mind. It was already strong enough. She just needed a way to communicate with the symbol she'd latched onto, to know that it respected her and accepted her as she was and, most importantly, was aware of what she was trying to do and cared about whether she succeeded.

Lynne is by no means "fixed," as her family had defined that process, nor is she completely healed. Depression is not a head cold or a sprained ankle. It doesn't work that way. But for sure she's been transformed, from the hopeless, self-loathing product of an emotionally abusive family into a highly accomplished woman with purpose and ambition.

I did not save Lynne Mills' life; she saved it herself, when she decided that IRONMAN was a life raft and reached for it with both hands. That I was able to lend a hand by being part of IRONMAN is one of the high points of my life.

S OMETIMES, I BECOME A PART of people's lives without even knowing about it. I learned about Matt and Kym Dildine's ordeal from a letter Matt, an attorney, sent me only after it was all over. The purpose of the letter was to ask me to meet with the family for a photo at the 2015 IRONMAN Arizona. On the way to making the request, Matt gave me the background as to why it would mean so much to them.

Two years before, in 2013, Matt had signed up to do his first full IRONMAN race, at Lake Tahoe. His wife, Kym, was as thrilled at the prospect as her athlete husband. With Kym's full support, Matt dove vigorously into his training, and the two of them talked frequently about hearing "You are an IRONMAN!" at the finish line. (Sometimes family members are more eager to hear those words than the athlete. I never want to disappoint a Mom or Dad or they will for sure let me know it!)

A few weeks after signing up, they found out that Kym was pregnant with their third child. Two days later, they found out that Kym was also pregnant with their fourth child. They talked it over and decided that Matt should carry on with his goal of competing in Tahoe.

But real life, as it often will, intruded on those plans. Early in the pregnancy, they were told that the twins had a very rare condition that would likely take the life of one while leaving the other significantly developmentally impaired.

There were only six doctors in the U.S. who were qualified to treat the condition. Over the course of two months Kym underwent several surgeries, but none of them worked. As a last, desperate measure, Kym was hospitalized under a protocol that called for her to be confined to a bed, wired up to monitors, for ten weeks. Even then, the Dildines were told that the best bet to get a positive outcome was to terminate the more troubled of the two twins in order to save the healthier one.

That was not an acceptable option for them, so they declined.

Matt was beside himself with anxiety. He had tried to keep up his training but with his wife now confined under such trying conditions, he tore himself up, feeling like a bad husband, a bad father, a bad lawyer, a bad friend and, of course, a bad triathlete. He told Kym he was going to quit training and give up on the race.

Kym was having none of it. Knowing how much it meant to Matt, she made IRONMAN a goal for both of them, as well as a symbol for the family, because they were all suffering tests of endurance. Kym was stuck in a bed, away from the day-to-day life of her family, for a miserable ten weeks. Their two children were enduring parents who were riddled with anxiety and uncertainty and not operating at full capacity for them, and they had no idea if or when life would return to some kind of normal.

And the unborn twins were in the worse test of all, fighting just to stay alive and come into the world.

That September Matt went to Lake Tahoe alone. By that time, the notion of him becoming an IRONMAN had become so important in the family that he was too nervous to sleep the night before the race. He felt like he was racing for them all, to the point where he'd begun to believe that if he didn't finish, he'd not only fail his family, he'd doom the twins. There's pressure, and then there's *pressure*.

Fortunately, Matt finished, in what he recalls as one of the most memorable experiences of his life. Kym watched him come in, on-line from her hospital bed, and shared his moment of triumph.

In his letter, Matt passed off the entire race in all of two sentences, because he was anxious to fill me in on the best part. A few weeks after he finished Lake Tahoe, the twins were born. They were extremely premature, badly underweight, but otherwise perfectly, gloriously healthy.

Matt wrote, "At the end of every race, every athlete longs to hear you say those four incredible words: 'You are an IRONMAN!' During our summer of hardship, my wife and I told ourselves that one day we would take our babies home and say 'We are an IRON FAMILY!' For this reason, and to remember our family's test of endurance, we named the twin who had to fight hardest to survive Reily."

I nearly dropped to the floor when I read that. I'd never been so flattered in my life. (The dropped "l" was purposeful, to make it sound less like a last name.) And these people wanted to know if they could take a picture with me? Uh, yeah, I think I could manage that. Matt and Kym wanted to frame it and put it in their son's room so his namesake could remind him of the story of how he came to be.

I could show you the picture, but I'd rather show you the one of the "miracle twins" the night before Dad went off to do another IRONMAN race.

The troublemaker on the right is Reily.

Matt Dildine

IFIRST MET JILL KOSKI at IRONMAN Wisconsin in 2017. Head IRONMAN sound and video technician Dave Downey had made a short video about her, and I said to him, "I gotta meet this woman." He introduced me to her at the welcome ceremony and I suggested we meet at the finish line the next morning. It was still under construction and is on a beautiful site, the state capitol serving as a dramatic backdrop.

I found a spot on a cement bench and Jill showed up a few minutes later. She was in her early 50s, with blond spiky hair, and obviously fit. After we said hello she gestured to a building right behind us near the capitol. "Isn't that the jail?" she asked.

Half a dozen thoughts shot through me at once, the foremost being, *Oh, God… how stupid could I be? Of course it's the jail!* I'd chosen the worst spot imaginable for us to meet.

Jill had spent eight years in prison.

I started to mumble an embarrassed apology, but she stopped me with a huge laugh. "That's funny as hell!" she said, and that told me a lot of what I needed to know about Jill Koski.

Then there was the rest of it. Until she was 39, Jill was a practicing psychologist with two undergraduate degrees and a masters in home therapy. Which made it especially ironic that she didn't know that she was bipolar.

"I was the same kind of person as my patients were," as she put it.

Despite her considerable accomplishments, she felt that something was lacking, and she didn't feel accepted. She was driven to strive for more, and the nature of her illness was such that, during the manic phases, she did it at 180 mph. "Rocketville Mania," as she called it. She just couldn't settle down. She started doing duathlons and triathlons. It helped a little, and it turned out that she was a pretty good athlete, but she was still revved up all the time. She also discovered the joys of shopping—acquiring things—and did it with a vengeance. In one week she bought a Harley Davidson and a BMW, both online. A terrible relationship with her mother didn't help, and the relationship with both her parents had taken a nasty turn when she let them know that she preferred women rather than men.

Still, she was leading a reasonable life. At least until she hit 39. A friend suggested a glass of wine now and again to help her relax. She'd shied away from alcohol because her mother was a raging alcoholic, but she was so amped up all the time, she gave it a go. "Now and again" quickly turned into "now," but it didn't do anything to settle her down, so she turned to prescription sleep medications to try to ratchet down the RPMs.

That was bad enough, but it wasn't felonious yet, so I asked her how she wound up in prison. She was scheduled to go on vacation with her partner, Laurie (nicknamed Lo), but her mother was facing surgery and she had to cancel the trip, even though her parents had disowned her when she came out. She was so angry, even thinking that somehow her mother had done this on purpose, that she went on a drinking binge, popped some Ambien and went to bed.

It took her weeks to piece together the story of what happened next. She woke up, fell down, broke her nose and ended up with her teeth cutting through her lip. There was blood everywhere. Scared, she tried to call Lo but it was 2:00 am and there was no answer. So she got into her car to go see her, managed to back it out of the driveway but only got twenty feet down the street before slamming into a tree. Neighbors heard the noise and came out. When they pulled her from the car she was stark naked. This was clearly something more than a random mishap, so they called the police.

It was her first DUI, but wouldn't be her last. Later she sat in court, shivering in confusion; this was usually where her patients sat. Why was she here?

She refused help from her friends and from Lo, and that relationship eventually cracked under the pressure. She kept drinking and doing drugs and buying expensive things she didn't need, racking up three more DUIs in the process. Somehow, none of those resulted in prison time, but it wouldn't have mattered. Jill was just drinking to die anyway.

When she found out her father was dying, that was it. Enough. She called her mother to say goodbye. Frightened, her mother called an ambulance to Jill's place. Sure enough, she'd done it again, a combination of pills and alcohol. This time it was so bad it would be five months before she could recall that night.

Then, a fifth DUI, and by then the courts had had it with her. She was given an eight-year prison sentence.

It was a blessing, starting with enforced abstinence from drugs and alcohol. Once she got over the terrible pain of withdrawal and the shock of being incarcerated, Jill started attending daily therapy sessions. She also used her psychology background to help other inmates, giving her a joy she'd never known.

Lo came back and visited her. She saw the change that was happening and believed that Jill could sustain a new life outside the walls. They got married four days after Jill's release on probation, 24 years after they'd first met.

That's when Jill decided that her transformation was not yet complete. "I needed to do something epic," she told me, "something that I would commit to and that would give me something to focus on. I wanted to know that I could accomplish something *big*."

The "something" was IRONMAN Wisconsin, and it was going to happen the morning after our meeting at the finish line. Her goal was 16 hours: two hours for each year she'd spent in prison.

When she arrived at the finish line the next day, I was nearly overcome with emotion. Most of the spectators had seen the video so they knew who she was when I told them she was on the way in. What none of us expected was that Jill would cross the line at 12:04 and finished fifth in the 50-54 age group. The roar from the crowd was unforgettable, the look on Jill's face priceless. And right in front of the Madison city jail, to boot.

I can't begin to imagine what it must have been like for her to mount the podium the next night, and she herself was never able to adequately describe it.

IRONMAN was Jill's proving ground, her final exam, the way she knew she was street-ready. She'd seldom been able to finish what she'd started unless it was geared toward her self-destruction, but she'd started and finished an IRONMAN triathlon, passing her exam with flying colors.

Which is not to say that she's any less driven than she was before. But now her efforts are directed in a positive direction. Jill's ancestry is Finnish, and her friends gave her the nickname Sisu, from the Finnish for "stubborn." That trait actually got her in a bit of trouble, at IRONMAN Florida in November, 2018.

That was going to be a big month for her. Not only would she complete her second IRONMAN race, she was also scheduled to go "off paper," meaning her probation was over and she'd be one hundred percent free. And there was also Lo's retirement party to plan.

Everything was going well until 80 miles into the bike, when she started to feel lightheaded. She plowed on anyway, and made it into T2, but wasn't feeling any better when the 26.2-mile run began. Regardless, no way was she going to start this special November off with a DNF, so she kept on going, walking most of the marathon. Amazingly, the race clock read 12:11 when I brought her in, only seven minutes off her "healthy" performance in Wisconsin. Lo put the medal around her neck, and then she went to the medical tent.

Later that evening I got a call that she'd had a heart attack and was in the hospital. I froze at the news, thinking, "This can't end like this!"

It didn't. Jill called to tell me that some enzyme that had acted up in her system had caused the lower part of her heart to react negatively. Scary, but not life-threatening, and it all got sorted out.

The new Jill went off paper, they got Lo's retirement party going, and she started thinking about her next IRONMAN race.

Don't you just love a happy ending?

THESE ARE BY NO MEANS ISOLATED STORIES. And it's not only amateurs who pulled themselves back from the brink of self-destruction. Lionel Sanders, one of the most successful and popular professional triathletes in the world, spent two years of his life fighting his demons with drugs and alcohol, two of the worst weapons in the human arsenal. They led him to a despair so bleak he contemplated suicide, but he used endurance athletics as the path back to normalcy. In 2013 he won his very first pro race, IRONMAN 70.3 Muskoka. He went on to win an incredibly long string of other half-distance events, and in 2016 set a world best in the full-distance IRONMAN race in Arizona.

When I think about these stories, and all the others I know about, I wonder about the stories I never heard. It's one of the things I think about when I watch people come across the finish line. There's no such thing as an easy IRONMAN race. They're all hard, with no exceptions, and every athlete has his own reason for undertaking such a difficult challenge. For some it's bragging rights and then back to the office on Monday. For others, it's a lifestyle and they return again and again to test themselves.

For people like Lynne, Matt, Jill and Lionel, it was a lifeline.

IRONMAN is often referred to as "Everyman's Everest." It offers an incredibly difficult challenge but, unlike free soloing or hang gliding, it is forgiving of error and doesn't pose a threat to life or limb. It's not a reckless pursuit.

But that touch of sanity that differentiates it from insane sports in which survival is one of the goals doesn't diminish its transformative potential. Failing might not kill you, but succeeding still carries tremendous power, as I've witnessed over and over again.

Nobody ever got to an IRONMAN finish line and said, "Gee, I'm sorry I did that."

But plenty have gotten there and said, "Gee, I can't believe I did that!"

And everyone comes out better than when they went in.

CHAPTER 14

Letter from a Schoolchild

IRONMAN occasionally invites local school kids to write letters to be put into the bags athletes are given at registration. Here's one a friend of mine found in her bag at IRONMAN Maryland:

Dear Athlete,

I understand that you are feeling nervous. Or you are feeling terrified. And I know how that feels.

All my life I feel sometime nervous or scared of what people will say, think, or tell me. And like you I'm trying to accomplish a goal too. My goal is to go to Salisbury, Morgan, or Maryland university. And I feel like I'm going to fail but like Frederick Douglas said, "If there is no struggle, there is no progress." So if you struggle it's ok and I know it is ok now and when you got into this race just know, you need to struggle to be great.

Best of luck, and do your best. I'm rooting for you, and best of luck.

CHAPTER 15

Veterans of the wonderful IRONMAN Wisconsin call it "Mad City," possibly because it's in Madison, the state capitol, but equally likely in reference to the wildly variable race conditions. It has to be in the top five of the hottest, rainiest, coldest and windiest IRONMAN races I've ever been to. But that's all part of the challenge, and it has that majestic finish line with the capitol building forming a stunning backdrop.

I never have a bad day at an IRONMAN event, just better days. With one exception, and that was race day at Mad City in 2015.

A Wisconsin National Guard Medic named Edward Schmitt was declared the winner even though he was the third to cross the line. That's because the first two were professionals, and this was not a pro race. While pros were welcome to participate, they weren't eligible for prizes. As the first age grouper across the line, Edward was the official winner. He held up the finish line ribbon, posed for photos, and I interviewed him over the PA to the delight of the crowd.

Except...the guy who came in just ahead of Edward, Rudy Kahsar, wasn't a pro. He used to be, but had given up his pro card and was therefore an eligible age grouper for this race. He was the rightful winner, and Edward graciously offered up congratulations despite his disappointment.

A little upsetting, to be sure, but that kind of thing happens once in a while, and it had nothing to do with why this was my worst IRONMAN day ever.

About an hour after the men's finish I welcomed the overall women's champ, Michelle Andres of Gull Lake, Minnesota. This was her fourth race here, and the age group record she'd set in 2012 still hadn't been broken. I interviewed her for the crowd, which went wild when she told them she was the mother of five teenaged boys.

There's something that really gets to people when moms cross the line. Everybody knows that they do the majority of work raising the kids—heaven knows my wife did—and when they can do that and race IRONMAN as well, it's just incredibly inspiring. And it's not just the age groupers: Some of the top pros have had babies and been right back on the circuit within a year. Meredith Kessler, Rachel Joyce, Liz Blatchford, Sara Gross and Mirinda Carfrae did it. Liz Lyles came back after *two* kids. These wonder women are true heroes and some of the best role models you would ever want your daughter, or son, to emulate.

Anyway, after calling in Michelle I needed to get back up to the announcer's tower, which not only had a bird's eye view of the finish line but was where the computers were that allowed me to call athletes in by name. There's an announcer's read mat about 50 meters before the finish line that picks up each athlete's bib number from a chip on his ankle. That information is relayed to the tower, where the finisher's name, home town, occupation and any interesting personal tidbits are displayed. How much of it I can tell to the spectators depends on how many others are finishing at the same time. (This is a great departure from the old days of looking at the finisher through binoculars, trying to read the race number on a bib that looks like it's been run through a Cuisinart after all those hours of racing, then looking up the name on printed sheets of paper. When we got a little computerized and were able to type the numbers in and have the names pop up, I thought it was the ultimate in technology. Then the read mat came along and did it all automatically. A real gift when you're trying to make sure you never miss a single finisher.)

The floor of the booth is about twelve feet above ground level, reached with a simple metal ladder that's really just part of the scaffolding. There's no slant to it, just straight up, and the "steps" are the same steel pipes as the rest of the structure. When you get to the top and your head is level with the floor of the booth, there's one more scaffold pipe about three feet up you can grab onto while you take the last two steps before swinging yourself inside.

With my notepad in one hand I started up the ladder, as I'd done a thousand times before. At the top I saw my two good friends, Philip LaHaye and Dave Downing, having a conversation in the tower just as I reached for that last rail and pulled myself up.

At least that was the plan. What actually happened was that my hand wrapped itself around thin air, as though the rail had dematerialized at the last second. Expecting that it would be there, I'd already let go of the lower rail and there was nothing connecting me to the ladder anymore. Almost before I even realized what was happening, I was in free fall, backward, heading towards the cement pavement below.

The world seemed to slow to a crawl. I don't know if it was my wrestling training that kicked in or some innate protective mechanism wired into my DNA, but I pulled my body into a 'V' so my head wouldn't smack into the concrete. In that position I could see that Philip and Dave had stopped talking and snapped their heads in my direction. We made eye contact, and I could see their hands start to flick out towards me reflexively, but by that time I was well away and looking at blue sky.

It takes just under a second to fall twelve feet. I'd read stories of people's lives flashing before their eyes in similar situations and always discounted them as exaggerated, but let me tell you: It's amazing how much can go through your mind. My first thought was, *This is it*, without having any idea what "it" was. Was I going to die? Be paralyzed or in a coma? I thought about my wife and kids, and then got mad and then sad and angry with myself over how many play dates I would miss with my 9-month-old grandson. How could I let this happen!

The shock of hitting the ground with my lower back was terrifying. The next thing I was aware of was lying on my side, out of breath and wondering how I'd gotten there. It must have lasted for only a second or two, because it occurred to me that I might have hit my head as well, and then I quickly became anxious to know how badly I'd been hurt. I think I also wanted to know if I was still in this world, and must have asked it out loud, because Melinda Downey, who'd come flying out of the sound tent and gotten to me within seconds, said "Yes, you are." I grabbed her arm in order to feel something and make sure.

The next thought that jumped into my head was that athletes were finishing and I didn't want this to interfere with their special moments. I looked around and was thankful that I'd fallen out of sight of the finish area and wouldn't disrupt the flow of things. I also started trying to move a little and decided that maybe it wasn't too bad, that I could shake it off and get back up the tower and into the booth and resume calling the athletes across.

By now people were all around me, urging me to stay down, but I thought my self-assessment was thorough enough to warrant trying to stand. When I was up on my feet, I got dizzy, so I felt the back of my head to see if it hadn't taken a whack but didn't feel any blood or bumps. The dizziness passed and I managed a few tentative steps. Dr. Lee, the race physician, and his nurse Mahgen had arrived. They insisted that I go to the hospital but, stubborn damned Irishman that I am, I was having none of it. I needed to get back on the mic. When they realized that I wasn't going to give in, they switched modes and tried to help. Mahgen, a true angel, got some ice and rigged up a wrap to hold it in place against my back. Dave Downing and his team quickly set up a ground level announcing station. I tried sitting but it didn't work, which was fine because I always announce from a standing position anyway.

We were all set. I picked up the mic, looked at the display on the laptop that had been brought down from the tower, and started to call the first finisher at the top. I got her name out, and her home town, but when I drew in a deep breath to belt out the four words I knew she wanted to hear, there was a stab of pain that nearly floored me.

Mahgen grabbed my arm to steady me, then she stared straight into my eyes. "Mike…"

"Yeah," I said. "We need to go."

I handed the mic to Dave and told him I'd try to get back. Dr. Lee called the ambulance over and in short order I was strapped to a backboard and loaded inside. Philip rode along and was with me every step of the way. I don't know what I would have done without him. It was awful not having any of my family around. Rose, Andy and even my brother Pat had been with me in Madison many times but they couldn't make it this trip.

When we got to the University of Wisconsin Medical Center, I saw a big wall clock. It read 6:00. There were still six hours to go in the race. I said to Philip that maybe this would work out. If I wasn't too badly damaged, they could wrap me up, give me some drugs for the pain, and we could get back in time for me to spend the last few hours bringing athletes across the line. He didn't even bother to respond, just shot me a look that let me know I was crazy.

For about four hours I was x-rayed, poked, prodded, interrogated and consulted over. Finally, they threw up their hands and said that, remarkably after a fall like that, nothing was broken. Reluctantly, it seemed, they said I could go.

Elated by that news, and seeing that it was now only 10:00 pm, I asked Philip to get us back to the race site as soon as possible. He shook his head but back we went.

After the relatively quiet ambience of the hospital, the carnival atmosphere at the finish line was almost surreal. Philip tried to protect me from getting bumped as we made our way to the tower. It was now 11:00 pm and Dave had taken over the announcing. He was doing it from the floor instead of the tower, and handed the mic over with a smile.

I read the first name and looked over to the finish line. This late in a race athletes arrive in dribs and drabs, so there was plenty of time and no chaos. As she approached the line I announced her name, then waited for her to step across. As soon as she did, I shouted, "You are an IRONMAN!"

It took every ounce of will I had to get the last syllable out. The pain that lanced into my back was overwhelming. I handed the mic back and it was all I could do to keep from crying, because I knew this night was over for me. When I went to the hospital earlier I'd thought there was a reasonable chance I'd be back, but this was it. Finished. I'd never abandoned an IRONMAN finish line in my life, or even contemplated what that would be like because it was unthinkable, and here I was doing just that. I couldn't push away the thought that I was betraying the athletes, cheating them out of hearing that call they'd worked so hard for. Many of them were in as much pain as I was, and I was walking away from them. It was one of the lowest points of my professional life and my dejection was bottomless.

I held it together as Philip walked me away from the finish to my hotel a block away, but once I was alone I totally lost it. Crying hurt my back but I just couldn't stop. Those athletes were still out there and I wasn't with them. Even though Dave is a total pro and does a great job, I had this picture in my head of an athlete crossing over the line all smiles, and the smile disappearing in disappointment when she didn't hear me call her name and declare to the world that she was an IRONMAN. I know that sounds conceited, but I'm keenly aware of what that call has come to mean to people and it was terrible to be a stone's throw from a finish line and not be able to do it for the athletes.

To be completely honest, I was also feeling sorry for myself, and I didn't want to wallow in it. As I tried to go to sleep, I loaded my mind up with images of IRONMAN athletes who'd suffered far worse than this and gamely fought their way back, guys like Brian Boyle and Matty Long. It was a sobering exercise, a way of slapping myself in the face and trying to quit pitying myself. I have to admit that it didn't work all that well. Maybe it would when the pain died down a little.

"Dear Lord," I said out loud, "help me come back from this, and thank you for keeping me here on earth."

My last thought before finally nodding off was that, hell or high water, I was going to be at the awards ceremony the following day.

OPENING MY EYES THE NEXT MORNING, I was afraid to move. I'd fallen asleep in the fetal position to ease the pain in my back, and it only took one tiny attempt to straighten out to tell me it wasn't going to happen. I didn't want to call anybody, because they'd all been up most of the night. It took a while but I managed to ease myself down the side of the bed onto all fours and then crawl my way to the shower, remembering to take my cell phone and put it nearby, just in case.

I stayed down on my hands and knees, and while hot water from the shower poured onto my lower back, I tried to visualize the awards ceremony. Once I got there, all I had to do was stand in one place and announce all the winners. No breath-heaving shouts required, and while I might not be able to generate quite the amount of excitement I was used to, maybe I could find the right words to compensate for my lack of physical enthusiasm.

I was already writing the script in my head and figuring out the logistics as I crawled out of the shower. Then my cell phone rang. It was the University of Wisconsin Medical Center. How nice; they were calling to check up on me.

"Mr. Reilly, you need to get back here immediately."

"Get back? Why?"

"Well...we found a fracture in your back."

A fracture? What about all those x-rays! "Are you kidding me?"

"Sorry, no. We took a closer look at the pictures after you left and there's a break."

Well, at least it explained the intense pain. At that point I had no choice but to call Philip and ask for his help again, any thoughts of making it to the awards now gone for good. By the time we got to the hospital they'd reviewed everything with great care and determined that I didn't need surgery. The break would heal on its own if I behaved myself and let it, and I should be in reasonable shape in about four to six weeks. They put me in a full upper body brace, gave me some stronger meds and bid me good luck.

By the time Philip took me to the airport and wheeled me on the plane, the drugs had kicked in and I don't remember much, other than some good Samaritan carrying my backpack off for me. I was so out of it that I couldn't figure out why my wife and Alan Rea, my neighbor and dear friend, were at the airport waiting for me. My first thought, still being a bit drugged up, was *What the heck are they doing here? I drove myself to the airport and have a car here, so I certainly don't need a ride.*

As I started to voice those thoughts to Rose, she held up a hand and said, "Pipe down! We're going in Alan's car." *Duuuhh.* Man, was I out of it.

The docs were right; a little over four weeks later I felt good enough to head to Hawai'i for my 27th straight turn at the mic at the world championship. I had a smaller, hidden body brace and didn't do as much dancing as I usually do, which was tough for me, but it all worked out. (Actually, I wasn't that smart. Every time I started to dance a little, Rose shot me a look from the bleachers that would stop a train. It sure stopped me.)

In retrospect, I shouldn't have kept the brace so well concealed. Jostling that I'd never even noticed before I noticed a lot now, and at one point an old friend I hadn't seen in a while and didn't know what had happened came running up prepared to give me a big old bear hug. I gave him a glare that must have looked murderous, because he backed off like I'd pulled a knife on him.

It all made me wonder if my higher power had a plan for me. Being there for athletes as their dreams come true is more than a job; it's my calling. Being deprived of it for even a few hours as I had been in Wisconsin hurt far more than the physical pain, and deepened my appreciation for the opportunity I was given. Maybe that was the point. After all, I'd gotten off awfully easy given how bad that fall could have been.

So I think—I *know*— it was a lesson: *Don't take this for granted; don't take anything in life for granted!*

Got it.

CHAPTER 16

Q: If you're at a party, how can you find the IRONMAN in the room?

A: Just wait. Eventually he'll come up and tell you.

As serious an undertaking as it is, IRONMAN has its share of humorous moments, some of them downright hilarious.

Although not everyone thinks they're so funny. One of my favorite incidents occurred at the inaugural IRONMAN Lake Placid in 1999.

This was a wetsuit-legal swim. (Wetsuits are only allowed if the water temperature dips below 76.1°F.) Removing a skintight wetsuit can be a pretty gnarly affair. Swimmers usually unzip their suits and pull the tops down as soon as they exit the water, which can be done while running. But the exit area looks like Grand Central station at 5:00 pm on Friday, and if athletes stopped and tried to take off the bottom of the suits, they'd be colliding with one another left and right, and possibly hurting themselves with the kind of strenuous contortions it can take to get out of the suit.

So a lot of race organizers stage "strippers" at the swim exit. While swimmers drop down and lie on their backs, two strippers each grab a fistful of neoprene and yank the suit off. That yank can be downright violent. Bystanders learn to stay well back so they don't get smacked as the suit slingshots backward, and everybody in the vicinity gets sprayed with the water that flies off at high speed. It's grand and glorious chaos and one of the most-videoed parts of any IRONMAN event.

I was calling the swimmers out of the water and shouting encouragement to the strippers. I just happened to be looking in their direction when a Japanese athlete dropped to the ground and stuck his legs up into the air. Two strippers did their thing and wrenched the guy's suit off with great gusto, when suddenly the crowd a) gasped, then, b) broke out into hysterical laughing.

Seems our young competitor had forgotten to put his biking shorts on under his wetsuit. There he was, on his back, stark naked, with a look on his face as though he'd been hit with a cattle prod. Undoubtedly acutely aware of a thousand cameras pointed his way, he tried to cover up and get the suit back on at the same time, which only made the whole thing twice as comical, and pretty soon he was laughing so hard himself he couldn't do anything right.

And, not for nothin' (you *Seinfeld* fans will love this), the water was cold. I'm just sayin'.

Finally, the guy threw the suit over his shoulder, cupped his privates and took off for transition, smiling all the way. When he finished the race, he was wearing shorts, but to this day I have no idea where he got them.

There's a good story from the 2015 IRONMAN Lake Placid that isn't exactly funny—far from it—but there's one visual that makes me laugh every time I conjure it up. The night before the race the third story of a building on Main Street where some athletes were staying caught fire. I was in the hotel next door, and by the time I smelled smoke and went out the back of the hotel, flames were shooting up from the roof.

I watched along with some athletes as two figures appeared through a window dragging a hose through an apartment and out to a back porch, presumably to get a better angle from which to spray the fire. When the guy in front opened the nozzle the spray was so powerful I didn't know how he could hang onto that hose.

Then I noticed something else. The guy in back was dressed head to toe in full gear, but the one in front was wearing shorts and a t-shirt.

My first thought was that this must be a volunteer fire department and this guy didn't have a chance to suit up. But even if that was so, why was he at the very front of the hose line?

Things got a little chaotic, with more trucks pulling up and lights flashing and additional hoses being hooked up to hydrants. After about half an hour I see a man and woman heading my way, and the guy looks a little familiar and he's wearing

Mike Reilly

shorts and a t-shirt...

"Hey!" I shouted. "Weren't you just fighting that fire?"

He confirmed that he was.

"But why were you dressed like that?" I asked.

"He's a retired firefighter," his wife said, "and there was no way he was going to not help."

Okay, very cool. "But why was he at the front with no gear?"

"Wasn't my intention," her husband said with a shrug. "They saw I had more experience than the other guy so they asked me to take the lead."

His name was Ken Meadows, from Babylon, N.Y., and he was there to do the race the next morning. But when he saw the fire, his training and instincts kicked in and he didn't hesitate to get involved. After he identified himself to the local fire chief, who realized he had an experienced pro on hand, the crew was glad to accept the help.

Ken paid a price for his bravery, as he suspected he might when he (literally) jumped into the fire without protective gear: By the time they got a mask and tank to him up on the second floor, he'd already breathed in too much smoke. While it wasn't life-threatening, he'd be unable to race the next morning. Race officials offered him, along with several athletes who'd lost bikes in the fire and couldn't race, free entry into an upcoming IRONMAN race of their choice.

"Does that include Kona?" was Ken's first question.

That October, he raced in Hawai'i.

At IRONMAN AUSTRALIA IN 2000, the joke was on me. Legendary race director and IRONMAN Hall of Famer Ken Baggs had invited John and Judy Collins to the 15th edition of the race. The two of them had key roles in the creation of the very first IRONMAN, on the island of Oahu in 1978. At the welcome banquet, my job was to introduce them, and then bring up John, a retired US Navy Captain who is frequently referred to as the Father of IRONMAN.

But let me back up to earlier in the evening. I'd been trying to think of a way to get the crowd warmed up and remembered Ken telling me about the different dialects throughout Australia. It's an enormous country, but with a relatively small population. Two of its largest cities are a continent apart with not a whole lot in between. It's not surprising that this kind of isolation would have led to the development of distinct dialects and accents. I decided to talk to the audience about how there was a similar situation in the U.S.

The audience was huge, one of the largest I'd ever seen. I started my verbal tour of America with California, doing my best to imitate a surfer boy/valley girl accent. This got a nice laugh, then I did New York ("Fuhgeddaboudit!") and Boston. I was on a roll now so I doubled down on Texas, which I'd saved for last because Aussies are nuts about Texas. Maybe it's the wide-open spaces and cattle ranches, or maybe it's the cowboy hats. I don't know, but there's a definite kinship.

"Some Australians think Texas is a separate country," I said. "Maybe that's because Texans think so, too!"

Laughs galore, so I pressed on, all about how everything's bigger in Texas — just ask any Texan and he'll tell you — including their legendary bragging about the Lone Star State. And did I mention I was doing all of this in a thick Texas drawl, complete with as many y'alls as I could get away with?

I milked it for all I was worth. Then, it was time to bring John up. Needless to say, I was extremely proud to be able to introduce him. "To help us celebrate the 15th anniversary of IRONMAN Australia, please welcome retired United States Navy Captain and the Father of IRONMAN...John Collins!"

As the audience jumped to its feet and began an ovation that would last over a minute, John strode onto the stage, all 6'5" of him, upright and every bit the Navy Captain. As he came close to me on his way to the lectern at the other end of the stage, I smiled and stuck out my hand.

John ignored it and walked right past me.

It was like getting socked in the jaw. Some in the crowd saw it, too. There was a discernible reduction in the noise level, which picked up again only when John reached the other lectern.

I stood there in shock, my face reddening. As soon as I realized my hand was still sticking out I put it down. Maybe John didn't see it? Maybe he was tired and inattentive after a long flight from the States?

I was still smiling because I didn't know what else to do. It was puzzling and awful at the same time.

John put up his hand for the clapping to stop and grabbed both sides of the lectern. "Thank you everyone for having Judy and me here as your guests," he began.

Hey, wait a minute! Was that...?

"We are honored to be a part of your 15th anniversary."

Oh, no!

John had paused and was staring right at me. "Mike, I got somethin' to tell you ya might not'a known, boy..."

Funny I'd never noticed that accent before. Was that a...?

"I am proud to say and let you know—" He paused again. It was an eternity. The crowd was as quiet as an empty church. "—that I am from the Great State of Texas!"

Oh. My. God. It was! It was a drawl! But I'd thought John and Judy were from Florida!

As my jaw dropped and a stupefied expression took over my face, the audience exploded with laughter. And let me tell you, if there was one crowd you didn't want to be humiliated in front of, it was a crowd of Australians. They're the best in the world at chiding their mates, and they couldn't get enough of John chiding me.

I hung my head as the laughter crescendoed. Then I looked over at John. He was laughing harder than anybody. As the crowd noise started to die down, he said, "Don't worry 'bout it, Mike. Evahbuddy knows Texans are bigger'n better'n ennabodda else!"

And they all started in on me again.

To say I was reminded about it once or twice during the rest of that week would be a monumental understatement.

There's a lesson in there somewhere. Maybe it was that—

Ah, fuhgeddaboudit. There was no damned lesson. But that wasn't the only time I had my face reddened in front of a race crowd. So in the interest of full disclosure, and as long as we're talking about Australia…

Remember back in another chapter I told you about how incredibly well the day went during my first announcing gig there? Yeah, well…there was this one little, tiny incident. As the 15-hour mark hit the clock, I let the crowd know that we only had two hours left, and let's make some noise, and let's keep the energy going and let's stay here right through midnight to cheer those athletes in!

Normally, this gets a tremendous reaction from the spectators, but all I got was two strong hands grabbing my shoulders from behind and turning me around.

It was Ken Baggs. "What the hell are you doing, mate!"

I stared at him in confusion for a second. "What do you mean? I'm revving up the crowd to go the final two hours!" *What was his problem?*

"This is Australia!" he shot back. "We don't do seventeen hours!" He sounded a little boastful as he said it.

What…!?

"Fifteen and a half, mate! We go fifteen and a half hours down here!"

Nobody had told me that. *Nobody*, not a single person the entire week I was there. I was in shock.

Then Ken started laughing. I'm pretty sure it was the look on my face that set him off. He clapped me on the shoulder, then turned and walked away, calling, "Fix it, mate!" over his shoulder. Somewhat gleefully, if you ask me.

As soon as I tried to "fix it" the whole crowd started laughing. I bet they thought the new Yank got pranked, and they were loving it, so I just stopped talking and stood there like an idiot as the fun-loving Aussies gave me an "all is forgiven" hall pass. The shorter race also had a side benefit: By the time midnight rolled around we'd already been celebrating a great day in the pub for over an hour.

As much as the Aussies enjoyed my brief humiliation, giving me as much grief as possible became a hobby, even a contest, among some pro athletes and staffers.

Starting with some of the earlier editions of IRONMAN in Lake Placid, Coeur d'Alene, Wisconsin and Florida, the sound guys began playing "Baba O'Riley" by The Who whenever I was brought up on stage to begin the festivities. I'm not sure how many in the audience caught onto the name connection (to me it will always be "Baba O'Reilly;" is it my fault The Who couldn't spell?) but it was the perfect "kick off the evening" music, dramatic and powerful.

Revved up by the music, I would run up on the stage and start pointing to people I knew, and then to the athletes, with both hands. I was excited, and that was my way of showing it.

Some of the top pros and race staffers, who'd seen me do it before, thought it was dorky. It put them in mind of Saturday Night Live's Dana Carvey and his immortal imitation of the first President Bush doing much the same thing. Warm, kindhearted bunch that they are, they started imitating me. And I don't mean just amongst themselves, like in a bar or something. I mean in the front row of tables at the ceremonies when I was walking on stage.

And since it was coming from the likes of "friends" such as Paula Newby-Fraser and Greg Welch, at first I thought this was in tribute to me, like, "Hey, Mike… right back at ya!" which would have been pretty cool.

Until one night when "Baba O'Riley" went on longer than usual and, as soon as it ended, someone yelled out, "I win!"

Win? Win what? Turns out that they'd started a contest to see who could predict how many times I'd point, the prize being free beer after the banquet. When I first did it, it was two or three times. But I always got a nice crowd reaction, so as time went by I did it five, six, seven times. I, of course, had no idea this was going on until that night when somebody yelled out, "I win!"

The guy who'd won was Dave Downey. He'd bet I'd point fifteen times before quitting. Dave was the sound guy responsible for the music, so instead of cutting off "Baba O'Riley" he kept it going until I hit fifteen, *then* he stopped it. Personally, I think that was cheating and he didn't deserve the free beer.

Dave and the other sound guys—and this includes my veteran announcing buddy Tom Ziebart—also liked to prank me at the finish line. There's a song by Lou Bega called "Mambo #5." It's not what you call…I mean…as songs go it's kind of…

Okay, listen: It sucks. It's a terrible song. I hate it. Everybody hates it. So what a treat when Dave takes over the PA in front of five thousand finish line spectators and says, "Hey, Mike: Here's your favorite song!" And then plays "Mambo #5."

You're a real riot, Dave.

I take a lot of ribbing, but what do I care? This is a great job!   Lee Gruenfeld/IRONM

W HEN I TOLD YOU EARLIER about letting Make-A-Wish kid Nicholas Purschke be the one and only spectator who ever called an athlete across the line, I didn't tell you how I learned that lesson.

That might have been the first time I'd handed an amateur a mic at the finish, but not the first time elsewhere in the race. The first time I did that was also the first time I realized there was an art to announcing.

It was at the World Championship in Kailua-Kona way back in 1992, the early days when I was still figuring things out. I had started a little bit of a tradition of bringing one or two friends out each year to provide some assistance and learn first-hand why I was so crazy about IRONMAN. I never tire of giving first-timers the thrill of witnessing the world's greatest endurance event.

That year I brought out one of my closest friends, Gary Baz, who was also best man at my wedding. We grew up together in Toledo, Ohio, wrestled on the same high school team, then after college in 1976 headed for the sun and surf in San Diego and have been there ever since.

During the marathon leg of the 1992 race, we were at the hot corner where runners approached from two directions, giving spectators a great view. And there were many, many spectators, all cheering loudly as the runners passed.

I'd been gulping down fluids at a furious rate owing to the heat, and I had to take a pee break.

Now, understand: Gary is not only one of the brightest guys I know, and one of the funniest, he's also the most verbally agile. An unrepentant extrovert, the guy can tell a story at the drop of a hat and keep you enthralled for an hour.

So it was with complete confidence that I let him take the mic for what I thought would be a few harmless minutes.

I'd no sooner gotten into the Porta-Potty when I heard what sounded like a funeral director with a hangover mumble something barely intelligible over the PA. I honestly didn't know what it was.

Then I heard it again, along with something else, which was nothing. The formerly raucous crowd had gone quiet.

Then again, and I could make out some semblance of a coherent sentence, like "This is number 565. This is number 267. This is…" But now it sounded more like the robot voice that tells you you've been placed on hold.

I hurried out, and was immediately accosted by one shocked wife named Rose Reilly. "Mike…"

"Yeah." I walked past her and was treated to glares from some spectators, while others were shrugging their shoulders, hands out to the side with astonished "What the…!" and "Do something!" looks on their faces.

Then I glanced over at Gary. He looked horrorstruck, the panicked look on his face that of a guy falling off a cliff and clawing for the ripcord. The hand holding the mic was shaking visibly.

To say I "relieved" him is more than a clever pun. More than twenty-five years later we still laugh about it, but it sure wasn't funny at the time. And I learned a lesson about blithely handing the mic over to the uninitiated. That's something to think about when you hear and appreciate seasoned professionals like Paul Kaye, Tom Ziebart, Joanne Murphy or Pete Murray: If it's effortless and natural, informative and entertaining, you're listening to a great announcer who takes his craft seriously.

And raise a glass to my buddy Gary. It took quite a few to settle him down that night in 1992.

An IRONMAN finish line is normally a place of great excitement, joy and merriment, but it's also a serious place. Despite the seeming chaos, it's a tightly managed scene, which is the only way to approach a situation in which over two or three thousand battered, triumphant and deeply emotional athletes are brought over the line in front of thousands of fans in such a way that each of them gets a moment in the sun.

Which doesn't mean that things don't go a little off the rails once in a while. Late in the evening at IRONMAN Arizona when only a few finishers at a time were coming in, a border collie came trotting down the chute, right in the middle of the carpet. His head held high, he was bouncing along like he knew exactly where he was, and belonged there.

The spectators, as you might expect, went crazy. And the more they cheered, the more fun this dog seemed to have. I got into it, too, spouting ridiculous one-liners, like "That's one doggone good finish right there," and "That's the secret to a good run: Four legs instead of two!"

While this was going on, a few runners came in, and I'll be dipped if this pooch didn't step aside politely as they ran by, then resume his spot in the middle like this was the most normal thing in the world.

As he came across the line, I yelled, "Bow wow…you are an IRONMAN!" A volunteer leaned down to try to put a finisher's medal around its neck, but the dog was having none of it. He kept running, nimbly dodging all the volunteers who were trying to catch him, and disappeared into the night. At the awards ceremony the next day I professed sadness that he hadn't shown up for the banquet, and announced that he'd won his age division and qualified for Kona.

Once at Coeur d'Alene a woman in the 45-49 division crossed the finish and immediately ran back out into the chute. Not part of the protocol but it happens; it's not uncommon for athletes to want to give a few hugs and high fives to friends and family before they hit the finish line. No problem there, but this particular lady did it *after* crossing the line, which was odd. But, it was late in the evening, with not a lot of people coming across, so we just let it go.

She ran out about 80 meters, turned around and ran back to the finish, smiling and waving to the crowd. She hadn't greeted anybody in particular along the way. Okay, whatever. Probably a first-timer dragging it out a little. Just for fun I called her name again (but didn't call her an IRONMAN).

Then she did it again. Smiling, waving, the whole show. This time there were other runners coming in so I tended to them and tried to ignore her, as did the crowd. I figured, "Third time's the charm," and surely she was done.

Nope. Out she goes again. And now I've had it. I could understand her wanting to keep reliving the moment but there were other athletes finishing and she was a distraction.

I've never had a stern word for anyone at a finish line. The only time I ever let even a touch of pique come into my voice is at the swim start when the pros drift over the line before the cannon goes off. Even then it's still good-natured and everybody gets it.

I wasn't about to get openly irritated with this lady but I was thinking, "Holy Toledo…what if she does it again!" and that I needed to get her out of there. So on her fourth go she's about five meters from hitting the finish line with a "Let's do this again!" look on her face. I glance at the clock and see that she's at 14:59 and some seconds, which is when I got an idea.

I said her name real loud—okay, maybe it was a little stern, but I got her attention—and then said, "If you go back again we're going to add all your back-and-forths to your finish time!"

The crowd broke out in laughter, but the smile on the lady's face froze, then disappeared. She looked up at the clock, as I hoped she would, and saw that she was just a few seconds from breaking the 15-hour mark. I kept quiet as she seemed to be deciding, and I had no idea what I'd do if she went back again. Finally, she walked across for the last time and into the hands of the volunteers, who whisked her away with more than their usual efficiency.

Okay, full disclosure: I did get a little harsh at a finish line, but only once. It was in Louisville. A male finisher stopped about ten meters before the finish line, leaned way down, and grabbed his shorts at the hips with both hands.

Another "Holy Toledo!" moment for me: Was this guy really going to moon the crowd? The mischievous look on his face told me that, yes, indeed, that was his plan. The crowd had gone quiet so they knew it, too.

No time for polite discretion now. "Dude," I said over the PA, "do it and you're disqualified *for life!*"

I had no idea if that would actually happen, but it worked. The guy straightened up and came across the line. I watched him all the way to the finish area exit…

Speaking of your butt hanging out in the open: My plane was late once coming into Australia. Fellow race announcer and Aussie native Pete Murray picked me up at the airport in an SUV and got us out of there as fast as he could. There was no time to stop at the hotel before the welcome ceremony and get into fresh clothes, so Pete said, "Change in the back, mate!"

Good idea, right? By then we were driving along a deserted road out in the bush somewhere and Pete really had the pedal to the metal. At just about the time when nearly all my clothes were off, he suddenly slammed on the brakes. I shot forward, flipping over on the way, until I landed in the front between the seats with my face pressed up against the windshield…

…eye-to-eye with the kangaroo Pete had hit the brakes to avoid running into. Startled, I yelped and jumped backward, and at the same time the kangaroo did the same thing, which startled me again. I ended up back in the rear of the car, pants and underwear around my ankles, feet up near the roof somewhere.

Pete, true-blue Aussie to the core, was choking with laughter and had to get out of the car to walk it off before we could get started again.

Thanks for not taking a picture of me in that car, Pete!

A T THE FIRST RUNNING OF IRONMAN Arizona in 2005, event director Paul Huddle arranged for a 14-year-old girl to sing the national anthem at the welcome banquet. He said the kid had a terrific voice and it would be a sweet surprise for the audience.

At the appointed time, I looked around but didn't see anybody who fit the description, and I didn't see Huddle, either. After a few minutes I decided that we couldn't wait any longer, and I began walking over to where the BCC guys were stationed, the people who handled sound at IRONMAN events. They always kept a recording of the Star-Spangled Banner at the ready for situations just like this. Halfway there, Tom Ziebart came up to find out what the hang-up was.

"Tom!" I called out. "You gotta sing the national anthem!"

"I gotta what?"

Tom has a great singing voice and I knew he could do it. The reason he reacted like that was that this particular song is a killer. It requires a very wide range, and if you don't start out at the very lowest note you can possibly sing, you're going to be in trouble when you get to the "free" in "land of the free." Even some well-trained, experienced performers flat out refuse to sing the anthem, and if they decide to tackle it, it's with a lot of preparation. And here I was asking Tom to do it on thirty seconds' notice.

But the man's got game, and he went for it, and he was doing a bang-up job.

Somewhere in the middle of it I looked over to the side of the stage and saw what appeared to be a mother and daughter. The mother was gesturing for me to come over to them. When I didn't, she gestured more forcefully, but I wasn't about to move during the national anthem, so I looked away, but not before noticing that Mom did not look happy and her daughter was on the verge of tears.

Tom nailed the high F and the audience responded lustily. Instead of heading to the lectern to start the program, I walked to the side of the stage and knelt down to talk to mother and daughter.

Mom pointed to the daughter, whose eyes were filling. "She was supposed to sing that!"

I apologized, but pointed out that they were late. Mom insisted that they'd been right there all along, which may have been true, but they hadn't told anybody.

"She has to sing the anthem!" Mom demanded.

"We just did it," I reminded her.

"Do it again with my daughter!"

I can't remember ever in my life hearing the anthem sung twice in a row, and it didn't seem right to do it now. The point of singing it wasn't to provide a showcase for the singer, and that's all it would be if we did it again. The kid was crying full on by now, and I felt terrible, but that was my decision. Things were getting uncomfortable, too, the whole crowd staring at us and wondering what was going on.

"I'm really sorry," I said, "but we have to get started." I stood up, shrugged apologetically and walked away, even as Mom continued to protest. A few minutes into the program, they finally walked away, dejected but resigned.

It took me a while to shake it off. It's an awful thing to disappoint a kid, and I remember thinking that I hoped she'd be able to get past it and that it wouldn't throw her off whatever musical track she was on in her life.

I needn't have worried. The kid's name was Jordin Sparks and two years later she won American Idol.

I WASN'T REALLY SURE where in the book to put the following story but there's a part that's pretty funny so I guess this chapter is as good a place as any.

One of my favorite personalities in the sport is a guy named Frank Farrar, from South Dakota and 90 at the time of this writing. A lot of athletes around the world have inspired me just by being present at an IRONMAN event, toeing the start line and then getting it done, no matter what. It's a lesson that ought to be taught by parents and teachers everywhere: Finish what you start! It's a cousin of the phrase, "Any job worth doing is worth doing well."

Another lesson is to be humble and not toot your own horn. No one epitomizes this better than Frank. I called him across three IRONMAN finish lines and had any number of conversations with him. "Pleasant guy," I thought, and always enjoyed our chats.

I had no idea until his fourth IRONMAN race that he used to be governor of South Dakota. Never occurred to him to mention it. Before that he was a three-term State Attorney General and, before that, a lieutenant in the US Army. He owns and still runs several businesses, and still goes to work every day in the same town (Britton, pop. 1,300) and lives in the same neighborhood he grew up in. His wife Patty always traveled to running races and triathlons with him, in the plane Frank owned and piloted. When she passed in 2015, they'd been married for 62 years.

When Frank was 63, he was diagnosed with cancer and told he had only two months to live. Not willing to limp submissively to his grave, he decided to jump off the high board and try something really hard. What he chose was triathlons. In the two months and 25 years since his fatal diagnosis, he's done over 325 triathlons, including 35 IRONMAN races, and he still flies himself around to sprint triathlons.

I brought him up on a few stages at welcome dinners. I remember one at IRONMAN Wisconsin particularly well. At first there was some polite applause owing to his age, but when I started going into his biography a deep silence fell over the room and I could see everyone staring at him in open-mouthed awe, drinking in every word. He told the story of how he got into triathlon straightforwardly, with no embellishments, and it was very moving.

"It gave me something new to do," he said. "It saved my life."

You can read a lot of inspirational philosophizing, but hearing it from a real champion and a true survivor is quite something else. This is a very special guy and everyone who hears him knows it…even if he doesn't happen to mention that he's an ex-governor. As you might have surmised, he's a good soul. You know it after just a few minutes of talking to him. He's full of kindness and concern for others, one of those guys who not only asks how you're doing, but is genuinely interested in your response.

Frank was a crowd favorite during races, too. He always had a smile on his face getting out of the water, then he'd hop on his bike and you could spot him a mile off because he rode bow-legged. He'd been severely injured in 1947 and was told his legs would have to be amputated. He refused. The medical technology in those days being pretty rudimentary, they drove nails into his knees to try to save his legs. I guess it worked, because there he was, albeit with knees pointed sideways. Not exactly an aerodynamic way to ride but he managed. Then on the run he wore these thick goggles that looked like a small snorkel mask, and he did a kind of half-shuffle ("I always have to remind myself to pick up my feet and not trip"), so Frank was easy to spot throughout the race and the spectators adored him.

He was always a late finisher, and anticipation heightened as the clock ran down. I got reports of his whereabouts and called them out to the crowd, receiving happy shouts in response.

At the race in 2007 I spotted him as he made the last turn in front of the Wisconsin State Capitol building. After the turn there's a bit of a downhill. Frank picks up a little speed, but he's still shuffling so it looks kind of precarious. But now he hears the wild cheering of the spectators and it brightens up his smile, and he picks up the pace again. As he gets closer, people on both sides of the fence lining the chute are straining over it to catch a glimpse of him. When he runs through the intersection at the last cross street before the finish, he's just about to step onto the red-and-black IRONMAN carpet. I call it the "magic carpet" because it seems to adore every footstep that lands on it. No matter how heavy and tired their legs, everybody looks like they're floating above it.

I'm out of the tower and down on the floor now, standing on that carpet just a few feet in front of the finish line. I want to make sure that Frank receives the highest and loudest praise possible, which is easy because the spectators are in a complete frenzy now. I yell out, "Here he comes!" and, impossibly, the noise gets even louder.

Hearing the sounds, Frank looks up, a dazzling smile on his face...

And catches his toe on the carpet.

We've all done it, stubbed our toe on something sticking up just slightly from the ground. Usually we make a small stumble and recover. But here's a man in his late 70s who's been pushing himself to the limit for well over 16 hours. So Frank went down. And I don't mean "down," like did a few stutter steps, dropped to a knee and rolled over. He went *down*, straight down, wham! Like an old oak tree struck by lightning and slamming into the earth. He went down so fast he had no chance to brace himself with his arms and hands to soften the blow. His stomach, chest and face hit the ground at the same time.

There was a collective gasp from the crowd, and then they went dead quiet, as if someone had pulled the plug on a stereo. They were in complete shock, and so was I. Rooted to the spot, I felt like a cement statue, incapable of movement.

Which was when I noticed that Frank wasn't moving, either. Not a twitch anywhere I could spot. I couldn't even tell if he was breathing. I shook myself loose and ran to him, a knot beginning to form in my stomach. He was still motionless when I got to him, his head to one side, his goggles on but cocked crazily on his head. I remember the fleeting thought that I hoped his wife wasn't seeing this. She was battling early-stage dementia and this could be overwhelming.

The crowd was coming out of its shock. I could hear mutterings of "Oh, my God" and "I hope it isn't serious" and "This doesn't look good."

I got down on my hands and knees and put my free hand on his back. It was only to make some comforting contact but I could feel a rapid rise and fall and realized he was breathing. Still, he had to be seriously injured, and I was anxious to find out how badly.

I put my face next to his. "Frank?" I said tentatively. "Frank, you okay? How you doing, buddy?" I heard some minor commotion nearby and assumed it was the medics on their way.

Frank's eyes fluttered open, then he looked at me. A good sign. He also smiled, or at least I thought so. I knew the crowd was waiting for me to say something, and I also wanted to give the medics some clues to his condition, but I couldn't tell what was happening yet.

"Frank, how're you doing? What's going on? Are you okay?"

He took a deep breath and let it out very slowly, like a prolonged sigh. "I'm good," he said. "I'm good."

What a relief to hear him speak. But Frank would probably say "I'm good" if he had a compound fracture. "You fell really hard, man," I said. "Are you okay?"

He took another deep breath, and closed his eyes. *Oh no...*

"I'm fine, Mike," he said. "But it feels so good to be lying down I just wanna stay here for a while!"

I blinked in disbelief, then threw my head back and laughed like an idiot, both in relief and at how funny this was. The crowd saw it and heaved a collective sigh, with a small smattering of applause and whooping.

Frank still didn't move. I waved the medics off; if they provided assistance Frank might be disqualified and I was sure now that he didn't need their attention.

But this wasn't going to do. I leaned down to yell in his ear. "Frank, buddy, you gotta get up!"

He sighed. "Feels *sooooo* good down here."

I picked up the mic and told the crowd what he'd just said. That got the frenzy going again, and that joyous sound got to Frank. He picked up his head and turned to look at the finish line, then he looked right and left at the spectators, who only got wilder and louder.

I took advantage of his semi-upright position to snake an arm under him and tug. He struggled to his feet, wobbly but determined, and eventually straightened up and stood on his own. As he took a few tentative steps, I looked at the race clock and yelled, "He's going to finish!"

I don't remember ever hearing a crowd that loud at a finish line. You could practically feel the energy pouring over the fence and into Frank, who kept up his teetering shuffle and started waving to the onlookers on either side of him. People were reaching out to try to touch him or high-five him, and I hoped he had the good sense to stay in the middle of the chute and not take any of them up on it. He looked like a breeze would knock him over.

"Frank Farrar of Britton, South Dakota..." I called as he neared the line. Then, "You are an IRONMAN!" as he stepped over it.

He raised both arms to shoulder height, not in triumph, it seemed to me, but in appreciation for all the support and obvious good feeling from the spectators. As volunteer catchers grabbed him and started leading him away, I wanted to say something but nothing came out. It might have been one of my most eloquent moments, just saying nothing, because what we'd just witnessed needed no narration. The crowd was imprinted with the image of a man they thought was done just fifty feet from the line, only to watch him cross a few minutes later, in one of the most glorious IRONMAN finishes they were ever likely to see.

I HAD AN ODD MOMENT leaving Wisconsin. I was in a taxi heading toward the airport. Stopped at a light, I looked out the window to my right. There was Frank, at the wheel of a rental car, with Patty in the passenger seat. I'd spoken to Patty after the race to see if she was okay. She was a touch confused, and worn out after a very long day as a spectator and somewhat thrown by the pandemonium, but she talked lovingly of seeing her husband finish. Sitting in the car, she had a pretty smile on her face as she listened to Frank speaking to her.

I started to roll the window down but the light turned green and we sped off. I thought, what a sight to see this humble man and his wife driving to the airport in a rental car. After all the noise and celebration and public adulation, this extraordinarily accomplished public figure was just like any other athlete who'd raced, getting himself to and from the event, hauling his own gear, accompanied only by the love of his life, with no pomp or fanfare. It was like seeing Craig Alexander and his wife all by themselves in that bar after Craig had won the World Championship.

I twisted around to watch as Frank turned off the main road and headed toward the private airplane ramp, where they'd climb into his little plane and head back to South Dakota.

I got a little emotional there in the cab, for reasons I can't quite explain. Was it because of the impact he'd had on so many people that weekend, followed by this lonely ride away from all the fussing over him? Was I wistful realizing that, ultimately, we're all in the same boat, whether you're an ex-governor or an 18-year-old trying to discover who you really are?

He had such an important lesson to teach us, as did other athletes in this book who faced seemingly insurmountable obstacles and overcame them by adding yet another challenge to their lives. Challenges define us, and they can provide a way to knock down other hurdles, tamp down the negative and teach us the beauty of overcoming difficulties. Frank Farrar has seen more challenges in his life than most of us will, and I believe it was facing those challenges head on that forged his character. When you talk to him, laugh with him, watch him push pain aside to get to the finish line, you feel inspired to do better yourself.

Thanks for getting up and finishing, Frank. And thanks for making us laugh like hell in the process.

A side note which makes me question whether there are accidents in the universe or just fate: I was editing the draft of Frank's story on a flight to a marathon in the Midwest that I was going to announce. Halfway there the plane experienced a mechanical problem and we had to land at the nearest airport. It was in South Dakota, a few gallons of gas away from where Frank lives. It was all I could do not to jump off the plane and go visit him.

I remembered something he said to me the last time we'd spoken: "My goal is to live to 100...unless I get killed by a jealous husband!"

CHAPTER 17

The Best Call I Ever Made

"**M**ike, what's the best call you ever made?"

I get this question all the time. It's interesting because, as long-time IRONMAN-watchers know, I don't play favorites. I try to keep in mind that every one of these athletes has worked hard, sacrificed deeply and suffered mightily. Each is deserving of a special shout-out and a rousing cheer from the finish line crowd. So aside from some details (e.g., "She just won the world title!" or "This 78-year-old beat the cutoff clock by over forty minutes!"), each gets a full measure of attention and enthusiasm. For a few seconds, they are in sole possession of the spotlight.

There have been some especially memorable finishes; hundreds, in fact. Who can forget the first time (after seven tries) that Mark Allen finally beat Dave Scott in the epic Iron War? What about Paula Newby-Fraser's eighth World Championship? Or Sarah Reinertsen, the first female amputee to finish Kona, on her second attempt? Calling those people across was thrilling, and I remember every second.

And then there was the time I called in a certain special corporate executive. It was Andrew Messick, CEO of IRONMAN, at the 2012 IRONMAN Mont-Tremblant. How cool is it that the guy who runs IRONMAN *is* an IRONMAN! And it wasn't just a one-off: I brought Andrew over the line three times at Lake Placid.

This may surprise you, but I do have a favorite. And I'm pretty sure no finisher, professional or age grouper, is going to feel disrespected or slighted when I tell you who it is.

THE FIRST IRONMAN TRIATHLON I ANNOUNCED was in 1989. My daughter Erin was six years old at the time, and her brother Andy was three. It never occurred to my wife Rose and me that I'd still be on the microphone when our kids were well into adulthood, with children of their own.

They grew up watching their mom and dad run and ride, and they understood what multisports was all about. They'd set up little triathlon courses in the neighborhood, using our driveway as the transition area, and invite their friends to race. Parents always wonder if they're bringing their kids up right, equipping them to make their way in the world with confidence and poise. Getting them to love a sport and commit to it is one of the best ways to do that, and we were delighted that our kids got into being active at an early age.

I like to think I was a little inspiring, too. Long before I started announcing IRONMAN races, I was on the mic at a local triathlon event. Erin, who was three at the time, whirled around to Rose as they were walking towards the venue and said, "That's Daddy!" She talked about it for weeks.

It's a competitive world out there, but it doesn't have to be dog-eat-dog. You can compete with style, grace and good humor, and there's no better way to learn that than through athletics. How many times have we seen Angels outfielder Mike Trout beat out a throw to first base and exchange a laugh with the first baseman before stealing second on the next pitch? Two boxers beat the living daylights out of each other for twelve rounds and then collapse into an embrace of mutual respect at the final bell. The runner-up at Wimbledon meets her opponent at the net and compliments her game.

Chrissie Wellington waits at the IRONMAN finish line to give second place a hug.

That's how we wanted to bring up our kids. We were all active, we ate well, we tried to impart the right lessons. Bringing up a kid is like building a satellite: You do everything you can while it's still on the ground and in your hands, because once you launch it into space, it's on its own and you can only hope you did everything right.

Erin and Andy diverged in terms of sports—Erin went through middle and high school as a gymnast, and Andy played baseball—but they pursued them with all the right attitudes. Erin ran the Boston Marathon in 2010 and seeing her face when she crossed the finish line was something I'll never forget. It wasn't a look of triumph; it was a look of accomplishment.

Turns out Andy had a knack for race announcing. He started joining me in the tower and handling the mic while I was on break. He has a great voice and appealing presence; I like to think he was taking after me but the truth is, he was his own man with his own style, and it worked. He loved IRONMAN, and a lot of his friends got into it as well.

Lee Gruenfeld/IRONMAN

Andy eventually decided to exploit his considerable talent for endurance sports marketing and turned his attention in that direction rather than race announcing.

Andy was with me in the tower at the 2012 IRONMAN Arizona. A few of his friends and work colleagues were in the VIP area in front of us. Sometimes when they caught us looking their way, they'd hold up their plastic cups and give us a hard time because they were whooping it up and hoisting brewskies while we were working. Nice bunch of pals! But while the suds looked inviting, there was still no place I'd rather be than where I was.

As the evening wore on and finishers kept pouring in, they started shouting to us that they were going to sign up in the morning for next year's race. This is an old story, people getting lubricated and inspired at the same time, thinking, "Boy, would I like to be one of those people coming across the line!" They know the IRONMAN mantra–*Swim 2.4. Bike 112. Run 26.2. Brag for the rest of your life*–and they want a piece of that.

And there's a phrase I've heard a thousand times: *I could do an IRONMAN, if I just did the training.*

I shake my head every time I hear that. It's the "if" that always gets me. The British used to say that wars were won on the playing fields of Eton. Well, IRONMAN races are won on the training fields. The race itself is tough, of course, but it's the training that wipes most people out. *Of course* you could do the race if you trained. But that "if" is everything.

Anyway, the *Let's-sign-up-right-now* 'tude usually wears off by morning. Except, right now, the shouts coming our way started changing. "You should do this, Andy!" they were yelling. My son shook it off with a smile, but the smile started fading after a while.

"Easy, there" I said. "You're getting caught up in the moment."

"Yeah, you're right." He dismissed it and we continued to call racers in together.

He was thinking about it, though, and then he said, "Dad, I think I'm going to do Arizona next year."

"You sure about that?"

"I don't know." He thought for a second. "Maybe."

The next morning, he told me that he and his buddies had signed up right there at the race site. I laughed and said, "Good luck!"

It wasn't going to be easy. It never was, but it might be particularly tough for Andy. He was in great shape, having played baseball all through college and then gotten paid for it after he'd graduated. But baseball shape wasn't IRONMAN shape. He weighed around 200 pounds and that was a lot of weight to be lugging around 140.6 miles in the Arizona desert.

But he was serious, as I discovered early in his training when he went on a long, tough climbing ride up Mt. Palomar in San Diego County with his old man. I was in decent riding shape and knew the mountain like the back of my hand, but it was a serious wake up call for Andy. I stayed in front all the way up to the top but he stuck with me the whole way, with no complaints.

He knuckled down to the training with the same kind of zeal he'd brought to baseball. As with all age groupers there was a lot of juggling, trying to balance it all with his full-time job, but he did it, and he did it well. And I was going to be in the tower when he finished.

Andy wanted to keep it all low-key but there was no way around everyone knowing what was happening. Aside from being my son, he was going to do the race with all those friends who'd signed up with him. All during race week people would come up to me. "Mike, what's it going to be like to call your own kid an IRONMAN? Do you think he'll even finish? Make sure you're not in the bathroom when he does!"

On race day, spotters apprised me of his progress. At the 11:20 mark I got ready to climb down from the tower and head to the finish line. I turned to my long-time announcing partner, Tom Ziebart.

"Tom, listen," I said. "We need to make sure that every athlete near Andy gets his call, and I'm going to lose it if I try to do it. So take special care with each one."

He promised he would. Rose was waiting under the timing clock with a finisher's medal. Erin was there, too, with her husband Andrew (which is what he goes by, thank goodness, avoiding family confusion with my son, Andy). She was unfurling a mylar space blanket to wrap around her brother against the cool desert air. The anticipation in the crowd was palpable. I felt like they were holding their breaths. Oh, wait: That was me.

Then we saw him coming down the chute. As soon as I spotted him, it was like everything had slipped into slow motion. There was another athlete right in front of him, and I heard Tom call him across. Andy hit the front edge of the carpet with 11:29 on the clock and a mile-wide grin lighting up his face. He put his arms out, ready to hug his family.

It took every ounce of strength I had to keep my voice from cracking. "Andy Reilly, from Poway, California..." I began.

Then he stepped across the line.

"You are an IRONMAN!"

As the crowd roared lustily, Andy fell into my arms and wrapped me in a bear hug. Then he grabbed his mom, and she put the medal around his neck. Erin wrapped him in the mylar blanket, a big sister protecting her little brother.

After a few seconds, the three of them began walking away, out of the finish area, two of the most important women in my son's life holding him up. (He hadn't yet added the third, his future wife Briana.) I stood there by myself, feeling a little lonely for half a second. *Hey, what am I...chopped liver?* But Andy's race was done and I still had a job to do. Athletes would be coming across for over five more hours, and they deserved my attention.

I looked wistfully toward the back of the finish area, where a big spotlight was shining down at the departing trio, the mylar blanket twinkling brightly, the strap of the finisher's medal visible around Andy's neck. His head was down, and both Rose and Erin were talking to him, telling him how proud they were. I hated seeing them leave.

One thing I don't do is call people an IRONMAN for a second time. But I badly wanted to do something before my family disappeared. And, hey: This was my own flesh and blood, right? Wouldn't I be forgiven one small act of self-indulgence?

"Andy Reilly..." I said into the mic. "You are an IRONMAN!"

As the crowd roared its approval, Andy raised his arm in the air and flashed a thumbs-up without looking back.

I climbed back up the scaffold and called racers in until the 17-hour mark. I couldn't stop thinking about my boy and how proud of him I was. It was like I was floating above the wooden floorboards.

And that was my best call ever.

CHAPTER 18

I'm the luckiest person in the sport, hands down.

It's hard to think of a job involving repetition that doesn't become tedious and make one jaded, bored or indifferent. How much sincerity and enthusiasm can a flight attendant muster up when offering pretzels for the millionth time? Do you really expect that ticket taker at Dodger Stadium to chat you up about how great it is that you're about to see a baseball game? How special can you be to the guy in the diner who's been slinging hash for fifteen years?

How do you think an athlete coming across an IRONMAN finish line looks to the announcer who's yelled, "You are an IRONMAN!" over 400,000 times?

Well, to *this* announcer, she looks like a mortal god who just lassoed the moon and wrestled it to the ground.

To me, their faces don't blur, their stories don't repeat, and it never, ever gets old. I look at every athlete and try to imagine their pain, their sacrifices and how it must feel to finally cross the line. I consciously remind myself that their race wasn't about these few triumphant moments coming down the chute under the bright lights in front of a cheering crowd. It was about hours of struggle, bouts of loneliness and many moments of doubt during the course of a very, very long day. And it was also about the hundreds and thousands of hours of swim, bike and run training that made this day possible.

I also think about their families. I know that spouses, partners, kids and parents are watching this finisher, either right here or on the real-time remote feed. They've sacrificed as much, and sometimes more, than their athlete did, and every one of them deserves to share this moment in the sun. I think of little Grace McDonnell, who told me (in no uncertain terms) that I was going to call her daddy an IRONMAN. There is no explanation she would ever understand about why I failed to do that. Grabbing a sandwich? In the Porta-Potty? Unthinkable.

If I have a few moments to say something personal about an athlete coming across the line, I learned long ago not to expect a response. Many don't trust themselves to speak; others can't find the words; some are simply too exhausted.

It doesn't matter. What I see in their eyes speaks volumes. And, as my friend Bryce Courtenay had put it, "What you are speaks so loud that what you say cannot be heard."

As it turns out, despite the lack of response, they can later recall every word I said, and often repeat my words back to me. Crossing the line seems to put people in a state of hyperawareness, as though, having worked so hard for this moment, they want to remember every single thing about it. Since it's my voice coming over the PA, I try to make sure the moment is as memorable as possible. I consider it a sacred responsibility.

What an announcer says *before* the finish can matter, too.

The power of mind over body is a well-known phenomenon. It's difficult to pinpoint because you rarely know when it's going to happen. One sure bet for seeing it demonstrated is to come to an IRONMAN finish line. At every race, virtually without exception, there are a handful of athletes who teeter towards the last few hundred meters spent, exhausted, battered, even delirious. There's nothing left in the tank, and some of them are barely moving or even standing. They've had it.

At close to midnight one of them spots the bright lights at the finish line. She hears the encouraging cheers and shouts from the spectators in the distance. She thinks back to all the work she put in, the sacrifices her husband and kids made, and all the visualizing the whole family did of what it would be like when she topped the summit.

She sees the lights and something happens. She reaches way down inside, searching desperately for a hidden reservoir. Somewhere, in a place she's not familiar with because nothing's ever driven her there before, she finds a few atoms of fuel. Or maybe her strength of will created them on the spot. Nobody knows, but suddenly the legs take a step, then another, and another. A minute ago she wouldn't have thought it possible. But she's moving now, and with each agonizing step the lights grow brighter, the crowd gets louder.

She looks up again and deflates, because the finish line still looks a hundred miles away. She's trying, but the muscles are depleted. The only thing pushing her forward is the fierce determination in her heart.

And it's her heart I go after as soon as I spot the struggle taking place. I'll stand right at the finish line where she can see me. I'll wave a towel over my head and dance. I'll shout out her name and every encouraging phrase I can think of over the PA, and I'll do everything possible to rev the crowd up to fever pitch.

Somehow, by some unfathomable alchemy, all the noise and energy zaps directly through her eyes and ears, into her heart and down to her legs. It's real, and you can literally see it happen. The crowd roars, she takes a step, the crowd sees that and roars even louder, and there's another step. The grimace turns into a tentative smile and the crowd goes out of its mind. Many of them had finished the race earlier and came back to cheer others in, and they want this as bad as she does. The energy is buzzing in the air now, and the connection between the athlete and the crowd is so strong it's like a tow rope pulling her forward.

She knows what I'm going to say when she steps over the line.

And then she's there.

I'M OFTEN ASKED WHICH is my favorite IRONMAN race. Well, it's Lake Placid. The mountain setting is unrivaled for natural beauty, and poignant reminders of two Winter Olympic Games are everywhere.

Wait: Actually, it's Wisconsin, with that amazing state capitol setting and down-home, mid-Western atmosphere. Hang on, no: My favorite is the Big One in Kona, the granddaddy of them all, stark, lava-strewn desolation set against a lush tropical landscape and brilliant blue ocean. Then again, how could New Zealand not be my favorite? Or Mont-Tremblant, or...

Okay, here's the truest answer I can give: My favorite IRONMAN event is the one I'm announcing right now, wherever that might be. The impact on me of announcing IRONMAN has been profound. I've got a ringside seat to the ongoing affirmation of the very best of the human spirit. Not only that, I become a part of it. I don't feel at all immodest in acknowledging that "You are an IRONMAN!" represents the certifying seal, the clarion declaration that something extraordinary has just happened. That's got nothing to do with me; I'm the herald, not the warrior. I'm not the one who did the training and the racing, which makes me doubly fortunate to share in the joy of accomplishment, and to contribute to it in some small way. The "audio diploma" I bestow is not just from me but from every person in their lives that loved them, supported them and believed in them.

Doing this race binds people in a way you hardly see anywhere else. Maybe it's the old story of uniting in a common struggle, but people come from all over the world—eighty countries represented in Kona is typical— and I've yet to see a hint of any nationalistic rancor or enmity rear its ugly head. If you could bottle this extraordinary feeling of shared purpose and mutual respect, there'd be no more war.

I'm in constant awe of the pull this event has. It's mind-boggling to find people like Super Bowl MVP Hines Ward, Indy 500 champ Tony Kannan, multi-time Olympic gold medalist Apolo Ono, Senator Kyrsten Sinema, actor-producer-director Sean Astin, major league baseball veteran, sports announcer and 11-time IRONMAN finisher Eric Byrnes, master chef Gordon Ramsey, and NHL-legend Pat LaFontaine stepping up to the start line. They've all been at the very top of their respective professions, have been showered with awards and accolades the rest of us can only dream about, and have nothing left to prove. They could relax, take it easy, put their feet up and rest on their considerable laurels.

But that kind of attitude is not what got them where they are. People like that are always looking for the next mountain to climb, and the lure of IRONMAN is irresistible. Watching them tackle it was incredibly inspirational, and actually led me to shape this book in a certain way. Originally, I wanted to address myself to people inside the IRONMAN community. But seeing the fascination that people from other walks of life have with it, and how motivating and healing it can be, convinced me that the lessons to be learned are universal.

If you know someone who you think might benefit from those lessons or draw a little inspiration from the stories you just read, why not pass this book on to them?

We're all juggling family life, work and our varied interests. We all face obstacles and moments of doubt, we all get into ruts, and we're all trying to figure out how to do the best we can with what we've been given. There are plenty of ways to do that, and I hope that this book has given you some notion of one way in particular, which is to set a goal that is dizzyingly difficult, immensely rewarding once accomplished, and lets you try again if it doesn't work the first time.

If you want to become a Super Bowl MVP, you have to be better than every other guy who wants that title as well, and you have to get a lot of breaks so that the trophy-winning plays come your way. Same thing for a heavyweight title or the FedEx Cup, or the US Open. The competition is fierce, and there's only one winner.

But if your goal is to be an IRONMAN, the only thing standing in your way is you.

It's one of the very few towering individual achievements that is attainable by ordinary mortals. Which is not to say it's easy. It's terribly hard. You have to put in an awful lot of work and make a lot of sacrifices. But if you do, you'll cross the finish line and have those bragging rights for the rest of your life.

The trick is to start. It doesn't have to be an IRONMAN triathlon, but start *something*. You might not be the fastest or strongest when you get to the end but you're going to be a whole lot faster and stronger than the ones who never tried. Starting is the key, and to start you have to overcome a lot of things: inertia, laziness and, more often than not, fear. Talking to thousands of athletes I discovered an interesting paradox: The best way to get over your fear of starting is to *start*. I've watched countless IRONMAN competitors approach the water on race morning in various states of anxiety, panic and near-paralysis. Every one of them tells me some variation of the same thing later: *As soon as that cannon went off, all the butterflies disappeared and I was happy, because that was exactly where I wanted to be.*

With every athlete I call across the line, my passion only increases, as does my optimism about the world. So many people driven to find the best within themselves, to undertake grand challenges, to push themselves to the outer limits to make it to the finish line? It leaves me full of hope, and full of gratitude for the opportunity to do what I do. It's an endless gift, and I owe an enormous debt of thanks to every athlete who gives me the privilege of making that call at the finish line.

E komo mai.

For those readers who can't see photos on their devices, we've posted all of the pictures in this book at www.mikereilly.net.

The website also contains links to videos, other resources and some stories that weren't included in the book.

Acknowledgements

Rose, where do I start? Your support, strength, and most of all patience, has given me the opportunity to pursue my dreams. You are the most loving wife, mother and Nene our children, grandchildren and I could ever have. Your critique and advice for me are no-nonsense and always spot on, even though I usually won't admit it at first. I'll never forget one of the best days of my life, when I first laid eyes on you in Mrs. Sheehan's science class freshman year in high school. We've come a long way baby! XO

Erin, my sweet and strong daughter who still amazes me every day. You are one of the smartest and most self-motivated people I know. Watching you be the wonderful Mother you are is a joy beyond words. Hearing the word Daddy from you still melts my heart every time.

Andy Reilly, my son and best friend! You have constantly been at my side helping and guiding your Pops on this book journey, and I could not have done it without you. You are the best son a father could ever have, and I learn more from you than you can imagine. And always remember—You are an IRONMAN!

Don, Pat, Kathy, and Peggy, supporting your brother in this project and everything I've ever tackled has been a lifelong guiding light for me. Mom & Dad did one hell of a job raising their brood and they, along with big sister Judy, are always looking down upon us with smiles on their faces.

The Serenata Families of the Reas, McMillins and McGills, your friendship and support means the world me. We are family never to be divided; our children and grandchildren will carry on the Serenata legacy. We are 'Ohana, we are Love!

Bob & Heidi Babbitt, thanks for putting this book idea in my head many years ago and being the best of friends. Our sport is lucky to have you, Bob, you are a legend. And NO, he didn't marry my daughter!

Rob Klingensmith, your guidance and advice are always spot on. Your knowledge never ceases to amaze me and you're the best sales person I know. Thank you, my friend and fellow Buckeye.

Andrew Messick, your support from the beginning, when I told you about this book, has never wavered. Thank you for your leadership and passion for what you do.

Gary Baz, high school buddy, best friend and best man at my wedding. Your constant words of encouragement reading the transcript, and your humor, kept pushing me to the finish line. Your support and friendship are immeasurable.

Jim Connell, USNA '75, another high school buddy of Rose's and mine, who read the entire manuscript and provided valuable feedback. You gave us some gems. One of the smartest guys I know. Thanks, Genghis!

Neal Tabachnick, your legal guidance has been amazing and critical. Conversations with you are the best and your concern for my success is heartfelt and true. And don't worry, I won't make you do an IRONMAN.

Therese and Fred Rzymek, thank you for your love and support all these years. Freddie, who would have thought a couple of grade schoolers from the Toledo Catholic Club many moons ago would head down the same endurance path all their adult life. How lucky are we.

Tom Ziebart, at my side for over 100 events. Your support, friendship and laughter make our long days together the best. Your work and commitment to triathlon and IRONMAN are legendary. Watching Kaitlyn and David grow up and now working in the business is priceless. You and Debbie should be proud.

Julia Polloreno, your read of my manuscript was incredibly helpful. You are the best at what you do! Mahalo from the bottom of my heart.

Kevin Mackinnon, your feedback on the book was extremely valuable. Thank you my Canadian brother.

Cherie Gruenfeld, our IHE, your "in-house editing" and advice kept this book on pace to be the best it could be. Your daily reading and valuable feedback of everything we wrote was a gift I will never forget. Thank you for being such a dear friend. You inspire everyone who comes in contact with you.

Many other people helped with this book, and the finished product is better for their valuable assistance: Rick Dressler, Bob Babbitt, Kevin Berg, Mattheiu Van Veen, Nick Paskiewicz, Stephanie Greenfield, Paul Phillips, Tony Svensson, Nils Nilsen, Sachin Shrestha, Jason Reinhardt, Aaron Ramirez, Jessica Kaye, Deborah Reeves, Michele Pinkas, Melinda Downey, Bethany Smith, Marilyn Reilly, Gary Roethenbaugh and Helen Gruenfeld.

Matt Long FDNY, my Irish brother from another mother. Being a part of your amazing life and journey is an honor for me. You have the strongest 'never give up' attitude I have ever witnessed. Remember girls, you are welcome at our Cali Casa anytime.

Diana Bertsch, you are a dear friend who constantly shows me the value of hard work and passion for your job. You provide the most amazing stages where dreams always do come true. Aloha for letting me be a part of your world.

Alan and Dena Rea, for over 30 years you both have been at our side, in friendship, support and helping raise our kids, and now grandkids. Rose and I are blessed to have you in our lives.

Melinda & Dave Downey, BCC, you have always made me sound better than I am. Your work is the best in the world and your passion for all the athletes is next to none. Can't imagine ever working an event without you.

Robbie Little, my flying buddy and worldwide photographer who has captured it all. Anything I ask you for, you deliver in abundance. You built a company that shows the world what the power of the smile is all about. Thank you, my friend!

Dave McGillivray, your friendship since our Saucony days has been one of the best constants in my life. Watching you continuously raise the bar shows me there should be no complacency in our lives. And, you're simply the best race director that I know. Boston Strong!

Fr. Dan "Iron Friar" Callahan, thank you for the heartfelt blessing you gave me and my book in front of St. Agnes Church in Lake Placid, July of 2016. It propelled me to finish it all.

Katherine Kelly Lang, your support for me and love for triathlon is over the moon. Thank you for introducing so many to our great sport.

Rob Wallack, your and Ann's support and friendship are very dear to me. All these years we've stayed close is one of the things in life I cherish the most.

Mike Plant, thank you for thinking of me and making that call to join you in 1989 in Kona. I will be eternally grateful.

Dave Deschenes and Sarah Hartmann, you both showed me what giving back really means. Thank you for that lesson.

Ken Baggs, your and Glenda's friendship means the world to me. Thanks for accepting this Yank down under all those years ago. The health and strength of triathlon in Australia is due in large part to your work and passion. Next Guinness on me, mate!

Whitey Anson, the foundation of your mentorship and work ethic has help guide me all these years. Taking a young sales rep under your wing, you showed me how to create a path to success. And all these years later how cool is it I called your son an IRONMAN.

Jane Patterson, your friendship, love, and support has always boosted my confidence. Your passion and job of directing IRONMAN New Zealand all those years was next to none. It was such an honor to call you an IRONMAN! And it's okay that you and Jennette laugh at me when Rose tells me to take out the trash!

Paula, Paul, Heather and Roch, you have always been there for me and IRONMAN is lucky to have you all still in the game, helping guide its path towards the future. Working an event with you is like being with my brothers and sisters.

John Duke, your friendship and support all these years have never wavered and your sales ability always amazes me. Laughter is the best medicine, so it goes without saying, you'll live longer than all of us.

Ben Fertic, thank you for inducting me into the IRONMAN Hall of Fame. The speech you gave was one of the most heartfelt I'd ever heard. I'll never forget it or your kindness.

Bill, Tom and Michael Begg, you are my Lake Placid Bro's and friends for life. Watching your families grow and finish so many IRONMAN races has been my honor.

Eric Gilsenan, our sport is much better off because you are a part of it. Thanks for your constant support, buddy. You are a true friend.

Ian Hepenstall, I'll always cherish working with you all those years in New Zealand. You are a legend and a great mate.

Graeme Hannan, for pushing to bring me to Australia long ago and introducing me to the amazing passion of IRONMAN in Oz. Plus, who would have ever thought our boys, meeting when they were eleven, would be groomsmen in each other's wedding.

Marc Roy and the entire Sportstats timing team, you have been invaluable in providing information critical to my book. Working alongside you all these years has been a blast.

Graham and Sue Fraser, from day one you gave me your support and the stage to do my thing. Your vision put us where we are today and I'll always be grateful. Standing at the start of IRONMAN Lake Placid 1999 with you, Graham, was one of the most emotional moments of my career.

Lew Friedland, your vision, leadership and foresight in 1999 led the way for the expansion of IRONMAN events in the United States and abroad, introducing thousands of people to our sport.

Mike Rouse, my brother and a man who inspires me every day. What you have come from, accomplished and succeeded at could fill four lifetimes. Never stop doing what you do; people everywhere depend on your guidance.

The amazing three degrees of separation in finding Dan Trone, the first person I ever called an IRONMAN. A massive Mahalo to Scott Tinley>Jimmie Black>Jay Larson. Way to go, boys.

Bart Yasso, you have always inspired me to reach new heights and never quit! Your inspiration has guided hundreds of thousands of athletes to be winners.

Larry White, slinging running shoes with you in our shoe dog days and throwing tennis balls around, were some of the best times I ever had. You still make me belly laugh, my friend.

All my friends and workmates from ACTIVE and EVENTS.COM, you know who you are. We grew up together and the bond we all have is priceless. Nothing pleases me more than seeing so many of you achieving great things in life and business, including many IRONMAN finishes. Never stop living the dream!

The hardest working group of people I know and have ever been involved with, are the endurance event roadies (the "carnies"), the men and women who, weekend after weekend, plan, set up, maintain and break down race sites all over the world. Some of them work over 40 weekends per year, sometimes around the clock, making sure race courses are safe and clear for athletes to achieve their dreams. They are out there on race day in the shadows, never looking for accolades. When someone tells me how hard they work at their job I just smile to myself, because I witness firsthand, at every running, triathlon and IRONMAN race, what hard work really is. Mahalo to each and every one of you! And Godfather Bohannan, you know you're my #1 carnie!

The hard working, incredible race directors I've had the pleasure to work with over the years: You don't receive the praise you deserve. You are, and have been, the backbone of endurance sports, and we are a thriving business because of you. Thank you Dave Christian, Ryan Richards, Diana Bertsch, Ken Baggs, Jane Patterson, Valerie Silk, Sharron Ackles, Dave McGillivray, Graham Fraser, Jeff Edwards, Greg Borzilleri, Wayne Reardon, Dominique Piche, Janette Douglas, Rick Kozlowski, Matt West, Mark Knutson, Roch Frey, Philip LaHaye, Neil Finn, Geoff Meyer, Gerry Boyle, Joanna Jordan, Lyle Harris, Ryan Griessmeyer, Nick Curl, Ben Herbert, Carl Smith, Gina Thomas, Shane Facteau, Buzz Mills, John Conley, Christine Adams, Ellen Flanagan Larson, Kai Walter, Ben Rausa, Paul Huddle, Tim Murphy, K. Reid, Debbie Baker, Steve Borowski, Tim Brosious, Shane Smith, Mac Cavasar, Rob Wallack, Jan Caille, AJ Sills, Scott Langen, Judy Stowers, Jamie Pitblado, Tom Cooney, Adam McDonald, David Ray, Judy Stolpe, Bill Uncapher, Kathy Loper, and last but not least, Lynn Flanagan, the first race director to hand me a microphone. See what you started, Lynn? Mahalo from the bottom of my heart. XO

To each and every person I've had the honor to work alongside and has had the guts to pick up a microphone to go live. Thank you Tom Ziebart, Whit Raymond, Paul Kaye, Mike Plant, Pete Murray, Cameron Harper, Brian Ashby, Mark Bone, Dave Downey, Eric Gilsenan, Greg Welch, Michael Lovato, Joanne Murphy, Alain Cyr, Jacques Galarneau, Rudy Novotny, Fitz Koehler, Werner Damm, Steve King, Tammy Barker, Shannon Spake, Mike Ribbitt, Tracy Sundlun, Peter Beckerleg, Don Ryder, Tony Lugo, Dave Latourette, Dave Kappas, Ann Wessling, Ken McLaren, Belinda Granger, Creigh Kelley, Dave Ragsdale, Vinny Finneran, Kevin Mackinnon, and Andy Reilly. Always remember the five P's to success - Proper Planning Prevents Poor Performance!

To each person in every story of this book, thank you for letting me into your lives and most of all welcoming me in your families. The bond we have will be everlasting, and long after we are all gone your shining examples of love, perseverance, positive attitudes and success will teach many to never give up.

Last, but certainly not least, LEE GRUENFELD, you are an amazing man and dear friend. From the beginning you and Cherie (well, maybe Cherie more than you at the onset) have supported this book. Your guidance, writing and humor have made me the luckiest author alive. Not one time did we have a disagreement or cross word. Our collaboration every day was a joy and I can't wait to get started on our next project, whatever that is!

About the Authors

MIKE REILLY, the official "Voice of IRONMAN" worldwide and a member of the IRONMAN Hall of Fame, the USA Triathlon Hall of Fame and the Running USA Hall of Champions, is the only person to have been inducted into all three. Mike has been involved in endurance sports for over 40 years and is one of the most prominent personalities in the field, having called over 400,000 athletes across finish lines with his iconic phrase, "You are an IRONMAN!" and countless hundreds of thousands more in other events. An IRONMAN Foundation Ambassador Team Captain and avid cyclist, he lives in San Diego, CA, with Rose, his wife of 44 years.

LEE GRUENFELD is the author of fourteen works of fiction and non-fiction, many of which have appeared on domestic and international bestseller lists, including the *New York Times*. His works have been translated into 13 languages and published in 22 countries. A columnist and photographer for the official IRONMAN Website, he has previously collaborated on books with heavyweight champion Evander Holyfield and ESPN Sport Science's John Brenkus. He lives in Palm Springs, CA, with his wife Cherie, a 13-time IRONMAN World Championship amateur title holder.

CPSIA information can be obtained
at www.ICGtesting.com
Printed in the USA
BVHW060116120619
550700BV00008B/510/P